D1306045

FOLLOW FOR NOW

FOLLOW FOR NOW

INTERVIEWS WITH FRIENDS AND HEROES

ROY CHRISTOPHER, EDITOR

Well-Red Bear

FOLLOW FOR NOW: INTERVIEWS WITH
FRIENDS AND HEROES

Published in 2007 by Well-Red Bear
4717 Stone Way N, Seattle, WA 98103

This book is licensed under the Creative Commons Attribution-ShareAlike 2.5 License.
To view a copy of this license, visit http://creativecommons.org/licenses/by-sa/2.5/
Or send a letter to Creative Commons,
543 Howard Street, 5th Floor,
San Francisco, CA, 94105 USA

Except "Terence McKenna: Struck by Noetic Lightning"
© Mark Dery 2006; all rights reserved.

Printed in Canada by Kromar
10 09 08 07 06   5 4 3 2 1   First edition

DESIGNED BY MCGUIRE BARBER DESIGN

Publisher's Cataloguing-in-Publication Data

Christopher, Roy.
    Follow for now : interviews with friends and heroes / Roy Christopher, editor.
       p.   cm.
    Includes bibliographical references and index.
    ISBN: 0-9776977-0-3 (pbk.)
    Contents: Roy Christopher—Eugene Thacker—Mark C. Taylor—Steven Johnson
—Howard Bloom—Manuel De Landa—Terence McKenna—Howard Rheingold—Rudy
Rucker—Albert-Laslo Barabasi—David Weinberger—Eric Paulos—Richard Saul Werman
—Eric Zimmerman—McKenzie Wark—N. Katherine Hayles—Geert Lovink—Brenda Laurel
—Peter Lunenfeld—Erik Davis—Gareth Branwyn—Douglas Rushkoff—Mike Ladd—Aesop
Rock—Pete Miser—Yoni Wolf a.k.a. Why? and Richard Adams of Hood—dalek—Weasel
Walter—Milemarker—Paul D. Miller a.k.a. DJ Spooky—Brian Coleman—Paul Roberts—Hal
Brindley—Doug Stanhope—Tod Swank—Shepherd Fairey—Steven Shaviro—Mark Dery—Steve
Aylett—Philip K. Dick—Adam Voith—David X. Cohen—Sean Gullette—Bruce Sterling.
      1. Interviews—United States. 2. Intellectuals—21st century—Interviews. 3. Intellectual life.
    4. Mass media and culture. 5. Science and the humanities.   I. Title.
CT120 .C49 2006
500.20—dc22

For Jack and Moms

TABLE OF CONTENTS

MUSIC

CULTURE

LITERATURE

Preface

THIS BOOK IS DECIDEDLY ECLECTIC. WHEN "CREATING CON-
tent" became a buzzing concept in the booming days of the web, I toyed
with the idea of "creating context" instead. The content of this book reflects
the changing interests of me and of my staff of friends. In spite of this
seeming haphazardness, my hope for readers is that they find threads that
run through the whole and provide some sort of relative cohesion. There
are themes that recur throughout these interviews, themes of self-reli-
ance, of resistance, of skepticism, of faith in technology, and, most of all,
of faith in the endless creativity of humanity. Some of these are due to the
fact that the same small group of people did the interviews, and some are
reflections of the Zeitgeist, but I like to think that still others are emergent.
Without getting too hoity-toity and self-aggrandizing, I want to explain
what I mean.

In Brian Eno's *A Year with Swollen Appendices* (Faber & Faber, 1996),
he outlines an idea he calls "edge culture":

> If you abandon the idea that culture has a single centre, and imag-
> ine that there is instead a network of active nodes, which may or may
> not be included in a particular journey across the field, you also aban-
> don the idea that those nodes have absolute value. Their value changes
> according to which story they're included in, and how prominently.

Eno admittedly fashioned this idea after Joel Garreau's concept of the "edge city," which poses the idea that the life of cities has moved from the center to the edges, but applying the idea to cultural studies opens the gaps, points to the connections, illuminates the networks. The interviews in this book represent the nodes in one network, one view of recent cultural history. Following Kevin Kelly (who incidentally was my first interview subject for my site *frontwheeldrive.com*, but whose interview was cut from the final version of this collection — sorry, Kevin), I view the mind as an ecology. For any ecology to grow and flourish, it needs diversity. New stuff comes not from the well-defined fields of thought or disciplines, but from the space and interaction among them. Allowing authors, theorists, art-ists, musicians, skateboarders, and others to rub shoulders, *Follow for Now* attempts to cross-pollinate areas of interest so that new ideas can grow. The way that I see some of the themes in this pile of stuff as potentially emer-gent is in the fact that each person who reads this collection, or just parts of this collection, is likely to come away with something different than any other: a different network, a different view of recent cultural history.

As you may have noticed, in spite of what I've just written, this book does feign a semblance of organization. The interviews have been arranged topically according to categories of Science, Media, Technology, Culture, Music, and Literature. This arrangement isn't arbitrary, but I'm sure I don't need to mention that there's more than a little overlap among these catego-ries, and most of the interviews herein could easily fit under the banner of two or more. Nonetheless, they are provided to help navigate the eclectic mix of people and ideas herein. I am hopeful that the reader will find the fluidity of the categories to be more of a boon than a burden.

Within each category, the interviews are arranged in reverse chronological order, and since these interviews were collected over a seven-year span, dates are provided with each to help establish the historical context. Most of these people have gone on to do bigger things since the interviews were conducted.

At the very least, I'd like for this collection to provide a conduit to something new. There's a lot of ground covered in here, a lot of ideas discussed, a lot of music described, and a lot of other books and projects mentioned. At the very least, I hope you're compelled to check some of it out.

Acknowledgements

FIRST OF ALL, I MUST THANK ALL OF THE CONTRIBUTORS TO *frontwheeldrive.com*. I met Tom Georgoulias by chance online during a book discussion. From there, he started helping with the site and added invaluable insight and knowledge to its contents. Brandon Pierce came on in a similar manner and broadened the site's knowledge base a step further. Mark Wieman only managed to submit one interview, but what his contribution lacks in quantity it makes up for in quality.

The look of this book is the product of the talents of one Patrick David Barber. Patrick's gift for layout has been among my favorites for years and it was an honor to have his help with this project. Adem Tepedelen did the final copyediting. I worked with both Patrick and Adem some ten years ago at *The Rocket* magazine in Seattle, Washington. It was a great pleasure to work with them both again on this project.

I must acknowledge all of the interview subjects on *frontwheeldrive .com* and featured in this book; these people gave of their time, shared their ideas, and provided the vast majority of the content for this project. In addition, several of these folks have also gone on to become contributors and advisors. Special thanks to Doug Rushkoff, Paul D. Miller, Erik Davis, Steven Shaviro, Howard Bloom, Mark Dery, Peter Lunenfeld, Howard Rheingold, Shepard Fairey, Bruce Sterling, Ken Wark, Paul Barman, and Doug Stanhope. Thanks to Mark Dery for permission to reprint "Terence McKenna: Struck by Noetic Lightning."; thanks to John Brockman for allowing me to reprint "Douglas Rushkoff: The Thing That I Call 'Doug,'" which was originally published on his site, *edge.org*; and thanks to Paul D. Miller for "Manuel De Landa: ILLogical Progression" and "Bruce Sterling: Future Tense," which were originally published on his site, *djspooky.com*.

I think I read somewhere that it's traditionally the folly of the first-time author to try and thank everyone. This book is the culmination of many years of correspondence, and if it's about anything, it's about gratitude. I'll never be able to cover everyone I owe, so apologies in advance to anyone I leave out. Above and beyond just answering emails, endless questions, and requests for feedback, this book wouldn't exist without the patience, guidance, and friendship of the following: Kristen Hren Sensenig, Lissa Warren, Doug Sery, Matthew Byrnie, David Barker, Brian Coleman, Richard Nash, Steve Connell, Alex Burns, Ashley Crawford, Richard Metzger, Gary Baddeley, Matthew Bialer, Anna Bierhaus, Eduardo Navas, Lev Manovich, Benjamin Bratton, Michael Blythe, Jonathan Field, Mark Lewman, Brian Spitzberg, Andrew Feenberg, Peter Atterton, David Silver, Benjamin Neziru Jawarhalal Hiltzheimer, Kris Amblad, Eric Black, Mary Kidrick, Ryan T. Lane, Alice Marwick, Mindy Wieman, Sean Walling, Matt Bailie, Steve Mayo, Mike and Tina Nagy, Greg Siegfried, Benjamin Murphy Myers, Thomas Durdin, Scott Griffin, Daniel May, GNARL, Def Junkies, P.F.E., Billy Wimsatt, Paul Barman, Greg Chaille, Brett Erickson, Brendon Walsh, Andy Andrist, Matt Arnold, Art Kabelowsky, Lynn Shawcroft, Renee Morrison, Kerry Mitchell, Jodi Esry, Tim Mitchell, George Mortimer, Drake Witham, Alysia Wood, Jake Johannsen, Brian

Tunney, Taj Mihelich, Steve Machuga, Mike Leask, Brian Benson, Ron Wilkerson, Ronnie Bonner, Brad McDonald, Jared Souney, Mark Whiteley, Tod Swank, Chris Mullins, Gautam Sahi, Charlie Thomas, Josh Beagle, Chad Foreman, Jamie Thomas, Wei-En Chang, Marc Garris, Dave Carnie, Andy Jenkins, Spike Jonze, Lori Domiano, Bob Kronbauer, Mike Daily, Duane Pitre, Hans Fjellestad, Adam Voith, Alap Momin, Will Brooks, Hsi-Chang Lin, Rob Swift, Justin Broadrick, Mike Patton, Tim Baker, Ian McMullin, Lonnie Lynn, Jimmy Jael, Killyou Meyou, Joe Scudda, Ian Goldberg, Ian Bavitz, Jaime Meline, Chris Palko, Derek Murphy, Stewart Brand, Brian Eno, Jaron Lanier, Kevin Kelly, Douglas Hofstadter, Dan Dennett, Mark Frauenfelder, Cory Doctorow, Scott McCloud, Coco Conn, Peter Giblin, Cynthia Connolly, Jessica Hopper, Al Burian, Dave Laney, David Brin, Marc Pesce, David Pescovitz, Doug Kellner, Jay Bolter, Rick Silva, Cory Arcangel, Lynn Usery, Jim Gleick, Jay Babcock, Jeff Wiesner, Nils Bernstein, Jon Skuldt, Scott Giampano, Pete O'Dell, John Mohr, Bill Barbot, Kim Coletta, Aidin Vaziri, J. Matthew Youngmark, Lord Jeff Daniel, Aaron Berkowitz, Larry McCaffery, Matt Heckert, Phil Agre, Troy Johnson, Val Renegar, Martha Lauzen, Joel Davis, David Dozier, Kim Stringfellow, Charles Mudede, Eddie Rehfeldt, Sean Nelson, Eric Schmidt, Josh Kane, Arnold the Well-Red Bear, Seana Shiffrin, Sidney Brinson, Jessica Raetzke, Kelly Ann Catherine Xavier Lum, Laura Ancona (next time, Miss Laura!), Katie Newcomb, Lisa Corrao, Susan Payne-Mulliken, Melissa Tritt, Amy Kidrick, Mona Fahoum, Angela Robeson, Courtney Ryers, Kristina Robinson, Claire Putney, Alaina Nims, Jessy Helms, Nikki Fels, Shawna Warren, and, of course, the one and only Jenny Blythe.

I'd be totally out-of-line if I didn't thank my sister for always being there, and for taking piles of photos of me trying to capture one non-goofy shot of my goofy self. This book is dedicated to my parents for supporting me no matter where my path leads. There's simply no way I'll ever be able to pay that back.

Roy Christopher
Introduction: Flip the Script
by SELECTED INTERVIEWEES (2006)

HOW BETTER TO INTRODUCE A BOOK OF INTERVIEWS THAN AN interview? Douglas Rushkoff suggested that I ask some of the interviewees from *Follow for Now* to ask me questions. I attempted to choose a broad set of people so that I might get a broad set of questions. I'm sure you will agree that I succeeded in this, but my answers may have yielded altogether different results. After answering these questions, I have an even deeper appreciation for all of the time and thought the interviewees gifted to this project.

ERIK DAVIS: *You have opted to put material successfully created for the web into a book. Why? What are your reasons — intellectual, emotional, tactical — for going Gutenberg in this day and age?*

ROY CHRISTOPHER: Well, I have to give credit where credit is due: Eric Paulos called me a few years ago and asked me why I didn't publish my site *frontwheeldrive.com* as a book. By then, the site had grown into a sizeable archive of interviews, so I considered it seriously. The idea had entered my head before that, but it had been the most fleeting of thoughts. His initial push was the impetus for the book you now hold in your hands.

The original design for *frontwheeldrive.com* was to host brief but in-depth interviews. It seemed that, as the site grew, so did the length of the interviews. I don't know about you, but I don't enjoy reading large tracts of text on the screen. Putting them into a book allows portability, ease of reading, and puts them in a different context. The hypertextuality of the web made each interview sort of an island, not only on *frontwheeldrive.com*, but on the web itself. *Follow for Now* houses them in one place, as a snapshot of the thinking that occurred on and through *frontwheeldrive.com*.

Certainly, part of the reason is selfish. I'm a bibliophile, and this is a book that I wanted on my shelf. Sure, *frontwheeldrive.com* has been around since 1999, but the nature of the web is still ephemeral, and I wanted a concrete document of these interviews, ideas, and the work put into compiling them.

STEVEN SHAVIRO: *What are the larger effects in the world, of the ideas you explore in this book and with these interviews? Are human lives being changed by them, in any meaningful and significant ways?*
RC: While there may not be a lot of directly earth-shattering revelations in the interviews in this book, potentially life-changing ideas abound. New and different ways of thinking about the world, about living in that world, about the future, about humanity, about technology are found throughout. I have learned more from these interviews and this project than most anything else I've ever done. Here's hoping I can pass at least a little bit of that on.

HOWARD RHEINGOLD: *Young people don't read newspapers. What is the future of journalism?*
RC: I don't know, the MoBlog? I think you'd know the answer to this one better than I.

If the newspaper was McLuhan's "warm bath," then the web is our hot shower. The serendipitous arrangement of the information in a newspaper is expanded and amplified online. Whoever can come correct with the news and information in the fastest, sexiest manner will determine the future of journalism. I can't say through what communication channel that will be, but whereas our parents read the newspaper, our children certainly won't.

HOWARD BLOOM: *Think back to when you were five, ten, sixteen, and twenty-two. Then tell me the passion points, the imprinting moments, the stories that shaped the curiosities that forced you to love these idea-makers, to do these interviews, and to write this book.*

RC: I grew up somewhat isolated. We moved constantly, but my family typically lived in the hinterlands of the South, so, early on, I rarely had neighborhood friends. Forced to entertain myself, I occupied my mind with writing, drawing, and reading.

By age ten, I found BMX and skateboarding. The influences of these activities and their surrounding cultures cannot be understated. As an offshoot of riding bikes and skateboards, I started making my own 'zines by age sixteen, and there I learned how to turn interviews and events into pages with staples. By twenty-two, I was writing music reviews and band interviews for magazines.

The final shift to this book's contents came much later. I read James Gleick's *Chaos* at age twenty-seven, and that book blew my head wide open. I suddenly realized that I wanted to do so much more than music journalism. I started *frontwheeldrive.com* and sought out the scientists, artists, and writers that I thought were pushing things.

This book is a culmination of all of these things. BMX and skateboarding still maintain a presence, and all of the ideas represented are the ones that still keep my mind well-greased.

3

BRUCE STERLING: *What the heck does "Follow for Now" mean?*

RC: I chose the phrase "follow for now," which is lifted from the Public Enemy song "Bring the Noise," as the title of this collection to honor to the interviewees in this book. I consider the people interviewed herein mentors. I have looked to them — and continue to look to them — and their work for insights about what's going on in the world, and what will be going on in the future.

I'm also hoping that this collection will help inspire a new crop of thinkers to pick up the torch, a Fourth Culture, if you will.

PAUL D. MILLER: *Why are you always checking out hip-hop? What makes you include it in your work?*

RC: I think hip-hop is one of the most exciting things happening in our lifetime. Those of us in our mid-thirties have grown up with it, and I find that people our age are either very into it or totally despise it.

I like to think of research and writing in the collage style of hip-hop. In many ways, hip-hop culture is about taking what you have and making something more from it, something uniquely your own — kind of an extension of what Bucky Fuller called "ephemeralization" (i.e., making more with less). Viewed in that frame, this book is a mix-tape that I remixed with cuts from all of my favorite artists.

The short and less pretentious answer is that hip-hop inspires me. I will always love H.E.R.

DOUGLAS RUSHKOFF: *Deep down, don't you consider yourself superior — or at least more advanced — than the people you've interviewed here? I mean, you're from the next generation, aren't you? We're rear-wheel, if anything. You're the front-wheel, right? When will you give up on us and just drive?*

RC: No, I don't see myself as superior or more advanced. I look up to all of you as mentors. I mean, this book is interviews with you, and the best interviews in here weren't even conducted by me.

There are advantages to being of the next generation, but a lot of them stem from the fact that my interests transcend the gaps between yours, mine, and the next. I'm interested in culture, the evolution of technology, and, more specifically, technology's influence on culture. At the same time, I'm interested and involved in several youth subcultures. The collusion of these interests puts me in touch with research and innovations from forward-thinking elders, theory-minded peers, and cutting-edge progeny. This book contains some of all of these.

But, if you're ready for me to drive, then by all means, give me the keys.

STEVE AYLETT: *Are you happy, and if so, do you do that by evading certain facts of the world, or acknowledging them and doing things that compensate personally and are a balm, or something else? Is there a difference between the first and second strategies?*

RC: Yes, I am genuinely happy. I think there's a contradiction in these two strategies. They are different, and not necessarily mutually exclusive. In fact, in order to evade facts of the world, mustn't one acknowledge them? I use a combination of the two. That is, I acknowledge those things about the world that I do not like, then I evade the ones I cannot change, and I constantly strive to do things that compensate personally.

Without slipping totally into solipsism, I recognize that my immediate world is, in large part, of my own creation: My existence is a product of the choices I make. I love Richard Saul Wurman's idea of "designing your life." While I certainly can't choose every aspect of my days, I refuse to act as if I'm not in control of most of them. Owning that responsibility makes me happy.

FOLLOW FOR NOW

SCIENCE

EUGENE THACKER

MARK C. TAYLOR

STEVEN JOHNSON

HOWARD BLOOM

TERENCE MCKENNA

MANUEL DE LANDA

Eugene Thacker
Whole Earth DNA
BY ROY CHRISTOPHER (2006)

IF, AS MARTIN HEIDEGGER WROTE AND MICHAEL HEIM CLARIFIED, philosophy is to stay one step ahead of science, then art is to stay one step ahead of philosophy. Art has the most freedom as a form of exploration, as a method by which to find the limits of a domain of research. That said, Eugene Thacker doesn't necessarily consider himself an artist, but, as he told Josephine Bosma in an interview for *Net-time,* "I have always been interested in approaching things from a theoretical viewpoint, as well as exploring the same issues in, for want of a better term, an artistic domain. Sometimes getting different results, sometimes seeing what you can learn from doing those kind of activities."

Thacker's unique blend of artistic methods, theoretical viewpoints, and science fiction-minded research has yielded two books about the overlap of technology and biology, more specifically, the human genome and the digital computer. As DNA becomes code and code is entered in networked databases, well, things are getting hairy — on a global scale.

Thacker's books, *Biomedia* (University of Minnesota Press, 2004) and *The Global Genome* (MIT Press, 2005), explore just how hairy.

ROY CHRISTOPHER: *Why is biotechnology now an inherently global phenomenon?*

EUGENE THACKER: Well, biotech is "global" in a few senses of the term. If you take the example of the field of genomics — the mapping of the genomes of various organisms, etc. — it is global in the literal sense that the institutions — universities, biotech labs, research centers — are not only spread out across First-World countries, but many of them are directly linked to each other, either as consortiums or public-private partnerships. Also, the actual technologies used involve not only "wet-lab" tools but, increasingly, information- and computer-based tools. In fact, the internet has become one of the cornerstone research tools for genomics-based research. My colleagues in bioinformatics tell me that there is a lot of genetic research that is almost totally done in the computer; networks, databases, and "gene-finding algorithms" are the new tools of biology today.

So, the mapping of the human genome is a "global" effort in these senses, because it is a network of labs in many different countries, and it involves the actual utilization of information networks. But, genomics is also "global" in the more political sense, because what they call the "international" human genome-sequencing consortium really means mostly U.S.-based labs (many with partnerships in the private sector), with a few other labs in Europe and Japan. Again, if we stick to the case of genomics, the knowledge being produced from all this research tends to flow into either medical therapies (the most risky venture), novel drugs (thus involving multiple patents and partnerships between biotech start-ups and "big pharma"), or diagnostic technologies (e.g. DNA chips for genetic screening — the safest investment). And, as you might guess, the access to any of these potential medical benefits will certainly come at great cost — and their health benefits have largely yet to be proven; anyone who's had to take prescription drugs knows that there are as many side-effects ("adverse drug reactions" or ADRs) as there are benefits!

So the book is really about trying to understand these trends: on the one hand, an integration of traditional biotechnologies with computer and information technologies, and, on the other hand, the increasingly "global" organization of the biotech industry.

But really, if you want the truth, the book began from a rather science fictional image I had — that of a giant cell stretched across the planet, forming a dense, fibrous network. Sort of like *The Blob* meets *Tron*. To me, that was what bioinformatics was like — all this information concerning genes, proteins, biochemical pathways and interactions, itself stored on servers spread out across the globe, like one network mapped onto another network.

RC: *I wonder if you could expound on your closing thoughts in* The Global Genome *regarding pop culture being the site in which to understand biotechnology (Appendix D,* The Global Genome*).*
ET: Well, part of that is due to my background in cultural theory and, I'll admit, my affinity for SF and horror. But in all my writing on biotech and the life sciences I've always tried to refuse any hard-and-fast distinction between science and science fiction as a way of understanding the different ways in which futures are extrapolated from a given present situation.

It's pretty obvious, if one looks around, that the life sciences and biotechnology have pervaded popular culture. A great way of demonstrating this is to look at all of the re-makes of Cold War-era science fiction and comics: *Spider-Man, Hulk, X-Men, Fantastic Four,* etc. It seems to now be a requirement to somehow put genetics in the stories, even if it really doesn't make any sense (which is often). I'm less interested in what the director "intended" to mean by this than what it means culturally that genetics, biotech, and even nanotech are always found in SF. One thing it means is that these sciences and technologies are normalized in a way that the general public going to a film will "accept" their inclusion as a matter of course. Certainly there are always SF geeks who dispute the technical accuracy of how the genetic mutation actually creates the superhero or villain, but on a general level these technosciences have become a part of a certain cultural imaginary. So the question is "What conditions had to be in place such that these particular technosciences could become normalized as a part of a certain world-view?" Perhaps this process is somewhat parallel to the normalization of medicine and public health practices themselves.

So I think that popular culture is relevant, not because I believe that films should educate and moralize, but because there is actually a great deal of ambivalence in pop culture's treatment of technoscience. We can't live without it, and yet it seems to be our downfall. The movies that moralize about the ineradicable human spirit do so using the most advanced computer graphics and special effects. There's also a sense in many of these films, books, and comics that we as a culture are not quite sure what to do with all of this information and all these gadgets. It's almost as if the greatest challenge posed to SF now is finding something interesting to do with all the technology that exists.

RC: *The literal "pathogenic qualities of information" (e.g., the anthrax virus being sent through the postal service) are a new development, but all of these overlaps between biology and information tend to beg the question about where we draw the line. As biology becomes information in the form of DNA, and information becomes pathogen, where does the text actually begin and end?*

ET: This is a complicated issue. With the genetic "code," there certainly is a sense in which, yet again, "there is nothing outside the text." And I think that one can use this position tactically to critique the fetishizing of "code" over the materiality of information. But I also think there's a lot to take from media studies and science studies on this issue as well. For instance, a code is not necessarily a text, and the genetic code is not even really a code, if we stick to the classical technical definitions from Claude Shannon or Norbert Wiener.

From a biological perspective, DNA doesn't have a grammar, and it only "means" something not in itself (e.g., genes for "X") but rather in the network of relations in which it partakes, and even then, one cannot talk about "meaning" without talking about materiality, relationality, and "expression" (to use Deleuze's term). Any college-level biology textbook states this: one has to look not just at discrete "genes" (a term over which there is really no consensus), but instead at gene expression network, metabolic pathways, membrane signalizing cascades, etc.

And then there are also historical questions to consider. Even though the notion of a genetic "code" is now commonplace (so much so that computer-generated DNA models appear in every show on the Sci Fi Channel), we have to remember that there was a long, discontinuous process through which this metaphor was established as such. During and after World War II, the same period in which mainframe computing was developing, there were a whole host of metaphors besides the genetic code; there were indeed textual metaphors, scriptural ones, metaphors borrowing from the telegraph or typewriter, metaphors dealing with cryptography and secret writing, metaphors relating to cartography, architecture, and music. So the question that historians ask here is how did this one particular metaphor take hold? What is its relation, for example, to the parallel development of computer and information technologies? What interests does it serve? What kinds of instrumental configurations does it enable? What can one do to the body through this metaphor?

If metaphors are concepts that we forget are metaphors, then it seems important to remind ourselves of the tropic nature of such central concepts as the genetic "code." Not only does this invite us to think otherwise (to think about alternative metaphors), but it is also an invitation to rethink the entire relation between metaphor and materiality itself.

RC: *Advances in biotechnology have allowed for a quite literal reading of Foucault's ideas of "biopower" and "biopolitics."*

ET: Yes, and you're absolutely right to point out that this is a literal reading of biopolitics and biopower. This also is a complicated issue. The "literal" can be limiting here because we remain at the level of content (e.g., that anything pertaining to biology or genetics is "biopolitical"). The problem here is that we limit the domain of the biopolitical to these disciplinary fields, and it makes it hard to understand, for example, the role of policy, patents, or security as also being biopolitical. This is the approach taken by much of the recent discussion over Empire and multitude, specifically in its relation to labor, production, and the idea of the "common." There is a sense in which, for thinkers such as Negri, Virno, or Lazzarato, to link biopolitics with medicine or biology would be reducing it and excluding any consideration of political economy.

I agree with this. But I think there's also a way of understanding the "literal" differently. In a way, the question is not getting beyond the literal to some more fundamental truth, but perhaps the issue is not being literal enough. Foucault poses this problem in his lectures at the Collège de France. The specifics of medicine, public health, and the emergence of "biology" are all important to him — precisely because they are never just medical, health-related, or biological issues. There, in the weekly lecture format, you see him experimenting, trying different things, spinning out these topologies that are always heuristic. In other words, the format of the lectures allows him to avoid the search-for-truth demand that scholarly books are often branded with. There are some great passages where, for instance, Foucault talks about sovereignty as itself becoming more decentralized and even rendered as biological (e.g., his concept of "race war"), or the notion of "human capital" that is central to liberalism and biopolitics, or his comments on the role that urbanism and plague played in the "apparatus of security" and the management of flows and circulations.

RC: *With DVD players currently available in many vehicles, are we seeing the convergence of Virilio's "automotive speed" and "audiovisual speed"?*
ET: Virilio does mention "metabolic speed" as well, and I think about the way that global air travel has changed our experiential topos of the globe — for those of us who are able to be "flexible" and travel, of course. But Virilio's notion of "polar inertia" — that feeling of backaches on a twelve-hour flight going through the upper atmosphere at hundreds of miles an hour — still, but moving — perhaps this is an apt allegory for the biological changes that are happening via biotech? Virilio, though he talks about the body a great deal, did not talk about "biotechnical speed" — the capacity to regenerate cells, tissues, and even organs in the lab; the ability to make thousands of copies of DNA in a few hours; the ability to use "mammalian bioreactors" to produce medical compounds in goats or cows for human consumption; and so on. But then, of course, there's drugs. And coffee.

RC: *Where has your attention turned since writing* The Global Genome?
ET: Two threads, basically. One is a book titled *Necrologies* that deals with the idea of the "body politic," a concept that was formulated in Plato and then in late-Medieval political theology before being formalized in Hobbes and natural-right theorists. We don't use this term today, but I think the issues it raises are absolutely pertinent to contemporary debates over sovereignty and "bare life." My interest is really in the body politic as a corpse, and thus my term "necrology," which is simply the study of the "diseases" and decay of the body politic. I'm interested in looking at plague and pestilence because they are moments in which the metaphorical "diseases"

17

of the body politic (civil war, dissent, factionalism) fold onto the actual states of emergency caused by epidemics and public health issues. These are obviously current concerns, and it's frustrating because there's no real consensus about how much control our governments have to really prevent something like a pandemic outbreak. But it's also a very gothic book, about resurrection, plague, and the demonic.

The other thread deals with what I've referred to as "networks, swarms, and multitudes," or, to get even more verbose, "the political ontology of aggregate forms." I'm interested in networks (the technical model), swarms (the biological model), and multitudes (the political model) as massing, "complex" forms that raise very "ancient" philosophical problems — that of the One and the Many, that of Wholes and Parts, that which is living and that which is ordered. With my co-conspirator Alex Galloway, we've just finished a book called *The Exploit* that puts forth a critique of networks, and we're working on another volume dealing with mythological swarms.

And then I'm writing fiction. No, really. I've been doing this sort of writing for a long time, when I was involved with 'zines and alternative presses like Black Ice Press, and later on with hypertext fiction. But I'm finishing a novel called *An Ideal for Living* that is sort of experimental science fiction. It features a technical description of "Biomolecular Transport Protocol (BmTP)." Of course, from a publisher's standpoint "experimental" means "will not sell any copies" so I'm debating self-publishing and doing a gift economy model for it.

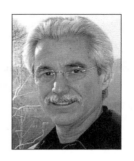

Mark C. Taylor
The Philosophy of Culture
by ROY CHRISTOPHER (2005)

MARK C. TAYLOR IS ONE OF THOSE PEOPLE YOU STUMBLE UPON and wonder why you were previously roaming around unaware. His countless books explore many areas of culture, philosophy, art, theory, and, most recently, commerce. I originally came across his work while doing research on artist Mark Tansey (Taylor's *The Picture in Question* [University of Chicago Press, 1999] explores the mix of messages and theory in Tansey's paintings). Having read his book *The Moment of Complexity* (University of Chicago Press, 2003) a few months ago, I was intrigued by Taylor's consolidation of seemingly disparate theoretical areas (e.g., postmodernism/ post-structuralism, chaos/catastrophe/complexity theory, network theory, the pixelated artwork of Chuck Close, etc.) into a new critical perspective. Not only that, but the book outlines how this new perspective can — and should — be implemented in education, a feat around which Taylor has organized the Global Education Network.

His latest book, *Confidence Games: Money and Markets in a World Without Redemption* (University of Chicago Press, 2004), brings together over three decades worth of research. And it seems he's just getting warmed up: Taylor has three new books on the way.

ROY CHRISTOPHER: *Your work crosses many disciplinary lines and encompasses many academic realms. What do you consider your field?*

MARK C. TAYLOR: The best way to describe what I do is the philosophy of culture. I am especially interested in the philosophical and religious presuppositions and implications of current cultural practices.

RC: *Tell us about your newest book,* Confidence Games. *What is this book's aim?*

MCT: *Confidence Games* draws together lines of analysis I have been tracing for more than thirty years. I have three major objectives in this book. First, to explain how art displaces religion, and then markets and finance displace art as the expression of spiritual striving during the past two centuries; second, to examine the interrelationship between postmodern philosophy and art on the one hand and finance capitalism on the other hand; third, to develop a model of global financial markets as complex adaptive systems. In the course of this analysis, the intricate interrelation of neoliberal economics, neoconservative politics, and neofundamentalist religion becomes clear.

RC: *You seem to have a visual counterpart in Mark Tansey. When and how did you discover his work?*

MCT: I first encountered Tansey's work years ago at MIT. I had just finished a visit to the Media Lab and in the elevator I noticed an announcement of an exhibition of his work in a nearby gallery. By the time I got there, the gallery was ready to close. But I saw enough to know the work was interesting. What intrigued me was that Tansey had gone through very similar stages in his work as I had in mine. He started with an analysis and critique of modernism, then examined deconstruction in considerable depth and finally turned to complexity theory. His pictures explicitly and implicitly explore these issues. Unfortunately, in recent years he has stalled and is no longer doing very interesting work.

RC: *How exactly is the Global Education Network working to implement your view of complexity and network culture into its program?*

MCT: I have experimented with new technologies in my teaching for more than fifteen years. I started by using teleconferencing to team-teach seminars with the University of Helsinki and the University of Melbourne. As the web became more extensive and reliable, I started webcasting my courses. When the college where I teach was not interested in developing these initiatives, I started Global Education Network with Herbert Allen, who is a New York investment banker. We have been trying to develop high-quality online education in the liberal arts, humanities, and sciences for people all over the world. I believe that networking technology is changing the structure of knowledge and eventually will transform the structure of education institutions. We are trying to develop new forms of education that more effectively reflect and utilize these technologies. Imagine a curriculum structured like a hypertext and an educational institution structured like a network and you will glimpse what I imagine.

RC: *Is there anything you're working on that you'd like to mention here?*

MCT: I have three new books that are at various stages of completion. The first is a book on religion and contemporary culture. While all of my books deal with religion in one way or another that is not always obvious to readers. It is now apparent to people that religion is not going away and they are trying to figure out what to make of it. There is a desperate need for responsible and critical thinking about religion today. This book is conceptualized, but I haven't had time to write it yet. The second book is entitled *About Nothing* and is a collection of essays on art and literature — William Gaddis, Mark Z. Danielewski, Joseph Beuys, Matthew Barney, James Turrell, Ann Hamilton, and others. This book is almost finished. The final project, which is finished, is a favorite of mine. It is a book of original photographs of bones. I took these pictures with a former student. The book consists of about 90 images with an essay and an aphorism for each image. The images are quite remarkable and are rather startling. The title of the book is *Mystic Bones*. As I write in one of the aphorisms: If you can't dance with bones, you are a nihilist.

Steven Johnson
No Bitmaps for These Territories

by ROY CHRISTOPHER with
additional input by JONATHAN FIELD (2004)

WHEN A FRIEND OF MINE LOANED ME STEVEN JOHNSON'S FIRST book, I had no idea what he was getting me into. On the surface, *Interface Culture* (Harper San Francisco, 1997) looks like most other books on the subject of computer interfaces, but how many times must I be warned not to judged books by their looks before I start to believe.

Johnson's books each tackle a different topic than the one before, but they all wander wide enough for you to see the color outside of the lines. Where *Interface Culture* seemed to be about interfaces, it was about, well, interfaces — but interfaces like I'd never thought of them before, in places I'd never seen them before. *Emergence* (Scribner, 2001) was about emergent phenomena and network culture, but again, in ways that I hadn't seen discussed before. Johnson writes about the signs of the times, but no one else sees what they signify quite like he does.

His latest book, *Mind Wide Open* (Scribner, 2004), is an autoethnographic romp through the neurobiology of his brain. It's not quite like reading a Charlie Kaufman script, but it's close. He also co-founded *FEED* online magazine, and writes for *Wired*, *Discover*, *Slate*, *Salon*, and many others.

I've returned to *Interface Culture* many times since that first read, and in turn, I asked Johnson to return with me.

ROY CHRISTOPHER: *I want to go back in time a bit to your first book,* Interface Culture. *Its title betrays the broad scope of the book, but in the meantime, the interface has expanded in our culture: Everything from media, to branding, to communication is, in effect, an interface. Did you see this expansion when writing this book?*

STEVEN JOHNSON: In a (slightly self-congratulatory) word: yes. There were a few things I think I ended up being wrong about, and more than a few that I failed to anticipate, but the general argument has held up very well over the eight years that have passed since I wrote it. The argument, simply put, was this: in a society where information is proliferating at an exponential rate, and where information is valued above all else, the tools we have to manage and filter that information — our interfaces — become the most important symbolic or "sense-making" form in the culture. It's not exaggerating things to say that Google is the defining mode of self-representation for our society, and Google is, in the end, just an interface to the web.

RC: *What are your thoughts on our political system as an interface? Everything in this country has evolved so much over the past century, except government. How well do you think it works in today's world so far as serving the public interest and public good?*

SJ: I tend to be an optimist about a lot of things, but the state of the government is not something that puts me in a half-full kind of mood. We're clearly in a transition phase right now, one that might well last another ten years, if not longer: a small and vocal (and well-publicized) part of the electorate has realized the power of information revolution, and they're demanding that politics be revolutionized accordingly. (Just today, one of the heads of Moveon.org announced that they had "bought" the Democratic Party in 2004 and it was time for the old guard to hand over the keys.) But a lot of us still think about politics the old-fashioned way: as a remote force over our lives that we can't control in any real way. I said after Dean imploded that his campaign was a classic study in the clash of two overlapping paradigms: the internet had transformed the way people raise money and mobilize supporters and that had led to Dean's spectacular rise in late 2003, but the decision that people made about who to vote for was still governed by the tradition of seeing someone on TV (or, if you were really lucky, seeing them in a town hall meeting in person.) And that created an imbalance — because all the early indicators revolved around money and activist passion, which created an artificial sense of Dean's inevitability. But the "actual voters" didn't really dig him.

RC: *As long as we're talking about interfaces, what about branding? What about the homogenization of the landscape where big-box retailers are concerned? This is a personal pet peeve, but I like to see different things in different places when I travel. I hate to see the same four stores, or the same coffee shop in every town. Is there any company you think is respecting regional culture even as they move in and set up shop?*

SJ: I'm sympathetic to what you're saying, but I think there's a risk of sentimentality here as well. I mean, Starbucks is everywhere, which means by a certain standard the world has gotten more homogeneous. On the other hand, the world is now filled with far more places where I can order a triple-shot iced latté with good espresso. Ten years ago the number of places serving a wide range of coffees was pretty small, outside the ten biggest cities and maybe a dozen college towns. But thanks to Starbucks, even airports and shopping malls now have a huge palette of coffee options to choose from. Same goes for Barnes & Noble. Their outlets regularly carry *Interface Culture* in stores, despite the fact that it never came close to being a bestseller. But you would have been very hard pressed to find a book like that in a nonmetropolitan/academic bookstore ten years ago. (And then there's the whole Amazon phenomenon, where everyone with a web connection now has access to the most obscure titles in print.)

So for the people outside the urban centers, I think the chains have largely been a force for more diversity, not less. The question is whether the chains are killing off the diversity in the cities themselves. I don't think anyone has done a convincing study of this yet. My hunch would be it's pretty much a draw: Soho is filled with J. Crew and The Gap now, but five blocks over in NoLiTa there are more small designers in one-room shops than there ever were in Soho. There are fewer indie bookstores now, but frankly, I don't need indie bookstores with Amazon. And there are like a thousand Starbucks in NYC, but all the classic small coffee shops I know of are still thriving.

RC: *In* Emergence, *you uproot the free-content-with-advertising model of mass media and propose an opt-in, information-exchange model. You envision a world of media with less ads, but rather a more open exchange of information between companies and consumers. As someone who cringes at ads filling every available space, I like the idea. Do you think there's a way to get past the privacy issues, or protect privacy, and still implement such a model?*

SJ: Amazon sends me email announcements when there's a new release that it thinks I might be interested in, given my past purchasing history. I'd estimate off the top of my head that they're on target about thirty percent of the time (often it's notifying me of something I've already purchased, though not from them.) That means that two-thirds of the time they're completely off base in anticipating my interests, but still I welcome those emails. I mean, what's the batting average of all the other advertising in my life — all the billboards and radio plugs and subway banners and random TV spots, not to mention the spam? It's a fraction of a fraction of a percent, if you add it all up. So when someone shows up and says, "thirty percent of the time, I'm going to point out something you really might want to buy," I say: "Great, keep it coming."

As for the privacy issues, I don't know. I worry about health and financial records — and personal information about my family — getting into the wrong hands. But I don't care about someone tracking the DVDs that I buy, as long they give me a one-click method of shutting down their recommendations if they're not working for me.

RC: *What's the new book-in-progress all about?*
SJ: It's a pure work of persuasion, arguing that popular culture, on average, has been growing more cognitively challenging over the past thirty years, not less. Despite everything you hear about declining standards and dumbing-down, you have to do more intellectual work to make sense of today's television or games — much less the internet — than you did a few decades ago. It will definitely be the most controversial of my books, but I think it's also going to be a fun read. It's called *Everything Bad Is Good For You*, and it'll be out in the U.S. in early May.

Howard Bloom
Mind at Large
by BRANDON PIERCE (2002)

WHEN ATTEMPTING TO EXAMINE THE ESSENCE AND INQUIRE about the idiosyncrasies of human behavior, where should one turn? The beaten paths of the past have lead us in the direction of archetypal models involving psychological studies and reflection on past human history. We have also ventured into cultural anthropological endeavors, as well as primatology and ethology. Howard Bloom has managed to swivel heads in a new direction. Many are now peering through the lenses of light microscopes, and catching a glimpse of our ancestors in action. Welcome to the world of primordial bacteria. Bloom's latest book, *Global Brain: The Evolution of Mass Mind from the Big Bang to the 21st Century* (J. Wiley & Sons, 2000), takes the reader on an evolutionary adventure where "time" seems to march backwards and forward simultaneously. Bloom dresses modern societies in anachronistic garb, and portrays our evolving communication culture in terms of vintage bacterial ideology.

The precursor to *Global Brain*, *The Lucifer Principle: A Scientific*

Expedition into the Forces of History (Atlantic Monthly Press, 1995) was the work that unleashed Bloom monstrous intellect onto the scientific world. He laid the groundwork for what was to become (is still becoming) a fluid science that shifts across boundaries, shapes to its new surroundings, and somehow holds its ground. Bloom takes an all-encompassing attitude toward his work. The bacterial derived theories are placed against the backdrop of geopolitics, particle physics, memetic phenomenon, and traditional evolutionary theory. They maintain an extraordinary amount of explanatory power.

A formal introduction of this man would include many honors and distinctions that would inspire a genuflection from anyone with an open, scientific, or creative mind. Bloom's wanderings from the reserved and stuffy halls of academia to the speedy, reality-warped microcosm of pop music culture and back have produced a frantic human being whose personality, passion, and research are equally unordinary.

BRANDON PIERCE: *You manage to articulate your theories quite broadly, injecting life into often prosaic scientific inquiry. Your ideas have profoundly changed the way readers view the world, with respect to ourselves, history, and human behavior. What can you stress about your ideas that will infect others with a sense of the importance of your work?*

HOWARD BLOOM: Be perceptually independent. Know a political or scientific cliché when you see one. Sidestep its rigidities. Try to see what others take for granted from unaccustomed points of view. Look for facts that are off the beaten track. Then come up with your own perspective. Pursue new insights even if they make you unpopular and politically incorrect. Try to inject new understanding into your own life and that of others. Use your empathy to understand as many other people as you can. Be curious. I don't know if that answers the question, but it's a way of life I believe in.

BP: *I am fascinated by biological frameworks that transcend boundaries, and this is becoming somewhat of a trend in the fields of social sciences and networks. You claim that we "inherit" our behaviors from bacteria, and I find this to be a recondite assertion and a bit hard to digest. What is the nature of this relationship or "inheritance," i.e., do you truly believe that the genes for bacterial communication, warfare, and group dynamics survive in humans and function in a similar fashion, or perhaps is this some sort of a default reaction to the stresses of the outside world?*

HB: Life existed on this planet for three billion years in just one basic form: single cells grouped in megacommunities. In other words, our ancestors were bacterial for seventy-eight percent of their time on earth. We share roughly forty percent of our genes with bacteria. More important, we share with them the basic stuff that allows all life on this planet to operate — the system of DNA. None of this was obvious to me in the beginning. When I first set out on a scientific hunting expedition for the roots of war, violence, and the sorts of crowd frenzies that fascinated me, I looked where everyone else was looking — at the behavior of baboons, chimps, and indigenous human tribes. But none of the theories based on primate research or anthropology came close to explaining the sorts of mass emotions Hitler or the Beatles had stirred up. None came close to explaining personal passions. That's probably because movements like Osama's firebrand Islam or St. Augustine's heretic-hunting Christianity draw their flame from emotions like idealism and from frenzies of commitment and belief. When you take a closer look, these emotions are part of a crowd phenomenon — a group thing on a huge scale. Christianity swept the known world of St. Augustine's day. It was a movement fueled by the emotions of millions. So is Osama's Islam. Chimps, baboons, and hunter-gatherers don't cluster in groups of millions. Bacteria do. In fact, they gather in societies of trillions. And, like us, bacteria broadcast their chemical "feelings" as widely as they can. They communicate their experience using attraction and repulsion cues, chemicals of seduction and fear, chemicals of influence. Bacteria make war and peace using armies that dwarf ours. Bacteria wheel and tumble through the equivalent of mass mood swings. And bacterial colonies are group-brains, ultra-quick R&D centers, parallel-distributed processing machines. I started gathering information on bacterial battle, cooperation, and communication back in 1985. Then, in 1995, I contacted Eshel Ben-Jacob, the head of the physics department at the University of Tel Aviv. Eshel was doing extraordinary research on bacterial mass behavior, mind-blowing work. My experiences with human mass movements and his with bacterial colonies meshed so eerily it was crazy. The things I'd seen among humans helped explain what he'd seen under his microscope, and his work made sense of mine. It sounds a bit crazy, but it was one of those eureka experiences you're lucky to come across even once in your lifetime.

BP: *To truly understand a concept or argument, one must view the idea from all angles and superimpose the images to construct a complete understanding. This is certainly true of human behavior. Interdisciplinary work is crucial. Unfortunately, you must drag your coattails through a myriad of fields (biology, psychology, history, sociology, anthropology) upon which academia has a stranglehold. Do you encounter resistance from scientists who feel that you are not grounded sufficiently in their specialty or do not fully grasp their ideas to be able to make the assertions and connections that you do? How do you deal with this and navigate the seas of academia without lofty credentials from the inside?*

HB: That's a good question, and I'm not sure I know the answer. I started in science at the age of ten. By the time I was eleven, everyone knew I'd be a college professor. But things that didn't fit the academic mold fascinated me. I wanted to understand the exaltations of mystics, why poetry was so on target, why religion had its pull. When I graduated from NYU, I had four grad school fellowships in clinical psychology. By then, I'd spent more than half of my life in academic science. I wanted to jump ship. There was no way I was going to get to the blaze at the center of the human soul by putting together rinky-dink paper-and-pencil experiments using groups of college kids — the standard technique for psychological research. I was going to have to go where the wild things are — into the arts, the media, and ultimately into film, politics, rap, and rock 'n' roll. After fifteen years of fieldwork with everyone from Tipper Gore (we were at war with each other over censorship) to Michael Jackson and from Bob Marley to Aerosmith, Kiss, AC/DC, and ZZ Top, I pulled my notes together and went back into the scientific world. I figured my colleagues who'd done things the "legitimate" way would laugh at me, or worse. How do you get people to take fieldwork in punk rock, political activism, and hip-hop seriously? I was wrong. Only three people pounced on me. Yes, one did try to get me blackballed. But from nearly everybody else, I've gotten an awful lot of help.

BP: *You gave a lecture in the past entitled "Instant Evolution," which challenged the notion of the "Stone Age brain" trapped inside bodies that exist in a modern world. In other words, the milieu of urban existence has not induced any significant genetic alterations within the human body. Have your ideas on this subject evolved, or are you familiar with anyone making headway on theories of urban evolution?*

HB: No one that I know of has taken up the challenge. Here's the idea: it's a big mistake to think we evolved all our human qualities when we were hunter-gatherers like the !Kung San of Botswana and Namibia. I tried to make the case that we've done a fair amount of evolving since 10,000 years ago when our first Stone Age cities were founded, and that city living has literally gotten into our genes. The evidence started to come together when

33

I was researching my second book, *Global Brain*. Then I got a call from the Foundation For the Future asking me to participate in an elite symposium on cultural evolution . . . a meeting of the eight of us who were supposedly the top brains on the subject in the world. That gave me an excuse to do even more research. Then the journal *New Ideas in Psychology* asked to publish the piece, which gave me a chance to research it further. The evidence that piled up is pretty substantial.

I've heard other scientists use the key term from the "Instant Evolution" article, *Homo Urbanis*, which means they've read the piece and that it's influenced their thinking. There've been a lot of requests for reprints, mostly from scientists in Eastern Europe. And the *howardbbloom.net* webpage with the Foundation For the Future version of "Instant Evolution" is one of the most heavily hit pages on the site; it's had over 868,000 visitors. But, nope, I don't think anyone is doing additional research to test the validity of the concept.

BP: *China seems to be kicking up dust within your crystal ball, as you co-outlined in the most recent Disinformation publication* (Everything You Know Is Wrong: The Disinformation Guide to Secrets and Lies, *2002*). *Being a seer par excellence, could you hint at the causes, or ideas that underlie the many strategic moves that China is making?*

HB: *The Lucifer Principle*, my first book, says that humans are pecking order animals. Twins gestating in the womb together will duke it out for dominance. The winner will take over the central living room of the uterus, and the loser will be shunted off to the side. This is fact, not fiction. Then, when kids are small, they'll play one pecking-order game after another, from King of the Castle to cops and robbers. In the process, they'll work out a dominance hierarchy. One kid will usually come out as the leader. Another typically emerges as the leader's sidekick. One becomes the group clown. And at the bottom there's some poor schnook the group picks on. All this is provable fact. But *The Lucifer Principle* says that human groups battle for dominance, too. The fight for the number one position in the hierarchy of groups has been going on since the beginning of history. The Athenians fought the Spartans for top-dog rank among the Greeks. The Greeks fought the Persians for number one position in the Mediterranean and Asia Minor. Then along came the Romans and knocked both of them off the peak.

Meanwhile, in Eastern Asia, China's been number one for 2,200 years. Until the mid-1800s, China felt that it was top-dog on the planet. In fact, it regarded itself as the center of the earth, the "Middle Kingdom." Then along came the Europeans with their steam-driven gunboats and humiliated the Chinese. Now the Chinese are ready to climb back where they've always known they belong — to the top. We in the US also want to be number one. But the Chinese will give us stiff competition. They led the world in science and technology for 1,600 years. We've only led it for ninety. They led the world in education, scholarship, and publishing for 2,000 years. We've only been ahead in those fields for roughly sixty years — assuming that we've ever led at all. We led the world in technological and software piracy from roughly 1811 until the 1890s. The Chinese lead the world in techno-absorption and techno-theft today. Add to that a population four times the size of ours, plug in the high value Chinese civilization places on hard work, and you've got a nation that could easily outstrip us in twenty years if we don't stay very much on our toes.

BP: *Can you tell us about some scientists, authors, or other humans who inspire, stimulate, or are strongly respected by Howard Bloom, people who's ideas mesh with yours or help thrust your work forward. Are any of these people involved in your Paradigm Book Series?*

HB: Albert Einstein gave me reason to live when I was a kid. Let's face it, unathletic geeks who read two books a day at the age of ten are not exactly popularity magnets. But Einstein was absent-minded like me (your average decapitated tortoise has a better memory than I do). He was a fashion-deadhead, like me. And he was slightly on the messy side. There were no role models in my hometown of Buffalo, New York. But Einstein made being strange and loving ideas seem okay.

Today, my favorite stimulators and co-agitators are: Eshel Ben-Jacob, who's one of the world's top physicists but can't keep his hands off research on bacterial information-processing, brain-cell self-assembly, nanotechnology, and lord knows what all else; John Skoyles, the British neuroscientist and evolutionary theorist whose new book with Dorion Sagan, *Up From Dragons*, I executive edited; Peter Richerson, the cultural evolutionist, with whom I bat ideas around via email pretty regularly; David Smillie, a zoologist/psychologist at Duke University; Lynn Margulis and Dorion Sagan, whose ideas on biology, evolution, and synergy are incredible; Richard Dawkins, author of *The Selfish Gene* (Oxford University Press, 1976), whose ideas I often disagree with, but who makes disagreement a joy, not to mention a way to generate huge new insights; my mentor, Ted Coons, the neurobiologist who discovered what the hypothalamus does; and David Berreby, a brilliant science writer who gets my brain up and running every time.

BP: *Anything exciting on the table for the Group Selection Squad or news concerning the Paleopsychology Project?*

HB: We put the Group Selection Squad to sleep once its mission was over and we'd made it permissible to speak about group selection without literally risking your scientific career. That was back in 1998 or so. The International Paleopsychology Project is a great place to breed and test out new ideas. It gives its members permission to use every science, art, and political event known to mankind as a piece of the big puzzle, the big-picture way of understanding things. What I'd like to do but haven't had time for is this: to establish a new field called "omnology." You know how tons of people are interested in oodles of things, but know no one will take them seriously unless they specialize? Well, omnology's designed to give them permission to be curious about whatever excites them. Here's the manifesto:

We are blessed with a richness of specializations, but cursed with a paucity of panoptic disciplines — categories of knowledge that concentrate on seeing the pattern that emerges when one views all the sciences at once. Hence we need a field dedicated to the panoramic, an academic base for the promiscuously curious, a discipline whose mandate is best summed up in a paraphrase of the poet Andrew Marvell:

Let us roll all our strength and all
Our knowledge up into one ball
And tear our visions with rough strife
Thorough the iron gates of life.

Omnology is a science, but one dedicated to the biggest picture conceivable by the minds of its practitioners. Omnology will use every conceptual tool available — and some not yet invented but inventible — to leapfrog over disciplinary barriers, stitching together the patchwork quilt of science and all the rest that humans can yet know. If one omnologist is able to perceive the relationship between pop songs, ancient Egyptian graffiti, Shirley MacLaine's mysticism, neurobiology, and the origins of the cosmos, so be it. If another uses mathematics to probe traffic patterns, the behavior of insect colonies, and the manner in which galaxies cluster in swarms, wonderful. And if another uses introspection to uncover hidden passions and relate them to research in chemistry, anthropology, psychology, history, and the arts, she, too, has a treasured place on the wild frontiers of scientific truth

— the *terra incognita* at the heartland of omnology. Let me close with the words of yet another poet, William Blake, on the ultimate goal of omnology:

To see a World in a Grain of Sand And a Heaven in a Wild Flower, Hold Infinity in the palm of your hand And Eternity in an hour.

Struck By Noetic Lightning:
Terence McKenna
Meets the Machine Elves of Hyperspace
by MARK DERY (2001)

TERENCE MCKENNA DIED OF BRAIN CANCER ON APRIL 3, 2000.
He was 53. This article was originally published in the late, much-lamented
Australian cyberzine *21C* ("The Inner Elf: Terence McKenna's Trip," *21C*, #3,
1996) and later reprinted in the *21C* anthology *Transit Lounge* (Craftsman
House, 1997). Its centerpiece is a lengthy interview with McKenna, conducted in two epic sessions in 1996. As a rule, I maintain a zero-tolerance
policy toward New Age vacuity. Even so, I looked forward to interviewing
McKenna, whose writings and interviews offered unquestionable evidence
of a prodigious intellect, sweeping erudition, and a nimble wit. I was not
disappointed. A foeman worthy of anyone's steel, he proved to be as gen-
erous of spirit as he was intellectually formidable. Though some of his
ideas struck me — still strike me — as so much refried ectoplasm, I was
enchanted by his silver-tongued eloquence: equal parts Irish tale-spinning,
scholarly discourse, and Joycean river-run. And that voice: drawling, nasal,
sly with irony, suffering fools graciously, if not gladly. Like many, I'll think
of Terence on December 12, 2012, the portentous day his Transcendental

Object at the End of Time is supposed to arrive. Whether it will or not, he only knows.

On a rainy February evening in 1967, fueled by the mind-morphing hallucinogen dimethyltryptamine (DMT), Terence McKenna's ontological warp drive engaged, leaving a contrail of frozen light where his ego used to be. James Joyce would have dubbed the event an "epiphany." The psychologist Abraham Maslow would have called it a "peak experience." The sci-fi writer Philip K. Dick would have used the Platonic term anamnesis, the recollection of the absolute truths hidden within us. And a theologian would refer to it as a *metanoia*, or metamorphosis of consciousness.

In his lecture, "Psychedelics Before and After History," McKenna describes it as "a revelation of an alien dimension — a brightly lit, non-three-dimensional, self-contorting, linguistically intending modality that couldn't be denied." Imagine the inside of your cranium, redecorated with frescoes of the Marvel Comics cosmology by Jack Kirby, or a Disneyland "dark ride" based on a near-death experience as envisioned by Benoit Mandlebrot, or a virtual reality tour of God's cerebral cortex, hosted by the Lucky Charms leprechaun. McKenna recalled the episode in a recording of a 1987 lecture:

> I sank to the floor. I [experienced] this hallucination of tumbling forward into these fractal geometric spaces made of light and then I found myself in the equivalent of the Pope's private chapel and there were insect elf machines proffering strange little tablets with strange writing on them, and I was aghast, completely appalled, because [in] a matter of seconds . . . my entire expectation of the nature of the world was just being shredded in front of me. I've never actually gotten over it. These self-transforming machine elf creatures were speaking in a colored language which condensed into rotating machines that were like Fabergé eggs but crafted out of luminescent superconducting

ceramics and liquid crystal gels. All this stuff was just so weird and so alien and so un-English-able that it was a complete shock — I mean, the literal turning inside out of [my] intellectual universe!

This went on for two or three minutes, this situation of [discontinuous] orthogonal dimensions to reality just engulfing me. As I came out of it and the room reassembled itself, I said, 'I can't believe it, it's impossible.' To call that a drug is ridiculous; that just means that you just don't have a word for it and so you putter around and you come upon this sloppy concept [that] something goes into your body and there's a change. It's not like that; it's like being struck by noetic lightning." [Author's note: "Noetic" derives from the theologian Pierre Teilhard de Chardin's "noosphere" — the collective consciousness of humankind conceived of as a sort of philosophical virtuality.]

[What] astonished me was [that] . . . in the carpets of Central Asia, in the myths of the Maya, in the visions of an Arcimboldi or a Fra Angelico or a Bosch, there is not a hint, not a clue, not an atom of the presence of this thing," says McKenna. "This was more [multiplex] than the universe that we share with each other. It was the victory of Neo-Platonic metaphysics; everything [was] made out of a fourth-dimensional mosaic of energy. I was knocked off my feet, and set myself the goal of understanding this. There was really no choice, you see."

McKenna's quest led him to Nepal and Tibet, where his studies of Central Asian art and culture reaffirmed his belief that, contrary to Timothy Leary and Ralph Metzner's assertions in their switched-on version of the *Tibetan Book of the Dead*, the psychedelic experience had no strict corollaries in traditional systems of esoteric thought. Nonetheless, the pre-Buddhist shamanism of Nepal and Tibet, which involved the use of hashish and datura, had captured his imagination. Delving deeper into the subject, he traveled to the outer islands of Indonesia, where he spent a year in search of an indigenous tradition of magico-religious drug usage, supporting himself through the suitably surreal "blood sport" of professional butterfly collecting.

Finding none, he journeyed to the Amazon Basin in 1970, where the Waika and Yanomamo Indians inhale a powdered form of the visionary vine ayahuasca. "The dominant motif is a flood of visual imagery that, try as one might, one cannot recognize as the contents of either the personal or the collective unconscious," he says, in "Sacred Plants and Mystic Realities," an interview included in his book *The Archaic Revival: Speculations on Psychedelic Mushrooms, the Amazon, Virtual Reality, UFOs, Evolution, Shamanism, the Rebirth of the Goddess, and the End of History* (HarperCollins, 1992). "This was truly fascinating to me. I had made a thorough study of Jung and therefore had the expectation that motifs and idea systems from the unconscious mind would prove to be reasonably homogeneous worldwide. What I found, instead, with the peak intoxication from these plants, was a world of ideas, visual images, and noetic insight that really could not be co-mapped on any tradition — even the esoteric tradition. This was so fascinating to me that I have made it the compass of my life."

In the years since his fateful encounter with the self-transforming machine elves of hyperspace, McKenna has elaborated a personal cosmology which for funhouse logic and fever dream detail rivals the Palais Ideal of the "outsider" artist Ferdinand Cheval — a sprawling delirium of temples, towers, monuments, grottoes, spiral stairways, and statuary, fashioned from cement studded with pebbles and encrusted with shells. A born raconteur, he has fashioned his mental Merzbau on the New Age lecture circuit, where his effortless eloquence, encyclopedic erudition, and inside-out wit have earned him the benediction of the psychedelic High Priest himself, who dubbed McKenna "the Timothy Leary of the '90s."

Entertainment Weekly, an unimpeachable source on spiritual matters, lumped him together with Deepak Chopra, Tony Robbins, and Marianne Williamson in a round-up of "power gurus," and rave bands such as the Shamen have set his ruminations to billowing techno-trance music. His theories are expounded in his books (*The Archaic Revival, True Hallucinations, Food of the Gods: The Search for the Original Tree of Knowledge*, and *The Invisible Landscape* [Scribner, 1976], co-authored with his brother Dennis, a respected ethnopharmacologist) but McKenna's metier is the spoken word — stand-up philosophy that meme-splices Alfred North Whitehead and Alfred E. Neuman, delivered in a reedy, insinuating voice that sounds like Paul Lynde doing an impression of Don Juan (the Yaqui Indian sorcerer, not the legendary Spanish rake). Available on tapes with titles like "Having Archaic and Eating it Too" and "Shedding the Monkey," his lectures are tours de force of verbal virtuosity and pack-rat polymathy, leaping trippingly (in both senses of the word) from quantum mechanics to medieval alchemy, from the chaos theory of Ilya Prigogine to the neo-Platonism of Philo Judaeus. Elevating ontology hacking to an art form, McKenna brings Carl Sagan's worst nightmare to life: the reason, rhetoric, and technical vocabulary of science appropriated in the service of a unified field theory concocted from psychedelic Darwinism, fringe linguistics, and New Age eschatology.

Tens of millennia ago, he theorizes, climatic changes forced the proto-human primates of the African savannah to abandon their exclusively vegetarian diet for an omnivorous one. Following the vast herds of wild cattle whose dung harbored the insects that were undoubtedly part of their new diet, they cannot have missed the striking *stropharia cubensis* (magic mushrooms) growing in the cowpies. "The mushroom is a totally anomalous object in the grassland environment — it stands out like a sore thumb," asserts McKenna, in "Sacred Plants and Mystic Realities." According to McKenna, natural selection would favor the mushroom-eating apes, since psilocybin (the psychoactive ingredient in cubensis) has been proven to enhance visual acuity and stimulate sexual desire. Citing Henry Munn's essay "The Mushrooms of Language" and Julian Jaynes's *Origins of Consciousness in the Breakdown of the Bicameral Mind* (University of Toronto Press, 1978), he argues that psilocybin catalyzed the emergence of language in early hominids by expanding "their arboreally evolved repertoire of troop signals" into the hunting-pack signaling necessary for survival in their new environment. "It is reasonable to suggest that human language arose out of the synergy of primate organizational potential by plant hallucinogens," he writes, in "Mushrooms and Evolution" (from *The Archaic Revival*).

From there, it's only a silly millimeter to the edge. "Hallucinogenic plants may have been the catalysts for everything about us that distinguishes us from other primates, except perhaps the loss of body hair," writes McKenna. "All of the mental functions that we associate with humanness, including recall, projective imagination, language, naming, magical speech, dance, and a sense of religion may have emerged out of interaction with hallucinogenic plants." During one particularly memorable trip, the mushroom told him (his words) that it is literally not of this world, that, in fact, stropharia cubensisis is an alien symbiote whose spores were borne across the galaxy. If this scenario sounds strangely reminiscent of *Invasion of the Body Snatchers*, with its extraterrestrial "pod" plants, it's worth mentioning that as an "odd kid" growing up in a remote Colorado town in the 1950s, McKenna was an avid fan of the seminal science fiction magazine *Weird Tales*. In his defense, however, it should be noted that no less reputable a scientist than Francis Crick has advanced the theory of directed panspermia, which proposes that all life on this planet somehow sprang from extraterrestrial spores, possibly engineered by a higher intelligence. Alternately, suggests McKenna, the mushroom may be an intergalactic communications device, "allowing me to hear the alien when the alien is actually light- years away, using some kind of Bell nonlocality principle to communicate."

Ironically, in enabling our quantum leap out of nature and into culture via the abstraction of embodied experience through language, the mushroom set in motion an evolutionary telos that McKenna believes will culminate in a union of signifier and signified. In a cyberdelic variation on Marshall McLuhan's vision of *Homo Cyber* "retribalized" by electronic interconnectedness, McKenna envisions the magical reassembly of the primordial world- view shattered by language, like the shards of a broken vase flying together in a film run backwards. "[W]e will recover what we knew in the beginning: the archaic union with nature that was seamless, unmediated by language, unmediated by notions of self and other, of life and death, of civilization and nature," says McKenna, in a 1988 interview ("In Praise of Psychedelics," *The Archaic Revival*).

Humanity's post-Logos apotheosis will be precipitated, says McKenna, by the arrival of "the Transcendental Object at the End of Time." A cross between the enigmatic monolith from *2001: A Space Odyssey* and de Chardin's Omega Point (an evolutionary epiphany that marks the arrival of an "Ultra-Humanity"), McKenna's Transcendental Object is, in his words, a "cosmic singularity" — a term from chaos theory which refers to the transition point, in a dynamical system, between one state and another. Evolution, he asserts, in Douglas Rushkoff's *Cyberia* (Harper Collins, 1994), is poised to break free of "the chrysalis of matter . . . and then look back on a cast-off mode of being as it rises into a higher dimension."

The question of the literal truth or falsity of McKenna's theories is largely irrelevant, since they so obviously function as bedtime stories for cyborgs, spun from Arthur C. Clarke-ian sci-fi mysticism, New Age millenarianism, and the Dionysian "expressive politics" of the '60s (specifically, Norman O. Brown in *Love's Body*). Understood as theology, they take on almost conventional shapes: the fateful fungus and the tumble into language as the story of the fall of man; McKenna's visionary experience in "fractal geometric spaces made of light" as Saul's conversion on the road to Damascus ("suddenly a light from heaven flashed around him," Acts 9:3); and the Transcendental Object at the End of Time as the eschaton foretold in the Revelation.

Intriguingly, McKenna was raised in the Catholic tradition, a background he shares with one of his acknowledged influences, the devout Roman Catholic Marshall McLuhan. In *Escape Velocity: Cyberculture at the End of the Century* (Grove Press, 1996), I note that for McLuhan as for McKenna, the invention of the written word was the "separating membrane," dividing the "I" from the "all-that-is-not-I" and casting Western civilization into the postlapsarian world of isolation, objectivity, and rationality. His limning of this event in a 1969 *Playboy* interview sounds unmistakably like the Biblical allegory of the fall:

> The whole man became fragmented man; the alphabet shattered the charmed circle and resonating magic of the tribal world, exploding man into an agglomeration of specialized and psychically impoverished individuals, or units, functioning in a world of linear time and Euclidean space.

Elsewhere in the same interview, McLuhan holds forth the McKenna-esque hope that the psychic convergence facilitated by electronic media

> could create the universality of consciousness foreseen by Dante when he predicted that men would continue as no more than broken fragments until they were unified into an inclusive consciousness. In a Christian sense, this is merely a new interpretation of the mystical body of Christ; and Christ, after all, is the ultimate extension of man ... I expect to see the coming decades transform the planet into an art form; the new man, linked in a cosmic harmony that transcends

time and space, will . . . himself . . . become an organic art form. There is a long road ahead, and the stars are only way stations, but we have begun the journey.

Likewise, for McKenna, a self-styled "mouthpiece for the incarnate Logos," history will only achieve closure when the disembodying technology of language is at last re-embodied — when the Word is made flesh, in other words.

MARK DERY: *The ability to hold apparently contradictory ideas in one's mind is "the test of a first-rate intelligence," to quote F. Scott Fitzgerald. Even so, your attitude toward technology seems somewhat inconsistent. In your recorded lecture, "Shamanic Approaches to the UFO: Angels, Aliens, and Archetypes Symposium," you inveigh against it, maintaining that technology is a "demonic pact" that has led "to the present cultural and political impasse, [which] involves massive stockpiles of atomic weapons, propagandized populations cut off from any knowledge of their real histories, [and] male-dominated organizations plying their message of lethal destruction and inevitable historical advance." At the same time, in your lecture "Psychedelics Before and After History," you conjure a cybernetic Arcadia made possible by nanotechnology, where "the technological appurtenances of the present world have been shrunk to the point where they have disappeared into [nature] and . . . we all live naked in paradise but only a thought away is all the cybernetic connectedness and ability to deliver manufactured goods and data that this world possesses."*

TERENCE MCKENNA: I'm mistrustful of the dynamic at work in high technology, but you've probably heard me quote the French sociologist Jacques Ellul, who said, "There are no political solutions, only technological ones; the rest is propaganda." I believe that. I feel a commitment to democratic pluralism, but other than that, political solutions seem fraught with difficulties. I believe in what I call a forward escape, meaning that you can't go back and you can't stand still, so you've got to go forward and technology is the way to do this. Technology is an extension of the human mental world, and it's certainly where our salvation is going to come from; we cannot return to the hunter-gatherer pastoralism of 15,000 years ago. As far as the antithetical positions that you hung on me, I would just say, along with Oscar Wilde, "I contradict myself? I contradict myself!"

MD: *I'm not sure that there's a contradiction, since you seem to fall neatly on one side of the fence, for the most part — that of New Age techno-eschatology. Then again, there's an obvious contradiction in the fact that you vilify language and yet you're a virtuoso raconteur with a gift for wordplay.*

TM: Well, when I talk about the Logos I always invoke Philo Judaeus, who introduced the concept of the Logos into the Hellenistic world but who was unsatisfied with it and spent a great deal of time talking about the more perfect Logos, the Logos that goes from being heard to being seen without ever crossing over a definable moment of transition. In a sense, my position is that all of history is a making of the Logos more and more concrete. In the same way that McLuhan saw print culture as replacing an earlier, eye-oriented manuscript culture, my hope is that cyberdelic culture is going to overcome the linear, uniform bias of print and carry us into a realm of the visible Logos. I really believe that not only human society is involved in what could be looked at as a conquest of dimensions but that biology itself is, as well. This is the great overarching theme of evolution — this is why we go from being slime mold to having binocular vision and bipedalism and then adding memory and language at the top end of animal organization. It's because the thing which we are, whether you call it bios or Logos incarnate or whatever, is striving to ascend to higher and higher dimensions.

MD: *And if I understand you, that ascension leads inevitably to a state where the name for the thing and the thing itself are reunited in a sort of epistemological epiphany?*

TM: Exactly.

MD: *But aren't you chasing the same mirage intellectuals have pursued down the centuries, from Plato's "Allegory of the Cave" to Baudrillard's "Precession of the Simulacrum?" Isn't it in the nature of human perception that we see things darkly, rather than as they "really" are? And doesn't Heisenberg's uncertainty principle suggest that reality itself is a slippery concept? The notion of an ultimate reality seems to be an ontological illusion; the closer we get, the further it recedes.*

TM: Well, this may be true, but on the other hand, it's not that it's not real, it's that it's never realized; it serves as an arrow for the process. I mean, these problems were completely solved within the context of the sixteenth century, but that didn't end history, and now we're trying to solve the problems of the eighteenth and nineteenth century. When we do, I don't think it will usher in the absolute stasis of the eschaton; it will simply define a new cultural playing ground for us. But there's no question that as a result of the phonetic alphabet and Western religion and the growth of the ego and industrial power, we are facing a narrow neck. The world didn't end when Rome fell, but the *Roman* world ended when Rome fell, and what I'm trying to do is put a little spin control on the electronic world that is going to emerge out of the ashes of the assumptions of capitalism, communism, linear print culture, heavy industrial culture, and so forth.

MD: *Are you suggesting that even though we've passed into post-industrial culture, our worldview is still shaped by the mechanical paradigms of the industrial age?*

TM: Yes. Spencerian social theory and the economics of Smith and Keynes:

these are the thoughts that rule our society, and they're all nineteenth century. Ever since the birth of the atomic bomb and the electronic and psychedelic technologies that were emerging at the same time, we have essentially lived on the capital built up by these nineteenth-century ideologies. One of the problems with cyberculture is that these ideologies don't match our technologies.

MD: *What would an ideology better suited to our technological landscape look like?*

TM: Well, what these new technologies are doing is dissolving boundaries. The nation state, the monolithic party, and the nuclear family — all boundary-defined institutions of one sort or another — are legacies of the past; what we need is an ideology that is mercurial, shifting, nonstatic. And as long as we're talking about mercury and mercurial things, there is in alchemy (a pre-modern form of thinking) the idea of the coincidencia oppositorum, which means that you have to have ideologies which are able to accommodate positions which, within the context of the previous ideology, would've appeared contradictory. The very notion of noncontradiction is a notion that emerges out of the linear, print-created mindset; the whole sterility of that worldview is its inability to live with the presence of contradiction. And so it denies it, which creates the unconscious of a society where we've got serial killers running around. The world is not as simple as we desperately wish to make it within the context of the linear worldview.

MD: *The notion that we've said goodbye to the Gutenberg Galaxy is a McLuhanesque perception. You often invoke McLuhan, who built his historiography on a bedrock of technodeterminism. But is the presumption that our worldview is shaped by the technologies of our age the best way to analyze culture and history?*

TM: I think it's a good method, although I would hate to be caught saying it's always the way to go. I suppose the reason I'm so enthusiastic about psychedelics, at this point, is not because I think they're a sure fix, but because I really register the urgency of the situation. If this boat could have been turned around by mere hortatory rhetoric, it would have been turned around by the Sermon on the Mount. We don't have a lot of time, and the only thing that I have ever seen change a lot of peoples' minds in a hurry is psychedelics. So I advocate them not as the best solution but as a wild long shot that's the only game in town at this point.

MD: *Help me keep all the spaghetti on my fork, here; I'm having difficulty with the loose ends. You're saying on the one hand that what cyberculture needs is a brave new ideology consonant with its technologies, and on the other hand that you believe in technological solutions, which would seem to render ideology irrelevant. Doesn't this return us to the Carousel of Progress in Disneyland? Wasn't looking for technological solutions to what are essentially social or political problems the keystone of technocratic thinking in the '50s and '60s?*

TM: I think we've always had these two factions, one thinking that utopia was just around the corner with the next invention, and the other claiming things always stay the same. Again, it's a coincidencia oppositorum that things do stay the same but on the other hand they're changing at a faster and faster rate. So it isn't a matter of making a choice between these things; it's a matter of substituting a kind of Boolean logic where you can simultaneously hold both possibilities as potentially realizable even though in a different kind of logic they may appear incommensurate. This is the kind of world we're living in.

As an example of that, think about quantum physics, which is the basic metaphor of the new civilization: in quantum physics, you have ordinary logic, the either/or kind of logic we're all familiar with, and then embedded like raisins in bread dough in that logic you have what are called Isles of Boole — Boolean logic, incommensurate with the logic that surrounds it. That quantum mechanical image can be raised right up to the level of the macrophysical realm we're living in. Contradiction is not a problem; contradiction is the proof that you're actually dealing with the "real."

Science is in real crisis because the guy who works for some company developing products in an R&D environment and thinks of himself as a scientist has probably never read a work on the philosophy of science, and the philosophy of science is in deep, deep trouble. The Isles of Boole embedded in ordinary logic or the implications of Gödel's Incompleteness Theorem are the death knell for what most people think of as scientific thinking because they've allowed us to scratch down into the levels of reality where we confront not truth as it was assumed to exist in the nineteenth century but rather this magical coincidencia oppositorum. The world really is based on contradictions; nowhere is it writ large that the primate mind should be able to hold within its confines a correct model of being, and yet this is what science assumes.

The New Age has used the new physics to contest the traditional scientific notion of an objective, absolute truth and thereby legitimate its own worldview ever since Fritjof Capra's *The Tao of Physics* (Wildwood House, 1975).

MD: *It's my understanding that you make your living on the New Age circuit, lecturing at places like the Esalen Institute or the Omega Institute for Holistic Studies in upstate New York. Nonetheless, in an earlier conversation, you told me, "I am not New Age; I loathe all this Fall-of-Atlantis, color-therapy stuff — it's just bunk." Even so, in the Q&A sessions on your lecture tapes, you're very indulgent toward channeling, UFOs, and other notions dear to the New Age. In fact, in your taped lecture "Shamanic Approaches to the UFO," you say, "I have had contact experiences, I have seen a UFO very close, I have* *met with entities from other dimensions." In such moments, you adequately earn the label "New Age"; either that, or you're using terms like "UFO" and "entities" metaphorically, which makes me wonder if this is just a tactful way of not alienating paying customers.*

TM: Well, I do feel a distance between myself and the New Age, most of which is just menopausal mysticism. But let me break your question into two parts: First of all, whenever I mention channeling, I say that if you can do this without drugs, you're probably mentally ill. Now, the experiences of spinning disks in the sky that fill the supermarket tabloids are a whole other can of worms. Have you read Jung's book, *Flying Saucers: A Modern Myth of Things Seen in the Sky* (Fine Communications, 1997)? It's the best book ever written on UFOs; it appeared within two years of the first flying saucer sighting in 1948, and it essentially solves the mystery.

MD: *If I recall, your reading of Jung led you to conclude that flying saucers in the sense of extraterrestrial machines do not exist, but that they are a sort of phantasmagoric manifestation of the collective Id erupting into the mass imagination.*

TM: Well, there's more to it than that. This acceleration of history and technology that we are so intensely experiencing — and which we can look back into history and see has been going on for a long time — is, in fact, real, and we are being pushed toward what I call the Transcendental Object at the End of Time, which can be thought of as the ultimate tool in three-dimensional space. It's a higher dimensional object of some sort and either this thing is coming to meet us (which raises questions I can't answer) or we are summoning it out of ourselves. By virtue of its hyper-dimensionality, the Transcendental Object is acting as an attractor in the historical continuum. It sets off sparks or resonances that go back through time so that when the farmer in Iowa sees the spinning disk in the sky, he overlays it with his Fundamentalist religious upbringing, his reading of supermarket tabloids, and so forth; he dresses it in these culturally conventionalized ideas. But what it is is a true (again, this phrase) coincidencia oppositorum, the epistemic umbilical mark of reality; it is proof that there is a telos to the historical process. This planet is haunted at the higher levels by archetypes of various sorts and the entire historical thrust is toward confrontation with the Other. If you're living in the sixteenth century, it's conceived of as a visitation by the Virgin Mary; in the twentieth century, it's interpreted as friendly extraterrestrials from Zeta Reticuli. But in fact what it is is none of these things; in truth, it is the Other — that which cannot be reduced to anything familiar in our world — and the process of history is the shock wave which announces the eminence of this rupture of reality by this Transcendental Object.

MD: *You'll forgive me for being so mulish, but I've found a drill-bit insistence on hard facts to be a rather effective way of boring through opaque rhetoric. What, exactly, is the Transcendental Object at the End of Time? How did you arrive at this concept?*

TM: Basically, from reading Jung on alchemy. Do you know anything about alchemy?

MD: *A little; is your Object a cross between the Philosopher's Stone and the monolith in* 2001: A Space Odyssey?

TM: That's exactly it; Jung liked to talk about how, in the pre-scientific age, when people were naive about the categorical separation between mind and matter, they were able to imagine a migration of terms so that what was matter and what was mind would come together in something which was of the nature of both and neither. I would say that we are still epistemologically naive about the nature of mind and matter and that history is the effort to build a tool, and that tool is the self, and the self is this transdimensional vehicle; it transcends life and death, it transcends space and time, it is both here and there, it is both real and unreal, and so forth and so on.

So history does have a purpose and the revelation of this purpose is not that far in the future. In fact, the chaos of the twentieth century signifies that the historical process is coming to an end. We are now in a position to actually understand and confront this Transcendental Object at the End of Time and we are drilling toward it with psychedelic drugs and cybernetic machinery and so forth, and it is drilling toward us in its fashion (which is incomprehensible to us at this point).

At the same time, we're caught up in the nineteenth century desire to eliminate teleology from thinking about the world in order to keep Darwinism uncontaminated by deism. That has to be put aside because there is in fact a teleological attractor, and fields like chaos and catastrophe theory completely legitimize this kind of thinking in a scientific context which was not possible in the nineteenth century because they couldn't conceive of that.

MD: *With the aid of a programmer, you've produced a software package called Timewave Zero that illustrates your vision of the end of history — on December 12, 2012, to be exact — with the arrival of the ineffable mysterium tremendum that you call the Transcendental Object at the End of Time. Is your zero hour a poetic metaphor or an actual calendar date?*

TM: You mean how seriously do I take it? Well, as a rationalist I don't take it seriously at all. I mean, these things are models. On the other hand, I'm puzzled, because I have a whole theory about time that is a true theory — not a conversational theory, but a mathematical formalism, a fractal that describes the topology of temporality, which in Newtonian physics is assumed to be a smooth surface. I substitute for the traditional zero curvature a complex fractal dimension, and then I can see that all time that we have any data about, meaning historical or paleontological or whatever, can be mapped onto this fractal. But with a peculiar caveat: for the wave to fit the data, it must be generated from A.D. 2012.

MD: *But millenarians throughout history have fixed on arbitrary endpoints and adduced an abundance of evidence to support their prophesies. Inevitably, the great day comes and goes and history grinds on.*

TM: I'm well aware of the slippery nature of prophesy, and how once a prophesy is made, there is ample evidence at hand to support it. However, I think the evidence is that we are pointed toward a very tight choke point of some sort, and people who blithely assume that history will be a going concern in 500 or 1,000 years don't seem to have grokked the transformative power of technology. My Timewave Zero software places tools in your hands for you to decide whether this theory is just the product of too much psilocybin; it's a laboratory for moving this wave around and looking at it against historical data. This complex mathematical object is a touchstone for connecting a bunch of different data points that otherwise would appear completely unrelated to each other. I'm very aware of the selectivity of perception and the slippery nature of historical data, but if I could corner you with this software for a couple of hours, I could at least shake your faith that 2012 is going to be a year like any other.

MD: *Are there any parallels between your Transcendental Object and Tipler's Omega Point? [Author's note: In the weeks that elapsed between the two epic sessions in which this interview was recorded, I sent McKenna some articles by the physicist Frank J. Tipler which I thought might interest him. The essays in question set forth themes elaborated in Tipler's* Physics of Immortality: Modern Cosmology, God and the Resurrection of the Dead *(Doubleday, 1994), where he offers nothing less than a "testable physical theory for an omnipresent, omniscient, omnipotent God who will one day in the far future resurrect every single one of us to live forever in an abode which is in all* *essentials the Judeo-Christian heaven." Tipler posits an Omega Point (a term borrowed from the French theologian Pierre Teilhard de Chardin) of infinite density and temperature toward which the universe will collapse in a backwards Big Bang called the Big Crunch. The energy generated by this implosion could be used, he theorizes, to drive a cosmic computer simulator (think of* Star Trek: The Next Generation'*s holodeck) with infinite processing power — enough, certainly, to bring back to (virtual) life every creature that ever lived.]*

TM: I'm in complete agreement with Tipler and Teilhard de Chardin except that I'm willing to actually talk about the endpoint as imminent. I thought that Tipler's response to the German theologian ("The Omega Point as Eschaton: Answers to Pannenberg's Questions for Scientists," *Zygon*, vol. 24, no. 2, June 1989), was an incredibly creative piece of dreaming — all these ideas about computers of such size that the entire universe can be modeled raise the possibility of fairly apocalyptic scenarios. And the speed at which microminiaturization and computing power are going forward makes it not unreasonable that some of the scenarios that Tipler is talking about could probably be realized pretty much by 2012. The rate of technological acceleration in many fields is such that when you propagate all these curves forward into the future, you see that sometime after the turn of the century they seem to go asymptotic or become infinite. I would like to hear more from Tipler about his eschaton theory and know a bit about the background of this kind of thinking. The notion of an attractor seems to have re-legitimized teleology in science.

MD: *Yours seems to be a teleology of strange attractors.*

TM: You could call it that. Have you read *Process and Reality* by Alfred North Whitehead (Free Press, 1978)? That's where my whole metaphysic is drawn from; Whitehead has a concept that he calls "concrescence," and by that he means the eschaton, the Omega Point, the Transcendental Object at the End of Time. What I've done is simply take the Whiteheadian meta-physic and create a mathematical model that is consistent with his concept and then shown how it would work as a heuristic machine.

MD: *Don't you draw on Bateson as well?*
TM: I hardly know anything about Bateson, although I do occasionally use his phrase "the pattern which connects," but my intellectual roots are Jung, McLuhan, and Whitehead, and perhaps a little Thomas Aquinas, imbibed without realizing it as a result of being raised Catholic.

MD: *I'd like to re-attack the question of the New Age's relationship to science and technology. In* Strange Weather: Culture, Science, and Technology in the Age of Limits *(Verso, 1991), Andrew Ross writes, "If metaphysicians no longer habitually find themselves placed in the anti-science corner, it is because theoretical science in the wake of quantum physics has shattered the intellectual security of the mechanical picture of discontinuous time, space, matter, and objectivity." He goes on to note that some in the New Age community "have made common cause with quantum physics, finding among the more speculative adherents of that discipline a tolerance for mysticism that complements their own holistic metaphysics and a new raison d'etre for closing the gap between the two cultures." What do you make of such developments?*
TM: Before, science was based on calculability and sober reflection, whereas now it's based on premises which most people would find highly irrational and counterintuitive. I feel pretty comfortable being on the side of the philosophy of science but it's post-Newtonian, post-quantum physics science. I'm a little suspicious of the New Age's appropriation of the language of quantum physics, because I think most of these people couldn't solve a partial differential equation if their lives depended on it; they're just surfing on the obfuscation of quantum physics that its mathematical basis provides.

MD: *With all due respect, could you solve a partial differential equation?*

TM: No, but I don't call on quantum physics to support my point of view.

MD: *But you often wrap your ideas in the mantle of science by using scientific terminology.*

TM: There's science and then there's reason, and science has at times used reason, although at times its conclusions have been fairly unreasonable. Reason is a universal method for dealing with information, whereas science is an extremely culturally conventionalized method. I think there's a role for reason and the razors of logic, but this is a branch of formal philosophy, not a branch of science; science appropriates everything to itself and then we tend to genuflect before it, but what we really need is a relativistic approach to the true scope of science which is considerably less than it has claimed for itself. In the twentieth century, it's claimed to be the arbiter of truth in all domains when in fact it's simply the study of those phenomena so crude that the restoration of their initial condition causes the same thing to repeat itself, and that's a very small part of the sum total of the phenomenal universe.

The question of whether or not what's ultimately important about a scientific theory is its mathematical foundation or its popular misconception is an interesting one. You should take a look at Misia Landau's book *Narratives of Human Evolution* (Yale University Press, 1991), in which she argues from a lit-crit point of view that the theory of evolution is nothing more than a campfire story, with all the elements of good theater. It has someone of poor and humble and origins who goes a great distance in search of a great gift, forming alliances along the way and finally attaining this gift, but it brings him self-doubt rather than happiness, and so on. I view everything as narrative and science is simply a part of that; its reliance on mathematics is much less impressive to its high priests than it is to the rest of us.

MD: *So you make common cause with the post-structuralists to the degree that you view science as a text to be read closely for traces of culturally constructed, rather than empirically verifiable, meaning.*

TM: I'm a little uncomfortable being connected with deconstructionism, having just read Camille Paglia (anybody who read *Sexual Personae* [Yale University Press, 1990] would be uncomfortable being connected with those people!). But I think these critiques need to be done. Imre Lakatos, a Greek philosopher of science who wrote a very influential book called *Criticism and the Growth of Knowledge* (Cambridge University Press, 1970), talks about how certain theories which we accept as scientific have in fact been very reluctant to state the circumstances under which they would be proven false, which is what characterizes real science. Freudianism, for instance, is in this position: no Freudian has ever said what piece of evidence would be necessary in order to abandon Freud.

MD: *But isn't the question of falsification a moot point for someone interested in "reading" a discourse as reflective of cultural biases? The empirical grounding — or lack thereof — of Freudianism seems irrelevant, in such a context.*

TM: Well, I think you do have to ask this question of falsification, ultimately. For instance, in my own theory of time I've been very concerned to make it clear that if the historical continuum does not exhibit certain properties then the theory should be dumped.

What is interesting about the Timewave is that it seems to supply a map of historical vicissitude, a map that you can confirm for yourself by looking at how it maps the past, which then gives you a certain measure of confidence as you notice that it seems to map the immediate future astonishingly well. Where the cognitive dissonance enters into it is that all of these mappings only work if you assume a major singularity emergent on the 12th of December, 2012. That's such a screwy position that most people grow fairly uncomfortable with it. I mean, here is a formal mathematical theory which nevertheless has built into it a bearded character carrying a sign that says, "Repent, for the end is near!"

MD: *How comfortable are you with the stickiness of that position?*
TM: Well, I'm not entirely comfortable. On the other hand, if you look at the orthodox position on the universe, it's that it sprang from nothing in a single moment. You would be hard pressed to construct a tighter limit test for creditability than that! All I'm saying is that the singularity is more likely to spring from a very complex situation than to spring from what is a completely featureless situation, which is what the Big Bang says.

MD: *But you're turning a semantic somersault, there: Science's position is not that everything sprang from nothing, but rather that we do not know what the state of the universe was one picosecond before what we now theorize happened.*
TM: You're right; they don't say the universe sprang from nothing, they say we can calculate back to a moment when it was smaller than the diameter of the electron and then we can't calculate any further, and they call that last picosecond the prephysical era, indicating that it's somehow bad taste to attempt to push the laws of physics into that realm. But it seems to me that this is not a wit different from saying, "Let there be light," and resting with that. It's much more likely that the universe is driven by a singularity, but the singularity is of the nature of an attractor rather than an impelling force. Thus, it isn't a coincidence that at a high point of human history the singularity occurs; what I'm suggesting is that history is a phenomenon which announces the imminence of the concrescence: you only get language-using, technology-elaborating animals a geological nanosecond before the singularity occurs.

MD: *But what is the engine that drives that teleology?*

TM: Well, now we go on to Tipler's paper: It's this Omega Point that he's raving about. What's fascinating about Tipler's paper is that he's saying that physics supports the de Chardinian point of view, which is a theological point of view, but he, like de Chardin, makes the unnecessary assumption that the Omega Point is far away in time, when actually there's no way of making a judgment as to our distance from it based on what is present in Tipler or de Chardin. What I've come up with is a map of the temporal continuum which, when you have fitted its saw-toothed edges into the ebb and flow of historical vicissitude, enables you to look at the end of the wave and discover that far from meandering millennia or mega-millennia into the future, it actually comes to ground 21 years into the future.

MD: *What exactly will happen in 2012?*

TM: I've given a lot of thought to this and the answers range over a spectrum, from soft to hard. The softest version is: nothing at all. The Seventh Day Adventists believe the end of the world occurred in 1830, which is a *very* soft version; it can happen and you don't even notice! In the extreme, hard version, which maps Whiteheadian metaphysics onto Christian eschatology, the stars fall from heaven, the oceans boil, the dead rise, and so forth — in other words, a complete breakdown of ordinary physics.

MD: *But aren't you fudging the disprovability of your theory, given that the spectrum of possible proofs includes an event, on the extreme "soft" end, whose cultural reverberations are below the threshold of detectability? If nothing perceptible happened on December 12, 2012, how would an outside observer discern whether you simply got the date wrong, or the predicted event transpired but was simply beneath the threshold of registration?*

TM: Well, you need to move into the domain of what's called best-fit theories of curve matching. In other words, we have a curve — the Timewave — and we have a data field — human history — and what's needed is an impartial method of matching the curve to history. This is a difficult problem but not in principle an insoluble one; what makes it difficult on the face of it is that history is not a quantified data field — you don't get good agreement about what the vicissitudes of history really mean. However, there is a kind of vague consensus that you could use to guide you. If you had a thousand tenured professors of history and you asked them to name the ten most important turning points of the last 5,000 years, there would be a fairly high percentage of agreement on the Golden Age of Greece, the Italian Renaissance, the fall of the Roman Empire, and so forth as having global consequence upon all peoples that followed upon them. Eventually, what you would try to do is get a consensus by experts in the field of history and then get them to propose a set of variables onto which the original set of variables could be mapped and then the best-fit configuration of these two data streams should either indicate that 2012 is the end of the Timewave or indicate some other date as the end of the Timewave. So the answer to your question is that the comparison of these two theories lies in the realm of the quantification of historical data.

I don't incline toward the softer end of the scale, but I find the hard end of the scale, where you have the stars falling from heaven, equally hard to believe. I see the eschaton as a planetary phenomenon. I think the Timewave is a topological manifold of the unconscious of biology or something like that; I think the fate of this planet is entirely caught up in this 2012 end date. I'm willing to be the devil's advocate for that, to try to make it seem creditable, because the orthodox theory of history taught in the universities is one of what's called "trendless fluctuation," meaning that history isn't under the governance of any set of laws. Well, if that's true, then history is unique in this universe — the only phenomenon not under the governance of a set of rules.

MD: *The notion of an "unconscious of biology," by which I assume you mean some sort of planetary sentience, sounds like a New Age gloss on the Gaia hypothesis.*

TM: I've held different points of view about this. Sometimes I incline more to this theory that you're asking about, that the Gaian mind has somehow deputized a subset of higher animals called the primates to be the energy-garnering units in the global ecosystem, and then the question would be why? I'm interested in the phenomenon of these earth-crossing asteroids. Every solid body in the solar system clear out to the moon of Pluto is heavily cratered by cometary material and it may be that life actually has a kind of hyperdimensional proprioception, that there is an anticipation of danger on the planetary scale and so human beings have been called forth as a kind enzymatic response to this sense of danger, and the goal of human history is to use thermonuclear weapons to blow apart some very large object that would otherwise make a real mess out of things.

MD: *I'd like to end with a suitably facetious question: What do you consider yourself? Are you a psychotropic philosopher, a cartographer of altered states, a stand-up comedian for those whose neurons have been permanently rewired by psychoactive alkaloids, or . . . ?*

TM: I'm a cunning linguist (laughs).

POINTS OF REFERENCE:

Psychedelics Before and After History, a 90-minute tape available from Sound Photosynthesis, (415) 383-6712, POB 2111, Mill Valley, CA 94942-2111.

McKenna, Terence. *The Archaic Revival*. New York: HarperCollins, 1992.

Timewave Zero software, available from 48 Shattuck Square #147, Berkeley, CA 94704.

Metamorphosis, an eighty-eight-minute video of a "trialogue" between McKenna, the chaos mathematician Ralph Abraham, and the biologist Rupert Sheldrake on chaos theory, Gaian consciousness, "morphogenetic fields," and New Age eschatology, accompanied by fractal graphics and ambient techno, is available from Mystic Fire Video, 524 Broadway, Suite 604, New York, NY 10012, (800)292-9001, $29.95.

Manuel De Landa
ILLogical Progression
by PAUL D. MILLER (2000)

"The more consciousness is intellectualized,
the more matter is spatialized."
— *Henri Bergson, "Creative Evolution," 1911*

MANUEL DE LANDA WRITES FROM A STRANGE PATAPHYSICAL
world of disjunctions and fluid transitions — a milieu where writing about
ideas becomes a fluid dialectic switching from steady state to flux and back
again in the blink of an eye, or the turn of a sentence. His style of thinking is a like a landscape made of crystalline structures: rocks and lavas,
magmas and tectonic plates that dance beneath our feet at every moment.
And that doesn't even get to the shifting magnetic polarities of the planet
and the solar winds and celestial movements that surround our little third
stone from the sun. *A Thousand Years of Nonlinear History* (Zone Books,
1997) is like a cognitive labyrinth of false starts and dead ends, like an
M.C. Escher painting, or even more accurately, like Hieronymus Bosch's
carnival tableaux bereft of characters — the *mise-en-scene* displaces the

actors operating within it, and subsumes their identity. A shift in perspective takes place, creating a world where words act as a bridge across broken and fractured "times" that exist pretty much simultaneously. De Landa has given an overview of what he calls "historic materialism" and how the basic processes of the full environment we live in have shaped contemporary thought.

Writing about Manuel De Landa's work is difficult. It isn't the fact that his work is extremely well researched (it is), or the fact that much of it involves extremely precise investigations into different realms of theoretical approaches to the way we humans live and think in different multiplex contexts that themselves are part question part unanswerable — for lack of a better word — motif. There's always that sense that one thing leads to another and basically there is no discrete and stable form of inquiry: the question changes and configures the answer which again, reconfigures what was originally asked. And so the loops go on.

De Landa's first book, *War in the Age of Intelligent Machines* (Zone Books, 1991), was an instant classic; it encapsulated what so many different theorists were trying (without much success) to achieve — an overview of our time and the different historical cybernetic developments that created the milieu we live in. Call it morphic resonance, or material convergence, or hermeneutical fusion — yada yada yada — but you get the basic idea: the kind of "real" that theorists and philosophers such as Heidegger (of "The Age of the World Picture" essay fame) and a whole cast of people supporting the ideas and extensions of European rationality like Francis Fukuyama and Frederic Jameson have not only been crippling and distorting frameworks to view human history from, but have also divorced us from the physical processes of the world of flux and constant change that we are immersed in.

Written from the viewpoint of a cybernetic historian, De Landa's *War in the Age of Intelligent Machines* created a sense of "historian as actor as philosopher." The history of and relationships between humans and the machines we use to create our cultures were transformed into a continuum where the line dividing the organic from the inorganic blurs, and the end result is something altogether completely hybrid. *A Thousand Years of Nonlinear History* takes up where *War . . .* left off: with a critique of the material processes embedded in the migrations of not only human cultures, but of the geological, biological, linguistic, and memetic systems that have impacted on this planet and its inhabitants over the last thousand years. This includes teleology, contemporary constructions of identity, frameworks of philosophical investigation — in the flow of time like the old Borges poem "The Hourglass" says:

> all are obliterated, all brought down By the tireless trickle of the
> endless sand.
> I do not have to save myself — I too Am a whim of time, that
> shifty element

PAUL D. MILLER: *In* A Thousand Years of Nonlinear History *you point out that "human history is a narrative of contingencies not necessities, of missed opportunities to follow different routes of development." My question is this: history is always a framework of interpretation; do you feel that somehow we have moved into our frameworks, moved into the picture and lost the frame?*

MANUEL DE LANDA: One of the ideas that I attack in my book is precisely the primacy of "interpretations" and of "conceptual frameworks." Sure, ideas and beliefs are important, and do play a role in history, but academics of different brands have reduced all material and energetic processes, and all human practices that are not linguistic or interpretative (think of manual skills, of "know-how") to a "framework." The twentieth century has been obsessed with positioning everything. Every culture, given

69

that it has its own framework of beliefs, has become its own "world" and relativism (both moral and epistemological) now prevails. But once you break away from this outmoded view, once you accept all the nonlinguistic practices that really make up society (not to mention the nonhuman elements that also shape it, such as viruses, bacteria, weeds, or nonorganic energy and material flows like wind and ocean currents) then language itself becomes just another material that flows through a much expanded picture. Language, in my view, is best thought of as a catalyst, a trigger for energetic processes (think of the words "begin the battle" triggering an enormous and destructive process). The question of "missed opportunities" is important, since for most of the millennium both China and India had, in fact, a better chance to conquer the world than did the West, so that the actual outcome, a world dominated by Western colonialism, was quite contingent. Things could have happened in several other ways.

PDM: *What are your thoughts on digital art and its relationship to the different forms of communication in our dense and continuously changing world. Is there any return to the "comforts" of a "homogeneous" culture on the horizon?*

MDL: Here again we have two different answers depending on whether you believe in "conceptual frameworks" or not. If you do, then you also believe that there's such a thing as "the bourgeois ideology of the individual," a pervasive framework within which all artistic production of the last few centuries is inscribed. But if you do not believe there was ever such a thing, then history becomes much less homogeneous, much less dominated by any one framework, and hence you begin to look at all the different ways in which art has escaped the conditions of its production (which, admittedly, did include ruling classes as suppliers of resources). Put differently, once you admit that history has been much more complex and heterogeneous than we have been told, then even the "enemy" looks less in control of historical processes than we thought. In a sense, what I am trying to do is to cut the enemy down to size, to see all the potential escape routes that we have been overlooking by exaggerating the importance of "frameworks" or "ideologies." Clearly, if the enemy was never as powerful as we thought (which is not to say that it did not to say that it did have plenty of power) the question of the role of art (digital or otherwise) in changing social reality acquires new meanings and possibilities.

PDM: *How does your philosophy of history differ from those of previous philosophers? Do you feel affinities with any contemporaries on this subject? Deleuze and Guattari, maybe, with whom there's a sense of continuous, vertiginous change — a tacit admission that history is continuity, but seething, ebbing, and flowing continuity?*

MDL: There are two main differences between my philosophical ideas about history and those of previous philosophers. The first one, which is shared by many these days, is a rejection of Platonic essences as sources of form — you know, the idea that the form of this mountain here or of that zebra over there emanates from an essence of "mountain-hood" or of "zebra-hood" existing in some ideal world, or in the mind of the God that created these creatures. Instead, for each such entity (not only geological and biological entities, but also social and economic ones), I force myself to come up with a process capable of creating or producing such an entity. Sometimes these processes are already figured out by scientists (in those disciplines linked to questions of morphogenesis, like chaos theory and nonlinear dynamics) and so I just borrow their model, other times I need to create new models using philosophical resources — and people like Deleuze and Guattari have been very helpful in this regard. The other difference is my rejection of the existence of totalities, that is, entities like "Western Society" or the "Capitalist System." The morphogenetic point of view does allow for the emergence of wholes that are more than the sum of

71

their parts, but only if specific historical processes — specific interactions between "lower scale entities" — can be shown to have produced such wholes. Thus, in my view, institutional organizations like bureaucracies, banks, and stock markets acquire a life of their own from the interactions of individuals. From the interactions of those institutions, cities emerge, and from the interactions between cities, nation states emerge. Yet, in these bottom-up approaches, all the heterogeneity of real nation states can be pockets of minorities, the dialect differences, the local transience — unlike when history is modeled on totalities (concepts like "society" or "culture" or "the system"). In this latter situation, homogeneity has to be artificially injected into the model.

PDM: *One thing everyone seems to agree on is that there are so many different frameworks of interpretation available today that we have lost track of the world we inhabit: the "natural" has been displaced by the human; we as a species have altered the atmosphere of the planet, changed the composition of the oceans, even created seismic disruptions. There's an overwhelming sense of anthropocentric agency over determination: "There is nothing that man hath not wrought." How do you think this sense of über-agency so prevalent in philosophical, historical, and political discourse will change in the future?*

MDL: I agree that the domination of this century by linguistics and semiotics (which is what allows us to reduce everything to talk of "frameworks of interpretation"), not to mention the postcolonial guilt of so many white intellectuals which forces them to give equal weight to any other culture's belief system, has had a very damaging effect, even on art. Today I see art students trained by guilt-driven semioticians or postmodern theorists, afraid of the materiality of their medium — whether painting, music, poetry, or virtual reality (since, given the framework dogma, every culture creates its own reality). The key to break away from this is to cut language down to size, to give it the importance it deserves as a communications medium, but to stop worshipping it as the ultimate reality. Equally important is to adopt a hacker attitude toward all forms of knowledge: not only to learn UNIX or Windows NT to hack this or that computer system, but to learn economics, sociology, physics, biology to hack reality itself. It is precisely the can-do mentality of the hacker, naive as it may sometimes be, that we need to nurture everywhere.

TECHNOLOGY

HOWARD RHEINGOLD

RUDY RUCKER

ALBERT-LÁSZLÓ BARABÁSI

DAVID WEINBERGER

ERIC PAULOS

RICHARD SAUL WURMAN

Howard Rheingold
Virtual Cartographer
by BRANDON PIERCE (2002)

CULTURE IS DRIVEN BY TECHNOLOGY. CONTEMPLATE, FOR A moment, all of the devices that have changed your life in profound ways; or attempt a regress to your mental and physical state of being before the birth of the World Wide Web. Undoubtedly, you will notice your life is now inextricably linked to and tangled within technologies that pervade our daily experience (technophobes excluded). Our relationships, interests, and attitudes have all been cultivated by technological innovations made within our lifetime. Depending on the individual results of these developments, one can view the changes as mind-amplifying progress or a march toward a synthetic, controlled existence.

All of the above notwithstanding, Howard Rheingold is trying to give us a compass and a map, to help us navigate these times of speedy techno-social change and begin to understand where we're headed. There are people in this world who live in the future. They envision, design, and play with unheard-of devices; they organize physical communities that reflect their virtual connectivity; they live in a world that integrates technology and reality in novel ways. Rheingold knows these people. Hunting out the territories where technology meets human relationships is his business.

Smart Mobs: The Next Social Revolution (Perseus Books, 2002) is Howard's latest attempt to shine a flashlight into the future. This future is home to inhabitants that navigate daily life with devices that are literally remote controls for the physical world, devices that are electronically integrated into our everyday environment. Radio chips, reputation systems, wireless internet nodes, Global Positioning Systems, person-to-person texting, and wearable computers all contribute to a vision of commerce and communication at hyperspeed. How these developments will be handled, by government, corporations, and everyday people, is yet to be determined, and how these technologies will manifest themselves in society is yet to be clearly conceived.

In times where technological innovation is in overdrive, it is difficult to predict or prepare for the future. Governmental regulation cannot keep up with technological advances (you can't tame an animal that you can't catch). *Smart Mobs* wants to make us conscious of potential changes. Extrapolating trends into an uncertain future, Howard Rheingold is attempting to help shape it with socially conscious dialog.

BRANDON PIERCE: Smart Mobs *deals with the convergence, or overlapping, of multiple technologies. You argue that this new synthesis will manifest "emergent properties" that will be profound and unpredictable. Can you articulate this idea for our readers (i.e., why is the future of pervasive media and technology so much more than merely obtaining wireless internet access in the park or receiving baseball scores on your mobile phone?)?*

HOWARD RHEINGOLD: We've seen, at least twice before in the past two or three decades, the way the convergence of information and communication technologies have created new media that have had profound, widespread, and largely unpredictable effects. The television screen and the microprocessor made possible the personal computer as we know it. The personal computer is something that amplifies the ability of people to communicate, create, and do their work. It's not just a television screen and a microprocessor. It's an entirely new medium. In fact, it was regarded as a toy in its early days. The effect it has had on the way we do business and in the pursuit of knowledge, in academia, science, and medicine, have all been profoundly changed by the personal computer in ways that were not predicted. With PCs merging with communication networks (originally the telephone network with modems, but then over to cables and wireless networks) you get something that's not just a computer connected to a telephone; you get an emergent network, like the internet, which spawned the web and digital communication and all sorts of other phenomena which were not predicted beforehand. So we've learned something from this, but can we apply what we've learned to the future? We look at the internet, and it's been limited to the desktop, whether in a home or an office, but now, as we move on to devices we can carry, today there's mobile phones, maybe tomorrow there will be wearable computers and, for some, PDAs (personal digital assistants). That's not going to be just carrying the internet around; it's going to be an entirely different phenomenon.

BP: *You have participated in the dialogs that have cultivated consciousness and management of the consequences of techno-social revolutions. Despite our limited knowledge of the complex dynamics of change, are there any unifying themes or concepts that underlie revolutions such as these?*
HR: I think that it's not just our blind inability to forecast. In fact, if you look at what drove the internet's social communication, email was the killer app, along with newsgroups, mailing lists, chat rooms, instant messaging. These were just a huge driver of the internet. And with telephones, well, people like to communicate . . . socially. That's obvious. And we're

seeing with the early use of the new media, the text messaging and SMS messaging (20 to 30 billion messages annually, worldwide), that social communications are something that people value. If you look at what people have done with these various forms of social communications, the kinds of communication that technology can afford, the telephone allowed one to communicate with someone far away, in real time. The internet makes it possible to communicate with people you've never met, but with whom you share some mutual interest. Mobile communication is used mostly by people who already know each other, to coordinate their activities in real time, and although that seems fairly simple, that can lead to profound changes, because the way people organize their activities is really what drives the evolution of civilization.

BP: *In the U.S., wireless nodes are sprouting up quite quickly, accompanied by rapidly growing networks, while text messaging and G3 devices have yet to show their faces. Is there room in the U.S. market for both the G3 devices and wi-fi laptops to be successful?*

HR: The fact that text messaging has not taken off in America — the way it has in Europe, Asia, Africa, and starting in South America — has a lot to do with the failure of the American operators to market it properly. Unlike Europe and Asia, there were many competing standards, so you could not send a text message (or could not until very recently) from your phone to your friend's phone, if your friend had a different operator than yours. In Europe they had a standard, so you could send a message no matter who your friend's operator was. Secondly, in places where it has taken off, texting is cheaper than making a voice call, and the receiver does not have to pay anything, only the sender. Again, the American operators did not market it that way. The third thing is that in most places, texting first took off among teenagers. Again, American operators did not begin by marketing it to teenagers. They're changing that, but they started by marketing it to thirty-ish executive geeks. There may be other cultural reasons, but there's no way of finding out what those are while these major marketing obstacles are in the way.

G3 is how the phone companies refer to third-generation cellular phones, which have music and video capabilities. The infrastructure for doing that, centrally, requires buying expensive portions of the spectrum and installing a top-down infrastructure that's very expensive, and it takes a long time to install and to make it work. At the same time, other technologies are being utilized by armatures. People are using low-power devices to connect to the internet, and make small networks in their neighborhoods. These devices are selling at a million and a half per month. Telephone companies are laboring to build expensive infrastructures that might be too expensive for people to use, while people spontaneously build networks themselves, the way the internet was done. Wireless nodes are beginning to provide high-speed access to people in cites. The advantages are found in using the spectrum in ways that are not known or allowed.

BP: *The evolution of virtual reality technology has not mapped directly onto the path that you plotted for it. Do you feel that any aspects of that particular phenomenon are evolutionary dead ends?*

HR: I think clearly that VR has not taken off. I did say in my book that it would take 10 to 15 years for the processing power alone to be sufficient to provide an experience that could compete with what we're used to on television. So we're about 10 years into that period, and it's getting there. But clearly other things have happened in the world that have been much more important, bigger, and unforeseen. Once again, nobody predicted the web when I wrote *Virtual Reality* (MIT Press) in 1990. So I think it remains to be seen whether the technology will be able to provide a compelling experience, but I think the compelling use of the internet has come along that has been more significant.

BP: *Web theorists have suggested that the internet challenges many of our fundamental notions about time, space, self, etc. They exist differently in the virtual world. Web time has been called "sliceable" or "shapeable," custom fit for each individual (or possibly containing a myriad of distractions). How does your "softening of time" theory relate to, change, or enhance these previous theories?*

HR: There's some indication that the use of mobile phones to coordinate activities has changed those properties. People don't have set appointments; time has been "softened." It's not "I'll meet you at 1:00 PM wherever," it's "I'll send you a message once I get downtown this afternoon," and then people negotiate actually when and where they'll end up. Another change was pointed out by an urban planner by the name of Anthony Townsend. People are using their telephones and PDAs to get work done while in their car, walking down the street, or sitting in the park. These are times when they would not have been accomplishing tasks, business-related or social tasks, before. That means that people are doing more things than they were previously, and that speeds up the metabolism of the city. That might lead to good results for some people and bad for other people. We don't really know, but it's important to note that those changes are occurring.

BP: *Some opponents of wireless networks and virtual communities argue that we will emerge from the "age of instant access" as isolationists with underdeveloped physical and social skills. They talk of cities whose denizens devalue public spaces and natural communication and are totally dependent upon and useless without their mobile devices. What is wrong with this mentality? Can these mind-expanding gizmos enhance human interactions or enhance public spaces?*

HR: First of all, I don't know that I would argue that, in general, that people are becoming more civil to one another. Look at interactions that people have in traffic, or listen to talk radio. I think people are as impolite to each other as they have always been, but they seem to be more in a hurry, in general. But does that have to with technology, or the automobile, or skyscrapers, or capitalism, or suburbia? I think it's simplistic to try to nail it down to one cause. I think, however, that the problem is in generalizations. It's clear that while for some people, the internet, like many other things, can be a way of distancing oneself from other people. It's clear that, for many people, using online communication, just as their grandparents had used the telephone, is a way to connect with other people.

BP: *Dialectics are central to your work and your treatment of them is usually quite balanced. For example, "The bottom-up, grassroots forces of innovation and community clash and with and dodge the punches of the top-down control of the corporate world." Describe the sort of interaction that will need to take place or for these two opposing forces to work in some form of symbiosis."*

HR: There are a lot of different forces of conflict. There are existing industries and emerging industries. There are old business problems and new business problems. There are old ways of regulating public goods, and there are new ideas about regulating public goods. I think what I'm trying to drill here about virtual communication, using technology to communicate (as we did with the telephone, or the internet), is that people did not use it in ways that society had planned. So, we can see that telephone operators and cable operators . . . they have certain plans for what they would like to see with populations in the future, how they would like to see the populations of the future behave with regards to communication and technology. In general, I think we can see that Hollywood studios, the recording industry, electronics manufacturers, television industry would like to go back to the days of broadcasting, where people were consumers of content that was broadcast to them. The only choice you really had was changing the channel, never really creating content, unless you worked for one of the major studios. Now, when we look at the internet, we see that many people created it. Yet, the telephone companies created an infrastructure that was useful, computer manufactures created computers, but the internet was some "thing," like a shopping center that was built by a bunch of contractors. But it emerged from the cooperative effort of everybody, acting in their own self-interest. So, the PC revolution consisted of users. Bill Gates was one. The internet consisted of users. In the future, the user could become just a consumer.

I think what we need is not one side or the other, but a balance between the large scale infrastructure that can only be built by major corporations or regulated by national government, and the bottom-up stuff. I think citizens should be allowed more leeway, and new technology should be given an opportunity by better serving the people that use it, rather than the companies that sell it.

BP: ... *And for another example, "The liberating, creative, and opportunistic dimensions of the 'instant access' age are shadowed by the Orwellian image of a 'panopticon' of psychological imprisonment and privacy invasion. What factors are important in driving this dichotomy toward a healthy, humane solution? Will the tradeoffs (privacy for convenience) be worth it?"*

HR: This is a complex issue, but there is one simple way of looking at it: Who has control over information? The person who owns the information, such as whose medical histories it is, record of transactions it is . . . or others. People want to sell their products, and there could be a healthy market in this. All the merchants want to do is find people who are more likely to be their customers. Provided a method for doing this, that is what commercial interests want. People do not want to be bombarded with spam and junk mail. They see it as some form of identity theft, and they don't want people to spy on them any more than the constitution allows. So I think the question of future technology is who has control of these. Is there an off switch where you can turn off the information being broadcast about you, and if so, is the default mode on or off?

It's very difficult right now in California to pass legislation preventing banks from selling, not just your account information, but all the transactions that you make on your credit card (which is a big issue) to hundreds of thousands of other institutions. The California legislature has failed twice in the past two years to pass a bill about that because the banks spend a lot of money on lobbying. They spend a lot of money on politicians who then owe them something. So, although individuals say they care about privacy, the political process is tilted in favor of institutions that profit from having control of information.

BP: *Tell us about any new projects you have in the works.*
HR: In a couple of weeks I'm going to launch the *smartmobs.com* website, a resource center of all the resources that I did put in my bibliography, and a community blog of new developments related to the chapters in the book.

Rudy Rucker

by TOM GEORGOULIAS

Part One: Keeping it Transreal (1999)

RUDY RUCKER HAS A LOT OF THINGS ON HIS MIND. ALTHOUGH his day job has him teaching computer science and mathematics at San Jose State University, Rucker is a writer. He has written twenty nonfiction and science-fiction books covering such topics as higher dimensions, artificial life, and biotechnology. Called the original cyberpunk author by many, his self-described "transreal" writing style is akin to Kerouac's *On the Road* (Viking, 1959) and an issue of *Scientific American* after a run through the mince cycle on a blender. I recently had the chance to catch up with Rucker and discuss two of his most recent books, *Seek!* (Four Walls Eight Windows, 1999) and *Saucer Wisdom* (Forge Books, 1999).

TOM GEORGOULIAS: *I've been reading your new nonfiction collection* Seek!, *and I'd like to start with some computer-science questions for you. You write about simulated evolution to develop machines that are as intelligent as* *their creators, yet today's AI research seems farther from reaching the goal of intelligent machines than ever. What do you see as the missing link necessary to bring AI research up to speed with your visions of intelligent machines?*

RUDY RUCKER: There's a tendency to think that maybe if we can just throw enough hardware at the AI problem, then evolution can take care of the rest. Certainly that's how God went about making us. We evolved inside a planetary-sized round-the-clock simulation over maybe a billion years.

The catch is that there is such a great disparity between a desktop computer and a billion-year planetary analog computation. Even with the biggest imaginable kinds of increases in our computing power, our machines will remain very tiny playpens.

So rather than relying on blind evolution to build our intelligent programs, we get into trying to tweak the process. That's what traditional AI is all about, trying to find little top-down tricks to make a program behave more intelligently. But even in this kind of context, there are scads of program parameters that you don't really know the best values for, and this is where simulated evolution can help you.

Another point worth mentioning is that the stuff we are made of has been evolving all along as well. New kinds of organic molecules emerged, for instance. This is analogous to the fact that we are still feeling around for the best kinds of computer architectures, operating systems, and evolution frameworks. The evolution of robots is really happening at a number of levels. And it's not clear that we've really found the best kind of system to try and evolve a mind on top of. Neural nets, cellular automata, a soup of LISP strings — we don't know. We just have to keep trying.

One final, encouraging, thought is that, as our machines become networked into a planetary web, the collective power of our machines can experience some synergetic increases. Evolution takes a lot of machine cycles, and when we can distribute this kind of search to lots of users, we get a terrific speed-up. The trick here is getting people to run your simulation code. In my novel *The Hacker and the Ants* (Avon Books, 1999), the evolution code was a kind of virus that took over the chips in everyone's TV sets. What if every time users hit a particularly juicy porno site, their machine became co-opted into working on evolving intelligent software?

TG: *In your writings about cellular automata (CA), you mention how parallel processing hardware is best suited for running CA simulations. There are many supercomputers designed with parallel architectures, but for the most part engineers keep cranking out more powerful computers based on the von Neumann architecture. What are the final challenges left in designing parallel systems and how can they be overcome so that CA programs can advance even further?*

RR: Well, I too wonder what ever happened to the dream of parallel computing. About twenty years ago, the Connection Machine was supposed to be the big new paradigm, but before long they bagged it and got into making standard architecture workstations. I've never had a chance to do anything with parallel hardware. I have, of course, written a lot of CA code; usually the first thing you do is to set up a dual buffer system so that you can simulate the parallel updates of the arrays. And when you think about a CA rule itself, you are indeed thinking in terms of a parallel computation. If CAs ever found a really killer app, then the industry would be motivated to make parallel hardware to run them. Not that there isn't any such hardware at all, Xilinx of San Jose, for instance, makes some field-programmable gate arrays (FPGA) that are supposed to be good for running CAs. I recently read that a man named Hugo de Garis at Advanced Telecommunications Research (ATR) in Kyoto is trying to use them to evolve an intelligent robot cat called Robokoneko. We'll see what happens. A lot of times projects like this run into the wall of how much run-time it would take to actually evolve something truly interesting. The search spaces are just so superexponentially big. In any case, I've never tried using a FPGA myself. There's kind of a limit to how many new operating systems and hardware configurations you're willing to learn in one lifetime, and I'm getting awfully close to maxed out.

TG: *The use of computers and programs like Mathematica have rapidly advanced the field of mathematics over the last twenty years, bringing topics such as complexity, chaos, and CA to the front lines. What are some of the newer areas of research in math that have sparked your interest?*

RR: My favorites are chaos, fractals, cellular automata, artificial life, and higher dimensions. Anything gnarly. I love that computer science has made mathematics into something like an experimental science. I was never all that good at proving things, but I love doing computer experiments. Makes me feel competent. These days I'm wasting most of my time writing a book with the working title *Live Windows: Games and Graphics with Visual C++ and MFC.* I'd sort of like to just call it *How to Write Cool Windows Programs,* but Bill Gates has sort of uncooled the word "cool," hasn't he? In fact, whenever I write a novel, I do a search on the text when I'm done to make sure I didn't slip up and use the world "cool" in it anywhere. But here I am putting down Gates, and I'm writing a book using the Microsoft Foundation Classes (MFC)? Well, you gotta live in the real world. I want to see gnarly math things on my screen, and hopefully on lots of other people's screens, and the best way to get the things out there is with MFC. After awhile you even get to like it: kind of a Patty Hearst/ Stockholm Syndrome thing, where prisoners get to be fond of their jailers. MFC is where it's at. I just hope to God it doesn't fucking disappear before I finish my book.

TG: *Now tell me something about your other new book,* Saucer Wisdom. *Is it a novel?*

RR: *Saucer Wisdom* is a cross between a transreal novel and a popular science book of speculations about the future. It's my personal contribution to millennium madness.

Saucer Wisdom arose from three interests of mine. First of all, I have a lot of ideas about the course of future technology, and wanted to write a book about that. Secondly, I'm very dissatisfied with people's current ways of thinking about UFOs, and I thought it would be worthwhile to write a novel which treats them in a more interesting and amusing fashion. Thirdly, I like to write somewhat autobiographical books that give transreal representations of various periods of my life.

So *Saucer Wisdom* features a main character named "Rudy Rucker." Rudy is approached by a man named Frank Shook who's been frequently abducted by flying saucers, but rather than giving Frank Shook medical exams and lecturing him on world peace, the aliens have been showing Frank all sorts of things about our future. Frank gets Rudy to help work his notes up into a book, a book named *Saucer Wisdom*.

The main areas of future technology described in the book are communication, biotechnology, femtotechnology, and transhumanity. The material is presented in terms of stories about things that Frank and the aliens looked at. And I enhanced the text with fifty-seven line drawings (supposedly by Frank Shook.)

You might well wonder what "femtotechnology" is. This will be the science of transforming one kind of matter into another; for instance, of making air into gold or chicken soup. One of my motivations in writing any kind of science book is always to develop new things to use in my science fiction, so you can expect to see femtotechnology turning up in my forthcoming SF novel *Realware* (Avon Books, 2000).

Frank's stories are a grab bag of sketches and vignettes of little episodes from our future. And overarching these tales is the story of Frank and Rudy's interactions, which are none too serene. At one point Frank breaks into Rudy's house and disappears for two years. Frank and Rudy have their final meeting at — where else — the same Devil's Tower made famous by *Close Encounters of the Third Kind*. And after this meeting, Rudy has a dream in which he finally gains true "Saucer Wisdom." Check it out.

Part Two: Game Theory (2002)

WHEN I LAST SPOKE WITH RUDY RUCKER, HIS NONFICTION COL-lection *Seek!* and science-fiction novel *Saucer Wisdom* were just finding their way into bookstores. Since that time, Rucker has been hacking on a video game programming toolkit called the Pop Framework and keeping a low profile on the science-fiction scene. After bouncing a few emails with him, it was obvious that we needed to do another interview and shed some light on his latest projects. Rucker's going to need four slots on the bookshelves this year to hold his latest works: the computer science text-book *Software Engineering and Computer Games* (Addison-Wesley), a new science-fiction novel *Spaceland* (Tor Books), a historical novel *As Above So Below* (Forge Books), and a reissue of *The Hacker and The Ants* (Four Walls Eight Windows) are all being released in 2002. Here's what Rucker had to say about computer-science research, video-game programming, and what it would take to make a good Freeware movie.

TOM GEORGOULIAS: *What kinds of gnarly computer research (cellular automata, fractals, A-Life, etc.) are you actively doing these days?*
RUDY RUCKER: For the last few years, I've been putting most of my energy into computer-game programming . These days, this is the most exciting field. It combines a lot of things I like: virtual-reality graphics, artificial-life algorithms, artificial intelligence, computer art, street-wise attitude, simulated physics, obsession with writing code that runs fast.

Personally, I'm about ready to lay down my programming tools, though. I pretty much shot my wad creating the Pop game framework for my textbook *Software Engineering and Computer Games*. I did more programming on that than I've ever done. Writing science fiction is a lot more fun. You want a "frammistat" in SF, then all you have to do is describe it once, and if there's a problem with it later on, you just go back and change a few words. Quick revision cycles! The "building a cathedral out of toothpicks" aspect of programming does get old. At SJSU I'm teaching more graduate courses now and advising more master's degree theses. This means I can try to get students to do the programming work for things I'd like to see. One interesting project I have right now is that a student is extending my Pop game framework to use four space dimensions. He has a four-dimensional *Space Invaders* working pretty well, and I hope he can get a four-dimensional *Pac-Man*. One of these days I want to get a student, or someone else, to add cellular automata to the Pop framework, so we can have surfing on a CA wave. I'd like to see more chaos in games as well.

TG: *Now that Stephen Wolfram has released his long awaited book* A New Kind of Science *(Wolfram Media, 2002), which focuses on complexity and cellular automata, what do you think the net effect of the book is going to be on the CA field?*

RR: It should be a real shot in the arm. I was considering writing a jump-on-the-bandwagon book along the lines of "What Wolfram Said," but I found out it's already too late for that, which is kind of a relief. All I really want to do these days is write science fiction. As for CAs, I'll just settle for being one of the lesser-known "stations of the cross" for CA popularizers' Sacred Quest.

I read Wolfram's book through once, quickly, and I like it a lot. Many of the ideas are familiar to me from things he said back in the 1980s. But he pushes them a bit further, and he's really done the legwork in terms of checking out examples. I'm (very slowly) working on a longish, detailed review of the book for the *American Mathematical Monthly,* and I hope to use the book as a text in a course I teach at SJSU in spring 2003.

To rush and say much more now would be premature. John Updike once compared critics to "pigs at a pastry cart." Here's this mammoth volume that took a genius ten or twenty years to write, and people want to rush out quick-draw sound bites on it? "Gobble, gobble, tastes like prune!"

TG: *Since your desire is to focus on writing science fiction, what's your take on (pardon my lameness in using this phrase) "the state of science fiction"?*

RR: A science-fiction writer isn't necessarily the best person to ask about the field of SF. I tend to focus on my own little garden; I don't read a large number of other SF writers. It goes almost without saying that I love what Bill Gibson does in his books. Terry Bisson is a lesser-known writer whom I really enjoy. Paul DiFilippo writes wonderful stories. I wish Marc Laidlaw would start writing again. He's been swallowed up by the computer game industry; he works at Valve near Seattle, figuring out story lines for games like Half-Life. Though one could also say that he's simply switched to a new medium. But really I don't think there's any medium as rich as the SF novel.

In a novel you can do whatever you like and you don't have special effects budget issues. You can use beautiful language. You, as the author, get to create a novel on your own without dealing with producers. People can reread a novel, flip forward and back, dip in. It's a great medium.

I have a vague sense that it's about time for a new cohort of exciting SF writers. You could say we had the Golden Age guys in the '40s, the New Wave in the '60s, Cyberpunk in the '80s, so there ought to be something interesting in the '00s. But I'm not out there reading the magazines and the first novels, so I'm not the right guy to ask. Just at random, one first novel I did recently happen to read and like is Cory Doctorow, *Down and Out in the*

Magic Kingdom, due from Tor Books this fall. He does this next-generation thing of pretty much taking for granted certain far-out, science-fictional notions that I still think of as a big deal. For instance, his characters are online all the time via implants, which still strikes me as a kind of shockingly evil possible development. Why evil? How would you like to have Muzak, spam, telemarketing calls, political ads, polling, and surveillance going on in your head 24/7?

TG: *Your computer science textbook* Software Engineering and Computer Games *is coming out from Addison-Wesley this fall. Are video games a good way to teach computer science?*

RR: IMHO, having students do computer games projects is absolutely the best possible way to teach programming, graphics, software engineering, object-oriented programming, etc. I used to be into photography, and I managed to get hold of this very nice camera, a Leica M4. And I was constantly shooting pictures with it. And then I wanted another lens, and I went to a store that carried Leica stuff, and I found out that a lot of people were into collecting Leicas, like keeping them in glass cases. To me, a camera is for taking pictures. And a programming tool like Visual Studio or the JDK is for writing programs. Not for collecting different versions of, or for arguing about, or for comparing to other products. It's there to use. Writing a game is a nice big problem that makes you program a lot.

To take pictures, you need to have something you like taking pictures of. To learn how to write, you need to have something you want to write about. And to learn programming, you need something you want to program about.

It's very easy for a student to get excited about making a game work. A second win with teaching games programming is that the homework is very easy to grade. The game works or it doesn't; it's playable or it isn't. I've been teaching my sections of the Software Engineering course at SJSU this way for about ten years. Over the years I built up the Pop Framework so that students can build on it to make games pretty easily. I'm proud of the code. It's been used for about a hundred games now. I have some of the better ones up for download.

The Pop Framework is thoroughly OO, basically you just edit one file to overload a few methods and you've got your game: *Pac-Man, Asteroids, 3D Defender, Air Hockey, Soccer,* whatever. I used patterns and UML to try and get the design right. Graphically, I designed it so you can run the game inside a Windows window, instead of taking over the whole screen (which I've always considered to be morally wrong!). You can either use Windows graphics or OpenGL; switching between them is a nice example of using the Bridge pattern. It's all in the book. I don't think I'll ever write a textbook again, though; it's been an insane amount of effort. I do hope the book sells well.

TG: *I just finished reading* Spaceland, *your latest science fiction novel, about a Silicon Valley manager who is invited into the fourth dimension. Not only does the book nail the climate of the dot-com boom, the fourth-dimension experience is described extremely well and the story is funny to boot. What prompted or influenced you to write* Spaceland?

RR: The book is inspired by Edwin Abbott's 1884 book, *Flatland.* That book is a tale — not really a novel — about a two-dimensional character called A Square and about his difficulties in understanding the third dimension. Our situation is similar: we're three-dimensional creatures trying to understand the fourth dimension. The idea is that we can form useful analogies between A Square and ourselves. Four is to three as three is to two. Thanks to Abbott, I ended up writing two nonfiction books about the fourth dimension. And now I thought it would be interesting to make the fourth dimension work in a realistic novel. I call my main character Joe Cube. In *Spaceland,* I was particularly interested in working out how things would look if I could travel out into the fourth dimension. Nobody's ever pushed that notion very far before.

Flatland is set on December 31, 1999. A sphere from the higher (third) dimension appears, passing through *Flatland*. So when that day rolled around in reality, I wanted to have something amazing like that happen — I wanted a 4D creature to enter our world. That's the Y2K event I was really waiting for, and since it didn't happen in fact, I wrote it into reality.

Another thing I wanted to do in *Spaceland* was to depict my native Silicon Valley, kind of like the way I did in *The Hacker and the Ants*. So far, *Spaceland* seems to be doing pretty well. Just for fun I went ahead and posted my working notes for it on my page for the book.

The Hacker and the Ants will be reissued by Four Walls Eight Windows this winter, by the way, complete with a cover by my daughter Georgia's New York design company, Pink Design, Inc.

TG: *Was* Realware *really the final* *Ware *book, or can we fans begin quietly speculating on the fifth installment?*
RR: Hey, a series is never over till the author dies, and even then it might not be over. I'm as curious as you are about what happens to Cobb Anderson after he leaves Earth in that flying saucer.

But remember, there were nine years between *Wetware* and *Freeware,* so I'm not severely due for another *Ware till 2009. And maybe by then the market for a book of that nature will be stronger.

And, no, I'm not telling anyone yet what I would call it. Jinx, you know. Make up all the silly *Ware names you like, but you won't get the true name out of me. Vaporware, Shovelware, Stoneware, Silverware, Underware, Earthenware, Senileware, Noware — I've heard 'em all.

In the near term, I don't plan a sequel partly for reasons having to do with the publishing industry. Harper Collins, owner of Avon, the publisher of the *Ware books, was bought by a megacorporation called News

Corporation, which is the creation of Rupert Murdoch. If you're an author, over the years you find yourself being "bought and sold" a countless number of times. A mid-list author like me isn't exactly the juiciest part of any acquisition; I'm more like a piece of chewing gum stuck to the bottom of a shoe, something you pick up by accident. The News Corporation is bottom-line oriented, and I'm not viewed as a strong enough profit generator. My books earn out, and then some, but I'm no Stephen King.

This means that Avon has been quite resistant to books by me of late; they turned down *Saucer Wisdom, Spaceland,* and my forthcoming *As Above, So Below.* All of these were picked up by Tor Books, whom I now consider my primary fiction publisher.

Another bad sign from Avon is that they may be letting my *Ware books go out of print. I know *Wetware* is out of print, for instance. I find this especially galling, as a guy called Craig Nova recently published an SF novel called *Wetware* that, in fact, treats my pet themes. (Nova's publisher is owned by the Bertelsmann AG megacorporation, which seems to independent of the News Corporation, so I can't get totally shrill and paranoid here.)

In short, my problem with writing another *Ware in the next few years would be that I'm not at all sure Avon would want buy another *Ware just now, and I don't know if Tor would want to publish an "orphaned" series book. And they might both be right. When you drag a series on too long, I think the readership can drop.

Sooner or later, a movie of one of the *Ware books may get made. And then it would certainly be easy for me to sell another sequel, assuming I'm still alive.

On the film front, Phoenix Pictures had an option on *Software* for about ten years, but that died. I was annoyed when Phoenix turned around and then released a Schwarzenegger movie, *The Sixth Day,* using some of my themes, complete with a yuppie mad scientist called Drucker (as in "Dr. Rucker")! But I'd rather not rant about that here. Even as I type this interview, I'm inking a nice option agreement for *Freeware* with a Seattle outfit called Directed Evolution Networks.

A Brooklyn-based director named Mark Mitchell just optioned *Master of Space and Time* (St. Martins Press, 1984) as well.

Hope springs eternal in the human breast.

TG: *What are you hoping for in a *Ware movie? What do you want to see? And are you concerned about the way some of the story will be portrayed on the big screen? The moldies, drug effects, and moon city Einstein will no doubt produce some intense visuals, especially with the breakneck pace of Freeware's plot.*

RR: I'd like it to be hip and cool, as big as *Bladerunner* or *The Matrix*. The game they always play in Hollywood after dinner is to sit around doing fantasy casting. It would be nice to have Johnny Depp for Randy Karl Tucker and Matt Dillon for Stahn Mooney. Maybe Heather Locklear for Wendy Mooney.

One special effect I'd love to see them use would be to put live cellular automata onto the skins of the moldies. It wouldn't be that hard to do; I'm half tempted to write a demo myself. You'd run the CA in two buffers as usual, and every update you'd delete your robot's current texture object and give it a new texture object based on the bitmap in the CA buffer. Or you could do a low-tech version and simply use a computer projector to beam real-time CAs onto the skins of some guys in white rubber suits.

I would hate to see it get too violent; I thought that was the one weak thing about *Bladerunner*, that it's so vicious and bloody toward the end. When, in fact, Phil Dick's original book, *Do Androids Dream of Electric Sheep?* (Doubleday, 1968), was based on notions of empathy, kindness, and humanity. Mostly all they know how to do in Hollywood is kill things and blow things up.

I saw *Software* go through ten increasingly bad scripts, none of which I was allowed to write. By the end, the story wasn't even logical. I think a minimal, basic requirement of any SF movie should be that it's logical, that it's consistent, that it makes sense. Why is this so hard for producers to do? Don't they care? Can't they think? Do they think nobody notices? If they're spending twenty or a hundred million dollars on the movie, can't they pay a professional science-fiction writer a few bucks to go over the script and get rid of the holes? Why isn't that considered worth doing? Who knows.

There were some big holes in *The Matrix,* for instance, though I did really enjoy the film. The hole that got me was the notion that they were using those people in the toilet things for batteries. Like it's not too hard to see that the energy of keeping a person alive in a glass bidet is going to be a lot more than some millivolt trickle you get out of their nervous system. An SF writer could fix that easily. It's not raw electricity you're getting out of the people, man: It's psionic energy that you put into a quark resonator to convert into electricity. But you don't just pull wattage out of a person like C-cell battery, come on!

But in the end, if they make any kind of movie at all from one of my books or stories I'll be happy. I'll get money, and more people will read my books. Whatever they do in a movie, the books are what it's all about. The movie doesn't change what's in the books.

TG: *Are there any other projects or novels underway that you want mention before we wrap this up?*

RR: I've written a historical novel about the sixteenth-century Flemish painter Peter Bruegel. It's called *As Above, So Below,* and it's coming from Tor Books this fall. I think it's a masterpiece. No SF, though; I didn't want to drag this one in the gutter! Bruegel has always fascinated me. His early paintings of Hell are somewhat science fictional, his later paintings of peasants are wonderfully real. He often includes something vulgar, such as someone taking a dump. None of his works ever hung in churches. His landscapes show a profound sense of the cosmic divinity inherent in the world. His technical mastery is fabulous. He's deep and funny. He's one of my main men. His life isn't very well documented, so I got to make up a lot. I used reverse transrealism to deduce his life from his paintings. I'd like to write like Bruegel paints.

Currently I'm working on a longish SF novel with working title *Frek and the Elixir.* It'll take me maybe another year to finish writing it. It's an epic, light-hearted SF novel of biotechnology, suitable for young and old. I imagine flap copy something like the following:

> The year is 3003 and the tweaked plants and animals are quite wonderful — but there's only a few dozen species left. Nature herself has been McDonald's-ized. It's up to Frek Huggins, a lad from dull, sleepy Middleville, to venture out into the galaxy to fetch an elixir to restore Earth's biosphere. At least that's what a friendly alien cuttlefish tells him the elixir will do. But can you really trust aliens?
>
> For that matter, can you trust me?

Albert-László Barabási
Think Networks
by ROY CHRISTOPHER (2002)

WE ALL KNOW OUR WORLD IS HELD TOGETHER THROUGH A VAST network of connections, and we're all coming to realize that it's becoming more connected and interdependent with every passing day. The question is how? In what ways are we altering our lives with this network, and how do we deal with the negative aspects of the overwhelming connectivity?

Enter Dr. Albert-László Barabási and his new book, *Linked: The New Science of Networks* (Perseus Books, 2002). Underneath our online world of seemingly random connections, the cells of our bodies and our social ties lies a network of hubs and ever-growing links with surprisingly not-random patterns. Dr. Barabási digs deep into the world of links on the web, social networks, cellular connections, and other fields. He returns with a clear picture of how these connections operate and how they're re-shaping our lives.

Barabási is the Emil T. Hofman Professor of Physics at the University of Notre Dame, and teaches and directs research on complex networks.

His varied contributions have been featured and acclaimed in the media, including magazines such as *Nature, New Scientist,* and *National Geographic,* to name only a few. If he has one message to deliver, it is, "Think networks."

ROY CHRISTOPHER: *Can you give me a brief overview of the ideas in* Linked?

ALBERT-LÁSZLÓ BARABÁSI: For many decades we believed that networks are random. Whenever we had to face a very complex system, such as people are connected by social links (society), chemicals in the cell connected by chemical reactions, webpages connected by URLs, we assumed that the links are thrown randomly around. In the last few years we learned that this is not the case. Instead, networks hide wonderful order and are described by rather rigid evolutionary laws. These laws lead to the emergence of hubs, nodes with an extraordinary large number of links, that partly dominate real networks but they also keep them together. For example, on the web most people point to a few webpages, such as Google or Yahoo!; the web within a cell is held together by a few very active chemicals; in the economy, a few companies, such as IBM or Microsoft, have economic links to an extraordinary number of other companies. The number and the size of these hubs is fundamentally determined by the network's size, and they are responsible for a large number of rather unexpected phenomena. For example, sexual hubs are responsible for turning AIDS from a local epidemic into a pandemic and these hubs make the internet and the cell extremely resilient against failures. In short, the emergence of the hubs have completely reshaped our understanding of complexity in general. Probably the most interesting aspect of the network laws, is that just about all networks out there follow them. In addition to the sexual network, internet, and society, we and other have studies the structure of the language, the connections between comic book characters of the network of scientists connected by collaborations, and many other systems, and the same laws apply to them; the same structures emerge. This universality of network structure and evolution tells us that if we understand one network, we can apply this knowledge to understand all other complex webs out there.

RC: *Your book seems to explain away the role of chaos in the development of complex networks. Do you think the new discoveries in the behavior of scale-free networks will replace chaos theory as a way to understand large, seemingly chaotic systems?*

ALB: Chaos is talking about the interactions between a few agents, showing that even simple systems can behave in a rather complicated manner. Network theory does the opposite — it tells us that rather complex systems follow simple rules and laws. Network theory has allowed us to understand the architecture of complexity, a completely neglected area until recently. As networks are pervasive, we simply cannot ignore this message.

RC: *Mark Granovetter's idea of the "strength of weak ties" has intrigued me since reading Malcolm Gladwell's* The Tipping Point *(Little, Brown & Co., 2000). It seems such a simple idea that explains so much and to which I hadn't really given much thought before. Do you see this idea as one of the unsung traits of the behavior of networks?*

ALB: Granovetter's wonderful and rather influential insight, that weak ties play a key role in our social network, is still valid. Network theory has shown us, however, that there is a brand-new world out there beyond the weak ties that, without data, Granovetter could not even imagine addressing. The role of the hubs could not be appreciated until a few years ago, when we finally got real data on complex networks. Yet, following up on

Granovetter's insight is still a dream for us — while we have detailed topologies describing everything from the web to the collaboration networks, the strength of the ties in most of the cases is not available. This is one of the future directions for network research.

RC: *Tell me about your interest in "parasitic computing." Where do you see this area going in the future?*

ALB: Parasitic computing was a proof of a concept for us — to show that one could turn the whole internet into a computer, distribute a large computation on thousands of unsuspecting computers. For this we designed a way to turn anybody's computer into a slave for us, making them to unwillingly perform computation on our behalf. Do not worry — we did not use your computers. We just demonstrated on several computers that this is possible. The future of parasitic computing could lead us in many directions. It needs to be made efficient, and in this case it could turn into a mainstream distributed computation tool. For that to happen, we need to address the technical, ethical, and legal aspects of the process, which I believe could be worked out. It could also turn into an underground method for computation, where people will quietly use it. We published our results so that people are aware of the possibility, and we will have safeguards against it before it's too late. Finally, parasitic computing could simply allow us to think outside of the box. My collaborator on the project, Vince Freeh, is doing just that, and he has some wonderful ideas on the future of parasitic computing that will surprise many, I am sure, once he is ready to talk about them.

RC: *Is there anything else you're working on that you'd like to mention here?*

ALB: My interest has lately turned toward biology. I see cell biology as the area where network thinking would have the biggest impact in the near future. With the genome project finished, we have all the pieces, and we need to understand how the cell works as a whole. It is a wonderful challenge, with sure impact on everything from cancer research to drug development.

David Weinberger
Small Pieces
by ROY CHRISTOPHER (2002)

WITH NINETY-FIVE THESES THAT REDEFINED ONLINE MARKETS
and their prospective web consumers, *The Cluetrain Manifesto* (Perseus
Books, 2000) dropped a virtual bomb on the virtual world. David Weinberger
was one of its four authors. Therein he stated, "The web is viral. It infects
everything it touches and, because it is an airborne virus, it infects some
things it doesn't. The web has become the new corporate infrastructure,
in the form of intranets, turning massive corporate hierarchical systems
into collections of many small pieces loosely joining themselves unpredict-
ably." With his new book, *Small Pieces Loosely Joined* (Perseus Books, 2002),
Weinberger expounds on this idea. With insight and authority, he claims
— among other things — that the web hasn't been hyped enough.

ROY CHRISTOPHER: *Can you give our readers a brief overview of your
new book* Small Pieces Loosely Joined?

DAVID WEINBERGER: *Small Pieces* tries to get at why the internet has
sent such a charge through our culture. After all, from one point of view,

109

it's just a hunk of wires and silicon. Where does the exuberant part of "irrational exuberance" come from? The book treats the web the way we treat something like democracy; when we want to understand democracy, we look at how it affected a set of interrelated ideas, such as law, authority, citizenship, equality, and liberty. Likewise, *Small Pieces* looks at how the web is affecting the building-block concepts of the real world, including morality, time, space, perfection, knowledge, self, groups, and even matter.

RC: *The subtitle of this book* ("A Unified Theory of the Web") *is decidedly misleading. Can you explain your use of this phrase?*
DW: I liked the play between the dishevelment of the title and the tidiness of the subtitle. Either taken by itself is misleading, but the two together I hope are not: The book does attempt to say some coherent things about the effect of the web's chaos on our day-to-day self-understanding.

RC: *In the face of the boom and bust of web business, as well as the litany of online scandals (and the media coverage thereof), some might laugh at your claim that the web hasn't been hyped enough. How would you defend this idea?*
DW: The book says that the web has absolutely been overhyped for the wrong reasons and not hyped enough for the right reasons. The notion that it's going to make everyone a millionaire is and always was ridiculous. But the web ultimately isn't about business. It's about human connection. Humans are nothing without connection. Change the way we are together, and you change who we are. That's what hasn't been hyped enough.

RC: *You maintain that our attraction to the web is directly proportional to our feeling of alienation as a culture. What do you feel is causing this alienation in the first place?*

DW: What isn't? You could answer this question from every field of human study, from economics to psychology to politics. In the book, I look at it in terms of the concepts we use for understanding ourselves and our world. We have, in the West, 2,500 years of thought about time, space, and self that for lots of reasons has accepted dualism — the idea that there are two worlds, one mental and one physical, and we have to figure out how the mental could ever get an accurate representation of the physical. Further, we assume that the physical world is the "real" world. These ideas are the root of a lot of the alienation that *Small Pieces* discusses.

RC: *You draw on the philosophy of Martin Heidegger in your writing. Do you feel he's the most applicable, or are there any other philosophers whose work you feel would help us to understand what's going on with the web's infiltration into our culture?*

DW: Heidegger is especially important to the book because of two of his insights. First, his way of exposing the failure of dualism is rooted in a clear-eyed and simple view of experience, not in theory. We're on the web not because we care about some philosophical theory, but because of the quality of the experience. It's fun. Second, he constantly goes back to time as at the root of our understanding of the world. The web, as a virtual world, can't be understood through matter, so time becomes more important — time and connection.

RC: The Cluetrain Manifesto *seems like a book for "the average workaday type" disguised as a business/marketing book. Is this a fair assessment?*

DW: Definitely. We wrote it as a manifesto because manifestos hearten one's comrades. And I feel safe in speaking for my three co-authors when I say that we viewed *Cluetrain* as a way of talking about the effect of the web by taking business as our sustained example. But the same sorts of things are happening to just about every social institution.

RC: *Cluetrain claims that the web changes everything about business, where other self-proclaimed "experts" maintain that it changes nothing. What do you say to would-be detractors?*

DW: Pistols at dawn! The web is challenging just about everything about business, from its business models to its ideas about what competition means. For example, businesses have defined themselves over the past century based on control over information, and they have used the selective release of information as the main way they control their markets, employees, partners, and competitors. On the web, however, customers turn out to be the best source of information. Further, employees go home and have no compunction about going out on the web and talking straight, forgetting there's supposed to be a wall there. This gets at the very definition of a business.

RC: *Do you have any other projects that I missed that you'd like to bring up here?*

DW: Just: Give us this day our daily weblog! There are a couple of revolutions happening right now in the weblogging world. Social writing and idea development — true joint authorship in a truly distributed way. The development of highly voiced centers of knowledge that will twist the org chart around new axes. Grassroots person-to-person journalism that substitutes multiple viewpoints for the pretense of objectivity.

We're only at the beginning of the web journey.

Eric Paulos
ExperiMental InterAction
by ROY CHRISTOPHER (2000)

ERIC PAULOS IS A MAN RIDING THE EXPERIMENTAL EDGE BETWEEN humans and machines. His research in this area, both in his graduate studies in computer science and robotics at the University of California at Berkeley, and with renegade robot troops such as Survival Research Laboratories, is far more adventurous than most researchers in similar space dare to be. "Lethal, anonymous tele-obliteration," the "I-Bomb," and several types of tele-embodiment are just a few of his past projects. Danger is definitely not outside the scope of his work.

Soon to finish his Ph.D. in electrical engineering and computer science, look for him to continue to carry the torch that lights the dark area between humans and machines.

ROY CHRISTOPHER: *How long have you been interested in and involved with human/machine interfaces and robotics?*
ERIC PAULOS: I have to admit that my initial fascination was with the

machine — the motion, the intricacy, the precision, the simplicity. I'm one of those hands-on builder types always taking things apart to learn how they tick. But you get bored and restless after so long, at which point building your own creations is the only means to satisfy the madness. As for robotics I can clearly remember catching a documentary on PBS before I was even a teenager that mesmerized me. It showed people working on building running and hopping robots. Before witnessing that video it was inconceivable to me that there were actually people that society accepted (and even paid) for such activities. I sort of set it aside for many years but remember it strongly when I was choosing a graduate program. It was all too clear then what passions I should follow. It was also a short time after making that decision that I figured out the work I had seen was done by Mark Raibert and his team at CMU and the MIT Leg Lab. Maybe I'll actually cross paths with those hopping machines someday.

A combination of fortuitous events occurred almost immediately after I started graduate school. The web suddenly provided a revolutionary interface to people and data. It was obvious to me that this was the perfect tool to begin exploration of the human/machine interface. Not robot interfaces in the traditional sense (i.e., expensive, one-off systems requiring a highly trained operator), but interfaces that were inexpensive and globally accessible to anyone — tele-presence for the masses. This motivated much of the early work with Mechanical Gaze, Legal Tender, and the Space Browsing blimps. On a parallel track, it was at this time that I begin serious work with Mark Pauline of Survival Research Laboratories (SRL). At SRL I had access to perhaps the world's most diverse, bizarre, unique, and of course lethal machinery — a perfect arena to explore novel interface designs. Mark and I blended perfectly in our dark and wondrous thinking on so many of those early projects. Most notable during that time were the experiments in lethal, anonymous tele-obliteration.

RC: *When did you get involved with SRL?*

EP: My first involvement there was back in 1993. SRL is much more than it appears to an outsider. Certainly its grand vision and many of its brilliant ideas come from Mark Pauline, founder and director of SRL since 1978. But one of its hidden treasures are the many ragtag members of SRL. This group or family of people holds such a wealth of creative ideas and expert knowledge covering an overwhelmingly immense set of domains. Getting to know each of them over the years as colleagues, collaborators, and friends is something for which I am extremely thankful. SRL is one of the rare unique experiences in life. One that I know I will always cherish.

RC: *What are your aims with Experimental Interaction Unit (EIU)?*

EP: The EIU was founded to directly confront and explore the boundary between humans and machines. My interest in the machine has not diminished, but I have always found the narrow, almost nebulous, region of the human/machine interface to be most interesting. This is where the action and interaction takes place: the locus of communication and understanding, where the human meets the machine, the blurred boundary, the unknown, and epicenter of the unexpected.

There are endless permutations to explore, and recent experiments have examined only a small subset of these themes. For example, the work on tele-embodiment: human communication and interaction at a distance through various specialized mechanical tele-operated systems. Other projects such as the I-Bomb and Dispersion, research human action and reaction to accessible interfaces of more devious technological systems in our immediate future. Look for new projects along these themes. However, I certainly don't want to be complacent and predictable, so expect deviations in the publicly stated strategies to keep people (and adversaries) guessing.

RC: *What are your major educational/career goals for the short and long terms?*

EP: Right now my focus is on graduation. I'm nearing the end of the computer science Ph.D. program here at UC Berkeley. I recently took my final oral exams, and I'm now deep in performing final experiments and data collection for my thesis. I'm exploring many options: academia, research labs, companies, startups, etc. I really won't know which path I'll be taking until I spend some time visiting people, examining facilities, and understanding the goals of each individual choice. My long-term goal is clear: I want to insure that I continue my creative endeavors which help me maintain my sanity. At the moment, the area of personal tele-presence holds my passion and is ripe for investigation. But I believe it's still difficult to say where my major contribution will be.

RC: *Human/machine interfacing is one of the major growth points of computer science as well as psychology, ergonomics, etc. Where do you see your work fitting into the future of these fields?*

EP: These days I spend more time reading sociology and psychology research and literature than almost anything else. For years I've been examining the machine and now I need to catch up on understanding the human element. I'm fascinated with all of the human interaction experiments that sociologists and psychologists have been exploring. During regular meetings I've been having with them, we've found tremendous common ground and certainly equal enthusiasm for researching and understanding the personal and social aspects of computer-mediated communication and interaction.

The larger, looming long-term research issues center around online trust and persuasion. Experiments have shown that current online communication channels are inadequate at supporting means of capturing and exchanging trust. Similarly, successful persuasion online is almost impossible compared to direct face-to-face interaction. Something vitally important is missing. Computers and technology will make significant incremental advances in the years to come, but filling in the human communication and interaction puzzle is what I consider one of the major contributions.

I see my work in two parts. First, collaboration with social scientists and researchers to better understand the nuances and subtle cues necessary for rich human communication and interaction. Secondly, the design and implementation of software and hardware systems to facilitate some of the more important communication cues. Of course, there will be a tremendous amount of iteration through this process to improve these systems as well. This is an enormous project and no one person is going to get there alone so we're going to need new collaborations and interdisciplinary teams to make real progress. Do you trust me?

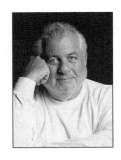

Richard Saul Wurman
Technology, Entertainment, Design
by MARK WIEMAN (1999)

WITH THE PUBLICATION OF HIS FIRST BOOK IN 1962 AT THE AGE of 26, Richard Saul Wurman began the singular passion of his life: making information understandable. Wurman coined the term "Information Architecture" in 1976 and in 1984 he created the Technology Entertainment Design (TED) conference and remains chairman and creative director. The next TED conference, TEDX in February 2000, will focus on understanding America at the millennium and will be accompanied by the publication of his sixty-sixth book, *Understanding USA* (TED Conferences, 1999).

MARK WIEMAN: *Information architects are in high demand at many internet-related companies. When you invented the title in 1976, did you anticipate how new media could affect the demand for such a role?*

RICHARD SAUL WURMAN: When I first came up with the term "Information Architects" in 1975, which was coincident with when I was national chairman of the AIA convention in Philadelphia in 1976, I decided to theme the conference and call it the "Architecture of Information" and start calling myself an "Information Architect." It seemed to make such sense to me that there was such a huge amount of information that nobody could understand — using myself as the model, and I couldn't understand stuff — that I thought that term would just catch on and overnight there would be a new field of human endeavor. Well, it didn't happen. So I was surprised that it didn't happen then. But now, in the last year particularly, there's been an explosion of people calling themselves information architects, and it's become ubiquitous. I'm surprised once again that when it took off, it took off so fast. I am, on a daily basis, becoming aware that people use it on their cards, use it on their stationery, use it on the internet, use it on their webpages. And of course, they don't even know where it came from. But it's a term that's of its time and people seem to identify with it. And it seems to fill in an important slot, as I thought it would many, many years ago — but of course I was wrong both times. One, that it didn't happen. And two, that it happened so fast.

MW: *Information designer Edward Tufte goes out of his way to emphasize the limitations of displaying complex information on computer screens as opposed to paper. Is he crazy, or are we still a long way from effectively using technology to enhance our understanding?*

RSW: Well, I think he's completely wrong. And he's completely wrong because of who he is. First of all, his books are terrific. But they're the books of an analytic historian. He is not a graphic designer. He is not an information architect. He doesn't have any ideas about graphics and what's going to happen in the future. He has documented the history of information design superbly, and he's done a very good analysis of it. But I think, since he doesn't have creative ideas about the future, he can't see how there will be amazing information displayed on the internet, done by very creative people, in the very near future. Are we stumbling around now doing things? You bet. Because we're finding our way. Much the same as when the movies first happened, when cinema first happened — they based it on old things, they made it look like stage plays. Well, we're just getting over the point where we're just putting diagrams on a screen. We're not taking the appropriate way of using dynamic information. We're using it to show off that we can spin things, and we're showing off things because we can do it, and everybody is bragging to one another about some cute program. We are going to get over that show-off stage very soon. We're going to be able to show things, and will show things, accurately, clearly, and using the medium for what it is. I mean, if you or anybody else is going through the stage that many of us are of getting fast downloads and speeding up your equipment, it changes your whole relationship with what you can see and how you see it. And I think his reflection is on things as he's looking backwards not forward.

MW: *You are a proponent of work as an extension of hobby. Please elaborate on this idea.*

RSW: The term "work" to me is a pejorative term. If you have to do something you don't like it's called work. Ditch diggers do work. You do work, work, work so you can take a vacation. So vacation and work have become opposites. As opposed to the idea that work is joy. As a designer, I think that the big design problem is designing your life. And if that's what you mean by hobby and that's what I mean by hobby, then my work is a collection of hobbies and things I want to do — that's part of designing your life.

MW: *The success of your TED conferences has been phenomenal. How do you explain it?*

RSW: TED is successful because it's not static. It's not a cookie-cutter conference where we have ten panels and fourteen speakers and a lunch paid for by IBM and everybody goes home. I've tried to make it a reflection, in real time, of what interests me. And I've tried to embrace my hypernormalcy — the fact that I'm more normal than other people, and what interests me, in all likelihood, will interest the audience. I don't pander to the audience by trying to present things that I think would interest them, but rather, as a committee of one, I try to have things that interest me.

Many years ago, after TED first started, I got less and less interested in boys and their toys and showing off just hardware and jumping through hoops, and seeing how fast we could speed up things, and how cute all our little hardware could be. I still have a passing interest in that, but the focus on the demo aspect of the conference has left a number of years ago and basically the theme is, "Why are we doing all this?" As we discuss why we are doing all this, it touches everybody. It's about not only high tech but high touch, which was the earliest pronouncement that John Naisbitt did in 1984 when he gave the keynote of the conference. And the more we don't have to come to TED, the more people are going to want to do it; the more they can not have to go to conferences and press the flesh, the more they'll want to talk to real people with real eye contact and look at connections — the connectivity between science and understanding and information. And the conference is really about understanding. Well, that's what the human spirit is about, understanding. As long as it's about understanding — partly understanding based on the growth of the information technology sector, the growth of the entertainment sector, the sophistication of the design sector — it's always going to be fresh and new and it's not going to surprise me. But that doesn't mean I'm going to keep on doing it forever, it just means that that's a much better theme than just showing off your wares. You know, "Look at me, look at me."

MW: *Can you explain the subject matter of* Understanding USA *in more detail?*
RSW: The working title was *Atlas of Understanding*. The actual title is just going to be *Understanding USA*. And there's going to be 350 pages of maps,

charts, graphs, and whatever works. Very easily understood, developed by the best information architects that I can find in the United States. They are responding to about 300 questions that I've come up with, 300 answers that we've researched here at TED, and trying to display them in a form that makes the complex clear. Much of this will have underneath it a dynamic set of statistics and graphs and charts, and that will be put on a website, and people will probably be able to download the whole book. But the website is not the book; the website will have its own life, and that's being developed by Bob Greenberg of R/GA Digital Studios, Ciaran Doyle from Intel, Curtis Wong of Microsoft, and myself, to be a really wonderful website of understanding, and a live website of updatable material that makes public information public about America. So to me, this is a very important turning point in the whole field of information architecture. Of course, almost completely ignored by the various organizations that talk about information design and the various graphic design groups in the United States, and the international design groups, for some reason. At the TEDX conference in February will be the greatest convocation of information architects ever, because all the dozen people and their staff who'll be working on the book will be there and making short presentations and even probably have a workshop.

MW: *Is there any aspect of your work, or any new project you're working on, that you'd like to bring up?*

RSW: My newest project, and I'll tell you for the first time because I haven't really announced it or sent out a press release on this yet, is a brand new, two-month-old publishing company called TOP. It's a joint venture; I own fifty percent of it and I'm the CEO and creative director. The other half of it is owned by a wholly owned subsidiary of the second largest health care insurance group in the country, United HealthCare out of Minnesota. United HealthCare has a subsidiary called Ovations, and the TOP comes from the Ovations press. We'll be developing, both in print and in electronic form, in the next five years, fifty single-issue books and websites on subjects from finance and debt and wills, to Alzheimer's and cardiac and diagnostic tests and care giving and care receiving, for people fifty and over — people in the second half of their lives. So that's my new hobby.

MEDIA

ERIC ZIMMERMAN

MCKENZIE WARK

N. KATHERINE HAYLES

GEERT LOVINK

BRENDA LAUREL

PETER LUNENFELD

ERIK DAVIS

GARETH BRANWYN

DOUGLAS RUSHKOFF

Eric Zimmerman
Play as Research
by ROY CHRISTOPHER (2004)

STEVEN JOHNSON CALLS HIM "THE LOU REED OF THE NEW GAM-
ing culture." Eric Zimmerman hops through the realms of game design,
academe, writing, game advocacy, and entrepreneurship as if he's playing
a game of hopscotch. And, in many ways, he is. He's spent the last decade
designing award-winning games, teaching at places like MIT, New York
University, School of Visual Arts, and Parsons School of Design at the
New School University, as well as writing continuously about gaming
— much of which can be seen in four recent books: *RE: Play* (Peter Lang,
2003), *Rules of Play* (MIT Press, 2003), *First Person* (MIT Press, 2004), and
Brenda Laurel's *Design Research* (MIT Press, 2003). In 2000, he and Peter
Lee founded the game development company gameLab, which develops
games for the computer and beyond. Zimmerman's work is based largely
on a concept of "play as research" — sort of a playful adaptation of Paul
Feyerabend's anarchist epistemology — and he's a strong advocate for this
concept in academic research, in game design, and in the workplace.

ROY CHRISTOPHER: *At gameLab, you've fostered a "play as research" plan. For the uninitiated, can you briefly lay out your tenets for a creative design research environment?*

ERIC ZIMMERMAN: In a game, the game designer makes the rules. But the game designer doesn't directly create the player's experience. The way that the rules play out — once people enter into the system and start playing around — is usually uncertain and surprising, especially if you've got a good game on your hands.

In creating a company culture, gameLab co-founder Peter Lee and I have carried this idea outward into thinking about how games are not just played, but made. In other words, for us gameLab is a structure that is designed to create unexpected and surprising staff experiences and resulting design artifacts.

On a practical level, that means a number of things: from a design process that emphasizes prototyping and iterative playtesting, to an office environment where each staff member has a monthly allowance to buy something — anything — for the company research library. Play should sometimes be undirected, and staff members are expected to spend about 10 percent of their time (half a day a week) playing videogames, surfing the web, horsing around with toys, and otherwise just playing.

RC: *Having worked in design for companies in various states of corporate control and clientele, I am completely sold on your ideas about the creative environment, but I'm also aware of the resistance or apathy to these ideas evident in these environments. How should designers go about convincing their employers of the import of a creative and stimulating design culture?*

EZ: That's a really tough one. In my experience, if the company culture isn't already healthy when you enter, very little is going to change it. I'd consider voting with my feet and finding another company that supports the kind of work experience you're looking for.

But I realize that's not always possible. So what to do? The key to creating a culture of design research is fostering relationships between the inside and the outside of the company — to find opportunities that let culture seep into the company and vice versa. If lobbying the higher-ups doesn't work, then just start doing. Try to organize a reading group, or a board-game night, or a movie field trip — even if your boss isn't officially sponsoring or condoning the event. (Remember, don't do these things gratuitously, but be strategic and make sure they're relevant to your work.) If you're lucky, the positive effects on your company's work and the office environment will be noticed.

RC: *In your essay in* First Person *you gallantly attempt to define specific terms about gaming and move forward in a sort of Wittgensteinian language game. Do you see these debates as an infinite regress, or is there a foundation in there somewhere?*

EZ: No and no. For a designer, the value of a concept or definition is not its scientific accuracy, but instead its ability to solve problems. So for me, attempts at definition don't aim to ultimately once and for all define a "game" or "play," or whatever complex term you like. Instead, it may be useful in part of a design process to be able to tell the difference between "game" and "play." Or not. Every designer has his or her own way of working and opinion about just what a "useful" concept is.

On a different level, I think that definitions are important for education, for critical debate, for scholars, for journalists, for cross-disciplinary research, etc. There's no doubt that in other design fields, such as architecture, there has been all kinds of exchange between "theory" and "practice." What I'd like to see in games isn't a single set of definitions, but whole ecosystems of competing ideas, concepts, and ways of understanding. That can't but help make better games.

RC: *We talk about gaming a lot in academia (i.e., "gaming" different scholarly situations). I've adapted my own ideas about it from James P. Carse's* Finite and Infinite Games *(Free Press, 1986). Do you find gaming metaphors spilling over into other areas of your life as well?*

EZ: In my scholarly work, I really do try to look at games as games, and not as something else. But games to me are so fascinating and complex it's hard not to apply them elsewhere. For example, a game for me is a model of a good friendship, relationship, or collaboration. The commonly accepted rules of games establish an agreed-upon "frame" for the playful, productive conflict of the game to occur. Without that frame, you've got raw conflict. With that frame, the spontaneous, creative, and ecstatic struggle of the game can take place. Of course, not everyone thinks that a good relationship is a context for productive conflict. But that's just the game designer in me, I suppose.

RC: *Is there anything you're working on that you'd like to mention here?*

EZ: Yes! Big things are afoot at gameLab. This fall, we'll be unveiling a brand new direction for the company. Sorry to be cryptic, but I can't yet tell you exactly what it is. However, I will say this: the work we do transverting rules into play doesn't just happen within a game, or as part of the company environment, but hopefully within larger social spheres as well. The idea is not just to play with a game, but create games that play with culture at large. When more games are doing this, then I won't have to be the loyal opposition to the gaming world — I can just be loyal. Stay tuned.

And keep on playin'.

McKenzie Wark
To the Vector the Spoils
by ROY CHRISTOPHER (2003)

WHEN VENTURING INTO NEW TERRITORY WITHOUT A PROPER map, McKenzie Wark is the kind of guy you want to have around. His intuition in such cases provides a beacon to the next viable vantage point.

Wark's intuition has shown up in his books, *Virtual Geography* (Indiana University Press, 1994), *The Virtual Republic* (Allen & Unwin, 1998), *Celebrities, Culture and Cyberspace* (Pluto Press, 1999), and *Dispositions* (Salt Publishing, 2002), among others. He was a co-editor of the Nettime anthology *Readme!* (Autonomedia, 1999) and, with Brad Miller, co-produced the multimedia work *Planet of Noise*. In addition, he has written for such publications as the late Australian cyberculture magazine *21C*, the rabble-rousing, subversive website *Disinformation*, the recent *CTRL [SPACE]* anthology (MIT Press, 2002), and countless other cracks and crevices of print and cyberspace. He is also a professor at the State University of New York.

Regardless of where you find his work, McKenzie Wark will direct you to that next place from which to see.

ROY CHRISTOPHER: *Let's get our terms aligned first: How do you define the term "hacker"? Do you include artists, software developers, and other so-called "knowledge workers"?*

MCKENZIE WARK: I think everyone who actually creates "intellectual property" could consider themselves part of the same class — the hacker class — and as having convergent interests. So, yes, that could include programmers, musicians, writers, and also engineers, chemists — all sorts of people who are culturally distinct. What we have in common is that we have to sell the products of our intellectual labor to corporations who have a monopoly on realizing its value. We invent the idea, but they control the means of production. The laws that used to protect us — copyright and patent — have been subtly changing over the course of the last few decades to protect corporate owners of existing "intellectual property," not individual creators of new ideas. And so I wrote "A Hacker Manifesto" to dramatize this emergent conflict.

RC: *I like the idea that the information world doesn't have an equivalent to the physical world's second law of thermodynamics, and that this idea represents true freedom. Is there a danger of this auspicious outlook failing?*

MW: The commodity economy runs on scarcity. It's all about making the wealth produced by labor the exclusive, private property of the few. At the moment it's hard to argue for the socialization of wealth. Some part of it needs to be social, or things just won't function at all. Every civilized society recognizes the need for socialized health and pensions.

But when we come to information, there's no need for it to be privatized. Economists call information a "nonrivalrous resource." Which is an oxymoron. Basically it is an admission that information need not be subject to the laws of scarcity at all. My possession of some information does not deprive you of it. The cost of making a copy is being reduced all the time.

So the one place where we can still entertain the idea of a release from scarcity is the world of information. It could have a quite different economy, or a non-economy. It is by legal artifice, the repressive force of the police and cultural re-engineering, that we are being persuaded of the necessity of a purely private economy of information, where Mickey Mouse is somebody's fiefdom in perpetuity, where nothing ever comes back to the public domain. I think we have to fight that.

But where Lawrence Lessig and others see this as a fight to get the law to recognize the common sense of a public domain, I think it is much more than that. We are up against a new and powerful class interest, which profits by the commodification of information rather than the manufacture of things. We have to resist this new interest with technical and cultural means, as well as through legal challenges.

RC: *The idea of education as slavery seems to be becoming more and more prevalent in intellectual circles. What do you think should be done about the education problem?*

MW: So-called critical theory in the universities becomes merely hypocritical theory if it doesn't deal with the fact that education is now part of the problem, not part of the solution. Education is about creating scarcity. Here in the United States we have the least democratic, most aristocratic education system in the (over)developed world. It is all about rationing prestige. It has nothing to do with seeking knowledge.

Knowledge too has to be released from scarcity and hierarchy. Forcing people to submit to twenty years of mental enslavement — all their childhood and young adult life — just to secure a reasonable standard of living is a status quo that needs to be challenged.

RC: *With information as commodity and media/communication as architecture, where should the hacker seek to gain/maintain power and/or control?*

MW: Firstly, it's a question of realizing that all intellectual creators are "hackers." It is about realizing a common interest that has nothing to do with choices of identity, culture, or taste. A class interest, in short.

Secondly, it's about realizing that our class interest confronts another class, one I call the vectoralist class. The vectoralist class controls the means of realizing the value of what we create. They control the vectors along which new information moves. A broadcasting network is a vector, but so too is a drug company. New information could be in the form of a digital file or a little pink pill. The form doesn't matter. What does matter is that the class interest of the vectoralists lies in making ideas a form of exclusive, perpetual, and global private property.

Thirdly, it's a matter of tactics. One can mount legal challenges to the enclosure of information in ever more restrictive intellectual property law. One can mount political challenges in uniting the various branches of the hacker class. Or one can mount a cultural challenge by showing that the interests of the public are not served by the exclusive control of information by a handful of corporations. And, of course, there is the technological strategy of creating new tools for sharing information freely. But really, it's a question of getting all of these tactics to work together, to create a strategy, perhaps even an alternative logistics in which information is free.

RC: *While reading* Virtual Geography, *I couldn't help but feel a weird sense of amnesia. I remembered all of the media events therein, but only as vague blips on the radar. How do we interject the idea of memory into the mediasphere?*

MW: As Guy Debord used to argue, the triumph of the spectacle is in the defeat of history and the installation of "spectacular time," which is purely cyclical. We no longer have history, we have fashion. Of course, history always crashes the party, but it appears as something inexplicable — the nightmare of 9/11 video footage on endless replay, defying explanation.

The temptation in media criticism, especially in America, is to claim a higher access to truth. All media is false, but one's personal experience of identity is somehow authentic. Politics is atomized into subjective feeling and turned into a species of moral judgment. This creates that peculiarly American pseudo-leftist language that is really about moral authority, a kind of weird mutant Puritanism.

An alternative is to take the great events that cross the media vector and freeze the frame. Look closely at the decisive images. Wind the tape backwards, looking for patterns. Play the whole thing in fast-forward to look at the rhythm of the edits. In other words, we can discover history within the media image, without making claims to an external, superior grasp on truth. Through the classic Burroughsian techniques of cut up, play back, repetition, we can produce our own knowledge of media as history, history as mediation.

RC: *Is there anything else you're working on that you'd like to bring up here?*

MW: I'm increasingly interested in the dual character of the vectoral empire. It has its engines of privatized information, but it also has its engine of vectoralizing military power. We are truly in the age of "infowar." Of course, real people die, killed by real bombs, but information over where those people are, how to target them with bombs — that's the new face of warfare. The new warfare is a suspected terrorist in Yemen being assassinated by a remote-controlled drone. It's the infrastructure of Serbia being jammed with strategically placed bombing that shuts down all command and control.

Now, the two faces of empire are closely linked in that they both run on the same vectoral technologies. There is a military-entertainment complex that turns civilian and military space alike into a game space for the calculation of moves, governed by arbitrary but nevertheless effective rules. We are in the middle of a great game, the goal of which is to subordinate history to reason. Not to Hegel's historical reason, but the logic of the game. And anyone who won't play by the rules is to be contained (Kim Jong II) or eliminated (Saddam).

To the vector the spoils.

N. Katherine Hayles
Material Girl
by ROY CHRISTOPHER (2003)

DIGGING DEEP IN THE TEXTS OF BOTH LITERATURE AND SCIENCE,
N. Katherine Hayles exemplifies the reconciliation of C.P. Snow's "two
cultures" better than anyone I know. Her refusal to concentrate on either
side of the fence, instead insisting on plowing new ground on both sides,
has lead her to some of the most intriguing research currently being done.
Looking at texts from all sources and angles, Hayles is always seeing new
things that others overlook.

In her recent MIT Press MediaWork Pamphlet, *Writing Machines*
(2002), she continues this analysis. Blending thinly veiled autobiography,
narrative fiction, literary critique, and other styles, she brings us into a
world where text, materiality, signifier, and signified come together and
come alive on the page. Her in-depth view of innovative texts, hyper-
texts, and experimental fiction (including an exquisite look at Mark Z.
Danielewski's postprint novel *House of Leaves*) leaves no doubt that she's
been working these fields for years.

ROY CHRISTOPHER: Writing Machines *incorporates many literary styles — autobiography, fictional narrative, critique, etc. — to great effect. Was it your initial intention to juxtapose these styles?*

N. KATHERINE HAYLES: Combining autobiography with theoretical analysis is one way of joining the personal with the political, analysis with life experience. Increasingly I see scholars and theorists trying experiments of this kind. To persevere in scholarship requires deep personal commitment. And where does this commitment, this passion, come from? Almost always from life experiences. Usually that connection remains submerged and private, but when it comes to light, it can be electrifying. In *Writing Machines*, I hoped to use the autobiographical narrative to illustrate what it means to make the journey from a print-centric to a media perspective. Profound changes like this never happen overnight. They more nearly resemble peeling away the layers of an onion, where one revelation leads to another, and that to another, and so on — a process that takes months and years. It is difficult to grasp this kind of process analytically, for its very nature implies a number of partial realizations that arrive slowly and often painfully. To know something on an abstract level is one thing, but to unravel all the assumptions and presuppositions bound up with it is something else entirely.

RC: *You've been analyzing the materiality of literature for years now. In reference to* House of Leaves, *you stated, "Focusing on materiality allows us to see the dynamic interactivity through which a literary work mobilizes its physical embodiment in conjunction with its verbal signifiers to construct meanings in ways that implicitly construct the user/reader as well." Can you elaborate on this statement?*

NKH: Despite rich traditions of combining the visual and verbal in artists' books, concrete poetry, and canonized works — from Blake's illustrated books to Pound's *Cantos* — there remains a widespread presupposition in literary studies that a literary "work" is an immaterial verbal construction, as if words floated in the air without having a tangible body. Strategies for understanding how words interact with their physical instantiations are still emerging, and much more work needs to be done to understand this more fully, especially with electronic media. In electronic environments words can swoop and fly, dance and morph, fade and intensify, change from black to red. How do these behaviors affect meaning, and how does verbal signification affect our understanding of these behaviors? Similar considerations apply to print literature, although here the interactions may be more subtle — but they are still important.

RC: *Rather than looking at the blurring dialectics between natural/unnatural and human/nonhuman, you've been looking at presence/absence and materiality/virtuality. Considering DNA as textual code and language as "writing in the mind," where does text end and materiality begin?*

NKH: Now that the sequencing of the human genome is approaching completion, molecular biologists are coming up against the full realization that DNA considered as a "code" or "text" is only a small part of the story. Understanding the relation of the genome to function — how and why genes actually work — requires an understanding of protein folding, a much more complex matter than simple sequence. The gene as text cannot account for these complexities; for that, the gene must be understood as an embodied structure in three-dimensional space. Similarly, the full complexities of language are increasingly related to the embodied complexities of the human brain as it has evolved over eons, as Steve Pinker, among others, has been arguing. In the twenty-first century, text and materiality will be seen as inextricably entwined. Materiality and text, words and their physical embodiments, are always already a unity rather than a duality. Appreciating the complexities of that unity is the important task that lies before us.

RC: *In* Chaos and Order *(University of Chicago Press, 1991), your self-referential analysis of the rhetoric of chaos theory tempted becoming fractal itself. Is language really able to exhibit emergent properties in the same way as other dynamical systems?*

NKH: Many literary texts use fractal structures to express and embody complexity, from the microstylistics of poetic effects between words to large-scale effects in novelistic structures. Language is certainly able to demonstrate emergent properties, though it may not always do so. I think a better way to state the question is to ask how and in what ways literary language demonstrates emergence. For starters, I recommend Joseph McElroy's *Plus* (Carroll & Graf, 1987), an experimental novel about a terminally ill person who agrees to have his brain extracted from his dying body and re-embodied as part of the neural network that pilots a spacecraft. The challenge that McElroy posed was devising a language for this posthuman condition in which normal thought processes have been profoundly disrupted and sensory inputs radically transformed. At first the narrator's language seems almost incomprehensible, but patient reading reveals strategic repetitions and re-organizations that instantiate emergent processes at work. This is one kind of strategy, but, of course, there are many others as well. To my mind, emergence is a rich concept that can illuminate the signifying practices of many literary texts.

RC: *Is there anything you're working on or new areas you're exploring that you'd like to bring up here?*

NKH: My book-in-progress is entitled *Coding the Signifier: Rethinking Semiosis from the Telegraph to the Computer*. It argues that signification works in significantly different ways in technologies that employ code, compared to natural language. Semiotics remains our most powerful and influential theoretical framework for understanding how texts create meaning, but it needs to be radically revised to account for how meaning is created within electronic environments. Returning to the theories of Ferdinand de Saussure, I compare his premises and conclusions to the realities of coding technologies, showing how coding technologies change the conditions for communication and require the introduction of new concepts. Then, through a series of case studies, I demonstrate how coding technology functions as a kind of trading zone where meaning-making becomes a negotiation between code and natural language. Following the fractures, ruptures, and tensions between these two different kinds of signifying practices, I explore how concepts central to human experience undergo reconfiguration, including subjectivity, agency, and free will. My tutor texts range from fiction by such diverse writers as Henry James, James Tiptree, and Stanislaw Lem to such computer texts as Karl Sims's simulations and Shelly Jackson's electronic literary work "Patchwork Girl." The book is under contract to the University of Chicago Press and, if all goes well, should appear sometime next year.

Geert Lovink
Tracking Critical Net Culture
by ROY CHRISTOPHER (2002)

WITH THE HIGHLY REGARDED AND WELL-USED NETTIME MAIL-ing list, Geert Lovink established himself as one of the few true leaders of sober, useful net criticism (a discourse he in effect cofounded). Now, with *Dark Fiber: Tracking Critical Internet Culture* (MIT Press, 2002) and the forthcoming *Uncanny Networks: Dialogues With the Virtual Intelligentsia* (MIT Press, 2003), he further expands his vision where others have fallen silent. Finally, with the end of the dot-com hand-waving, comes a voice for all of the fissures in the façade.

Lovink is one part activist, one part visionary, and two parts critical thinker. Peter Lunenfeld calls him "one of the great ones," and *Dark Fiber* proves it with insight, street cred, and wit to boot.

ROY CHRISTOPHER: *The openness (the ability for most anyone most any-where to participate) of the web has been one of its most touted aspects. You contend that this "openness" is being cut off by corporate interests. Could you briefly explain how you see this coming to pass?*

143

GEERT LOVINK: For most corporations the user is a consumer that needs to be monitored and, if possible, lured to buy something. This is a fundamentally different attitude from the user as "netizen," which is primarily seen as a producer. A good example of this are the weblogs and other open publishing tools. This silent revolution has not been developed by commercial entities. The new architecture of the internet is treating users by default as thread. Lately I've noticed that one can no longer switch on a terminal of some network and open a telnet session. Firewalls simply do not allow anyone to use this basic application. I do not want to blame the demise of the open internet on corporations only. Governments all over the world are acting as willing executors of corporate interests. Everyone is paranoid these days. Remember, it is American IT companies who help the Chinese government to censor and monitor their part of the internet. Apparently, they are more then happy to do the job. This sad fact proves that Gilmore's Law, which says that the internet is treating censorship as damage and will route around it, no longer works. ISPs are storing traffic data of their users, ready to hand them over to federal investigators. This is happening all over the world. I wonder how many of us are aware of this. In the meanwhile, the official internet ideology still talks about cyber freedom, as if nothing has changed. I guess at some point these contradictions can no longer be covered up.

RC: *What's really going on with blogging and collaborative text filtering that makes these areas so conceptually vibrant? This seems to be emerging as the next major focus of the study of the evolution of web use.*
GL: Weblogs are bringing the issue of open publishing and collaborative filtering to the next level. Weblogs are so much more sophisticated, compared to the relatively primitive, linear email-based, mailing-list software. There is a constant threat of information overload, these days. People don't surf anymore. For good reasons they have high demands on the quality of

computer-mediated communication. However, they do not want to hand over their online freedom. This is the background why open publishing tools such as weblogs have taken off so much. Users want to have a greater say about the information they receive and send out. Yes, they want to read carefully edited pieces and have reliable information on their screens. But at the same time, they do not want to give away the control over the medium entirely to commercial web portals. It's a fine line and software is playing an increasingly important role in the delicate balancing act between the internet as a professional medium and an open environment where everyone has a say.

RC: *You're the first person I've heard make mention of the fact that the "new media" won't always be new. Labeling seems to have quite a lot to do with the development of critical theory. With everything still on the move (even in our postdot-com era), net critique is still scrambling to describe and analyze its subject(s). Where should these energies be focused?*

GL: In his later work, Marshall McLuhan formulated the Laws of Media. By now everyone should be aware of them. There are cyclical movements, from mythology and hype to the creation of a market, followed by a mass acceptance and the subsequent "disappearance" of the technology into everyday life. We no longer see the refrigerator and vacuum cleaner. Literally. In that sense, the computer will also become part of the household furniture, apart from the fact that PCs are anyway getting smaller and lighter. The shocking fact here is not this particular development, but the blatant refusal by so many technology gurus and corporate consultants to admit this bare fact and communicate it to their clients. The terror of being positive has to come to a hold. But despite the dot-com crash and all the corporate scandals many still believe in the saga of a never-ending boom. We thus have to continue our cultural analysis in order to understand where this collective blindness, this unwillingness to analyze movements of markets and trends in society is coming from. Obviously many have a vested interest in a bull market. But why are so many still buying into those stories? We can only explain that with the tools of mass psychology. Venture capital models can only thrive on herd mentality. In that sense, the United States business culture is everything but individual and entrepreneurial. In short, Moore's Law may work for chips, but cannot be applied to the IT sector at large. Technology has its booms and busts, as well as anything else in society. The internet cannot be located outside of society. It is subjected to certain economic laws, and we all have to be aware of them.

Net criticism is not that different from theatre criticism or film reviews. What the IT sector needs is its own class of independent critics that are willing to stand up against the powerful interests of corporations and their governments. Great examples are *Cyberselfish* (PublicAffairs, 2000) by Paulina Borsook and Thomas Frank's *One Market Under God* (Doubleday, 2000). For me it all starts with the acceptance of negativism as a strong and creative force within society. As long as New Age is ruling over the corporate board rooms, not much will change. There is enormous need for investigative journalism outside of academia. It is not healthy to concentrate the public intellectuals within the walls of the universities. What new media need is a sophisticated vocabulary, shared by a great deal of its users. We have to accept that we are living in a techno culture. The core of today's arts and culture is deeply technological. We can no longer afford to separate the two. That's a very broad agenda for net criticism, I know. I purposely do not want to narrow it down to the critique of corporate power. Its agenda should be based on a broad cultural analysis, like that of Bauhaus, the Frankfurt School, and postmodernism. It is high time for the humanities to leave campus. Get technological! Build networks!

For me good critics are not outsiders but insiders. At the same time the supremacy of the engineering class has to be questioned as well. An engaged form of criticism can only happen if people are forced to debate. In order to get there we need more conflicts, more scandals, more public liability. I no longer believe in begging for interdisciplinary programs in which scientists, artists, and theorists peacefully work together. That soft approach has failed over the last decades. It simply did not happen. It should be part of a shift in IT culture to go on the attack.

RC: *Can you give an overview of what you mean by "tactical media"?*
GL: The tactical media was developed in Amsterdam in the "post 1989" years and is associated with the Next Five Minutes conference series. We tried to find an expression for our discontent with the existing definition of terms such as "alternative media," "subculture," and "underground." They simply didn't work anymore. For today's media activists, the designation "alternative versus mainstream" is no longer useful. Everyone is involved in "tactical" interventions in the mainstream. This does not mean that these people have sold out. There is no long march through the institutions. That's a romantic vision of the baby boom generation, at a time when there were still plenty of tenured jobs to be given away within the press and universities. Today everyone is more or less a freelance worker, permanently on the move. Work is a project. The whole idea that one has to "penetrate" the mainstream in order to do "good work" from inside the system is not valid anymore. But there is also a technological reason for this shift. Tactical media such as small radio stations, websites and mailing lists, record labels and 'zines are all thriving because of the enormous drop in the prices of hardware. This means that it is much easier to have your independent media infrastructure. It is no longer a political choice to remain in this or that ghetto. The so-called "antiglobalization" movement proves how broad concerns are over the environment and world trade. The backbone of these movements are sites such as www.indymedia.org. Activists these days try really hard to get beyond the lifestyle level and

address a variety of social groups. This capacity is partially due to better understanding of the workings of media.

RC: *In* Dark Fiber, *you call for a return of cybernetics. What void do you see being filled by a return to cybernetic thinking in IT culture?*

GL: Cybernetics was a unique form of science. We have a lot to learn from it, despite its mythological and speculative approaches and somewhat stubborn belief system. Unlike the present IT theories, cybernetics was deeply interdisciplinary and stood in direct contact with contemporary philosophy of its time. That link was lost in the '70s. Most engineers look down on cultural studies, postmodern thinking, gender issues, and post-colonial theories. The other way round is also true, of course. One of the great challenges of our time is the opening up of the technologists with other disciplines. Here I am not referring to spiritual levels. I am an enemy of New Age. I do not believe that the engineer has to open up and become sensitive for the "metaphysical." I am talking about society here. It would be such a step forward if technology would see itself as part of culture. We live in a technological culture. Society is not a user that "adapts" to the great inventions. Engineering culture is itself part of the bigger picture. Historically cybernetics was aware of this. Because of World War II and the fact that many of its practitioners were refugees, there was a critical understanding of social and political issues. Yet, I am not nostalgic. There will be new sciences in the future that will overcome the fear for humanities. The common effort called "net criticism" can only be one such attempt.

Brenda Laurel
Utopian Entrepreneur
by ROY CHRISTOPHER (2002)

WITH OVER TWENTY-FIVE YEARS EXPLORING HUMAN-COMPUTER interaction, Brenda Laurel is an unsung veteran of the field. Her doctoral dissertation was the first to propose a comprehensive architecture for computer-based interactive fantasy and fiction. Laurel was one of the founding members of the research staff at Interval Research Corporation in Palo Alto, California, where she coordinated research activities exploring gender and technology, and where she co-produced and directed the Placeholder Virtual Reality project. She was also one of the founders and VP of design of a spin-off company from Interval — Purple Moon — formed to market products based on this research. Her latest book, *Utopian Entrepreneur* (MIT Press, 2001), explores the struggles she dealt with at Purple Moon — attempting to perform socially conscious work in the context of business.

She currently serves as interim chair and graduate faculty member of the graduate Media Design program at the Art Center College of Design in Pasadena, California.

ROY CHRISTOPHER: *While* Utopian Entrepreneur *explores issues that emerge when one attempts to do socially conscious work in the context of business, it also illuminates sort of a dialectic between the two (the heartfelt work and the heartless business). Do you foresee a way that this conflict can be resolved in the context of capitalism?*

BRENDA LAUREL: To be frank, I'm no longer sure what capitalism means anymore. I see several problems with the "free market economy" that may prove catastrophic for societies and ecologies; for example: the degradation of some cultures and their environments by offering factory work as a substitute for agriculture, the privatization of health care and education, and unwillingness or inability of the government to regulate industrial pollution and waste. I do think that people who do good work that provides products or services of value can often make reasonable businesses out of those ideas.

There are certain issues — for example, the ability of people to earn an honest living creating content for the internet — that are not currently possible in our business climate, because they are resisted overtly and covertly by the publishing giants who profit from keeping "individual creators" in the role of contractors. It is also true that, due to the excesses of greed and moral laxness of the last several years, funding is extremely hard to come by no matter how good the idea, and there has been no perceptible change in the unrealistic expectations of the venture community (at least in the area of high-tech) on the rate of return on investment. It is worth noting that investors in alternative energy have a much longer horizon for return on investment, which makes their vital work possible.

RC: *The metaphor of "public good" or "the commons" keeps coming up in reference to the current peer-to-peer model of information exchange, where the simple sharing of bits is the raison d'être. There has yet to be a business*

model that could exploit this free exchange. Do you see a way to make P2P
work for business without killing the commons?
BL: Although I have been told strenuously by several people that it won't
work, I honestly think that an infrastructure for micropayments could
be created to support the sale of individual digital work that has value
to customers. Near-currency may also succeed eventually. The problem
with barter is that people are rarely willing to send a bag of groceries to a
content or service creator.

RC: *The narrative style of* Utopian Entrepreneur *reminds me of Ellen*
Ullman — thought-provoking and often simultaneously heart-breaking. She
said she struggled with the very personal stories in her book Close to the
Machine *(City Lights, 1997). While writing about your business experience*
and personal feelings, did you feel a pull one way or the other?
BL: No. I feel that personal experience must be revealed for the conclusions that one makes to have any credibility. I was remarkably restrained
in the narrative portions of the book, but I do think that they helped get
my ideas across. The audience for the book, I hope, is people who approach
their work with passion — not for what they can make, but for what they
can do or enable others to do.

RC: *The user interface has been a battlefield of theory, dogma, and experi-*
mentation for decades now. Users have been seeking better ways to create,
retrieve, and manipulate information while UI designers seem to be working
on the wrong problems in a lot of cases. What work do you see going on in the
conceptual space between human and machine that makes the most sense?
BL: Certainly work on speech recognition and generation has created
a wealth of new opportunities. The slow but steady degradation of the
notion of the machine as the thing to be used is helpful as well. For

example, a person does not want to operate a musical playback device; they want to listen to music while jogging — hence the Sony Walkman and its descendants. Focusing on the person, the situated context, and the desired result are the best ways to approach any interface problem. Also, I think that the rise of ethnographic and qualitative research is an enormous help to designers. As designers gain a more central role in enterprise, the situation will continue to improve. As my friend Aviv Bergman has said, "the machine is not the environment for the person; the person is the environment for the machine."

RC: *Is there anything else that you'd like to bring up here?*

BL: Only the work I did in real honest-to-goddess virtual reality (with head-mounted displays) back in 1993. There, the principle was that a person should be able to walk around in a virtual environment, because the sense of agency is imperative to a sense of immersion. Desktop VR was a very poor substitute and I look forward to the day when we use all the existing processing power with cheap, wide-angle stereoscopic displays to reinsert this important ingredient into VR.

Peter Lunenfeld
Critic as Curator
by ROY CHRISTOPHER (2002)

PETER LUNENFELD IS THE DIRECTOR OF THE INSTITUTE FOR
Technology and Aesthetics (ITA) and teaches in the graduate Media
Design program at Art Center College of Design. He is considered one
of the preeminent critics and theorists of the intersections of art, design,
and technology. *Afterimage* referred to his edited collection, *The Digital
Dialectic: New Essays on New Media* (MIT Press, 1999) as "the first printed
book you read about the virtual world that does not merely describe it,
but puts you there." *Snap to Grid: A User's Guide to Digital Arts, Media and
Cultures* (aka *S2G*) (MIT Press, 2000) has been covered everywhere from
Italy's *Flash Art* to Britain's *New Scientist*, the latter of which concluded
its featured review by saying that artists and designers working with digital technologies "now have their bible, their *Stones of Venice*, their *Ways
of Seeing.*" From 1998 through 2002, he wrote the "User" column for the
international journal *artext*.

Recently, he developed the Mediawork Pamphlet Series for the
MIT Press. These highly designed little books pair major writers with

contemporary graphic designers to produce "theoretical fetish objects" in the tradition of *The Medium is the Massage* and *War and Peace in the Global Village* — where Lunenfeld plays Jerome Agel to the Marshall McLuhans and Quentin Fiores of today.

ROY CHRISTOPHER: *Can you briefly explain "vapor theory"?*

PETER LUNENFELD: In *S2G*, I define vapor theory as "dialectical immaterialism, critical discussions about technology untethered to the constraints of production." I started thinking about vapor theory back in the days of VR, when otherwise sensible people got misty-eyed about abandoning their identities and moving into fully realized, photo-realistic virtual worlds. They were saying this at a time when most of the VR systems that I was seeing demoed had limited interaction in and among a small library of graphics primitives. The vapor theory bought into the short slope concept of technological development — that just because people wanted something (in this case fully immersive virtuality) to happen that something would indeed materialize.

RC: *Do you see this "flapping of the gums" subsiding with the recent fallout of businesses on the web?*

PL: I remember Biz Markie's old school rap that went through the usual enemies list of sucker MCs, claiming they all "caught the vapors." Within a decade of the VR boom and bust, venture capitalists caught the vapors and funded the new economy business plans of the dot-comedy.

RC: *With this fallout, the web (and the other "pop" aspects of computer science) has gone through what other relatively new areas of technological advancement (e.g., artificial intelligence) have gone through, but on a very condensed time scale. AI seems to have found its feet again (small and shaky as they may be). Do you see the web and other previously inflated* *digital arts going through a similar evolution (i.e., less hype, more real applications)?*

PL: I'm fascinated by the postutopian periods of aesthetics and technology. The utopian moment of a medium or field is intoxicating, of course — when the cinema or AI, rock 'n' roll or robotics, the portapak or the web, is going to change the world that very instant. But no one movement or technology can support that level of hype. Often, it's after the general public's attention has been raised and then dashed that artists, technologists, and yes, even entrepreneurs, can go back into the wreckage and make interesting, even lasting interventions.

RC: *Where many on the art side of the fence see all commercial forces as the enemy, you contend that art and economics are symbiotic. Given that artists of all kinds need money to do their work, isn't there still a line somewhere in there that shouldn't be crossed (for art's sake)?*

PL: I'm regularly misunderstood on this point. It's not that art and commerce are the same thing, just that all art exists in relation to the economic activity of its era. After Andy Warhol and Jeff Koons, it's impossible to speak of lines between art and commerce that "shouldn't be crossed," because, after all, that's one of the things artists do — cross lines. For thirty years or more, art historians and critics have been hashing this out, and it's pretty hard to ignore this fairly obvious point when you talk about the complex intertwining of art, design, and commerce in the realm of the digital. One of the reasons that these relationships were so contested in the boom years of the '90s was that a huge number of people came out of art departments, or trained themselves entirely outside of the academy, and took jobs as designers either to support their art — a quintessential day job — or just because that was the hot thing to do at the time. So, they called themselves designers without much in the way of exposure to the ethos of design as a profession.

RC: *Well, I'm one of those people. Thanks to computers, I've been doing print and web design professionally for almost eight years now. Though I've been through years of art school, grew up painting, drawing, and started making 'zines sixteen years ago, only a small fraction of this experience is used in my job as "designer." The frustrating part is that this division between designers who are involved in the discourse and designers who aren't is obvious, and the fact that industry that requires design work — for the most part — is completely unconcerned with the discourse. How can we bring the discourse inside the corporate walls?*

PL: At the risk of sounding like a workplace psychiatrist, I'd like to talk about the frustration you're feeling. Knowing something about the ways in which designers from earlier eras convinced their corporate clients of the validity of design research and experimentation might offer you, and others in your position, a way to approach these discussions. Certain designers have been able to shift the dialog from service to collaboration, staking out either new territory or reformulating the way the game is played (think Charles and Ray Eames). The computer democratized access to the tools of the professional designer, and brought about an amazing efflorescence of new styles and a deepened pool of people who, like you, consider themselves to be designers. Unfortunately, though, the democratization of digitization didn't go hand in hand with any kind of informed discussion of the history and discourses of design as a field.

RC: *Can you give me some examples?*

PL: Let's just talk about the web for example. With all the hype about Flash, and the concomitant backlash against it, this is precisely the time to revisit the debates about deep design versus styling. But, the very ones who should be talking about this haven't got the vaguest notion of who Raymond Loewy was, much less that as early as the '30s, he was talking about the designer's role in "reconciling" people to new technologies through exterior styling. I'm not endorsing Loewy's position by any means, but I'd sure like to talk it through with Flash partisans and their detractors. How about countering the banality of the Nielsen-Norman rap on web usability by recasting Adorno's condemnation of functionalism? In the '60s, Adorno was dealing with the unintended consequences of modernism's reductivism: the creation of boring and inhuman living spaces. Connecting the dots from these historical arguments to a staff meeting is tricky, but it can be done. Essentially, it's about making history, theory, and criticism viable in nonacademic environments.

RC: *Getting back to academe, Paul Virilio once said, "Play at being a critic. Deconstruct the game in order to play with it. Instead of accepting the rules, challenge and modify them. Without the freedom to critique and reconstruct, there is no truly free game: we are addicts and nothing more." Kodwo Eshun adopts the title "concept engineer" instead of culture critic. What's your stance on the role of critique and critics in this culture?*

PL: Hats (berets?) off to Virilio, but these days, even porn fans understand the importance of critique. The motto of the *rec.arts.movies.erotica* newsgroup is cribbed from Pauline Kael: "In the arts, the only source of independent information is the critic. The rest is advertising." And, sorry to say, if "the freedom to critique and reconstruct" guaranteed liberation from addiction, those guys in the trench coat brigade might be able to get up from their sofas, turn off *Edward Penishands*, and go out and meet some real people. I'm a big fan of Eshun's redemptive approach to criticism, but I'm not sure exactly what he means by "concept engineer." As a label, it doesn't seem that much more helpful than lumping critics along with doctors, lawyers, and software designers together as "symbolic analysts."

RC: *Can you talk about the relationship between a general social critique and the focus that you tend to put on art, design, and technology?*

PL: It's hard to argue with Christopher Hitchens' claims that the critic needs to live "at a slight acute angle to society" if you're doing politically motivated criticism. In the realm of aesthetics, though, there has been such an explosion of cultural production of all kinds in the past quarter century, that I'm less interested in the model of critic as scold — castigating producers for their errors — than I am of the critic as curator. The curatorial function is one which brings together and juxtaposes objects, systems, ideas, and people to make a case. The case I'm interested in making right now is that nostalgia for past glories is counterproductive, and that the contemporary world is in the midst of a ferocious pluralism of styles and media and aesthetics right now. There are wonders to be found in intriguing pockets, sometimes in full view, but often "at a slight acute angle." I hope that my methods and my writings can serve as something of a model about how one can curate compelling experiences with art and culture.

RC: *Whom do you read and respect writing about new media (or whatever else) these days?*

PL: I'm really interested in the work that's developing in Southern California. It's where I live, and I believe that people need to nurture local, as well as virtual, intellectual communities. Luckily, I'm in the right place at the right time. There's UCSD's Lev Manovich, of course, author of *The Language of New Media* (MIT Press, 2001), CalArt's Norman Klein who's been working on scripted spaces and special effects, independent scholar Margaret Wertheim who is writing and curating around the topic of outsider physics, and a passel of people from UCLA including film theorist Vivian Sobchack, Red Rock Eater News Service organizer Phil Agre, and N. Katherine Hayles, who holds a joint appointment in English and design/media arts. For fun, I've been enjoying independent publisher Tosh Berman's TamTam Books. Berman used to be the director of *Beyond Baroque*, the venerable Venice, California-based literary organization, but now he's putting out beautifully designed translations from the French of weird little books. The first three are Boris Vian's brutal noir *I Spit on Your Graves* (1998); Serge Gainsbourg's *Evguenie Sokolov* (1998), about an artist whose medium is farting; and Guy Debord's *Considerations on the Assassination of Gerard Lebovici* (2001), in which the Situationist reflects on being at the eye of the media storm that hit when Lebovici, his friend and publisher, was murdered mysteriously in the mid-'80s.

RC: *Is there anything you're working on that you'd like to bring up here?*

PL: I was trained as a film theorist, but haven't written about the movies in a long time. That's shifting a bit these days, and I've got an essay on "The Myths of Interactive Cinema" coming out in Dan Harries' *The New Media Book* (2002) for the British Film Institute. As a long-term project, I'm working on a new book about the aesthetics of information. Closer at hand, I'm putting together a collection of my "User" columns from *artext* magazine which I'd like to see come out in 2003. And, I'm continuing to put out the Mediawork pamphlet series.

RC: *What is the premise of your Mediawork pamphlets? What are you trying to achieve with these?*

PL: Mediawork pamphlets pair major writers with contemporary graphic designers to produce 100-page "mind bombs" in the tradition of McLuhan and Fiore's *The Medium is the Massage*. These "theoretical fetish objects" cover art, design, technology, and market culture with verve and impact. The first, *Utopian Entrepreneur*, written by Brenda Laurel and designed by Denise Gonzales Crisp, was published in 2001.

RC: *To be precise, it came out on September 14, 2001. What did it mean that a book written, and a series conceptualized, before the events of 9/11 were both seen, at least in part, as having something to say to that moment?*

159

PL: We almost cancelled the San Francisco launch event that the International Academy of Digital Arts & Sciences was hosting for us, but Brenda, Denise, and I all drove up from LA to the Bay Area on the fifteenth to confront a San Francisco as empty as I'd ever experienced it. There was a sort of doomed solipsism in the air, as though the attacks on New York and Washington, though 3,000 miles away, were the logical conclusion of the meltdown of the '90s. The Bay Area and Silicon Valley, as the former epicenter of all new, new things, were confronted by the triumphant resurgence of Ford administration dinosaurs like Secretary of Defense Donald Rumsfeld pulling back the curtain and reminding all us tech-heads who really runs this country. So, in the end, it was great to hear Brenda rally the troops and talk about a better future, and the still unfulfilled promise of (some) technology.

RC: *What's coming up?*

PL: In these slightly calmer times, we're finishing *Writing Machines*, written by N. Katherine Hayles and designed by Anne Burdick, for release in the fall of 2002. Paul Miller (aka DJ Spooky that Subliminal Kid) is writing *Rhythm Science* for 2003, and we're trying to figure out the best designer to pair him with, which is one of the fun parts for me.

Erik Davis
Mysticism in the Machine
by ROY CHRISTOPHER (2002)

SURVEYING THE OVERLAPPING REGIONS OF MYSTICISM, RELIGION, media theory, postmodernism, and cyber-critique, Erik Davis makes maps of new mental territory. His book, *Techgnosis: Myth, Magic and Mysticism in the Age of Information* (Harmony, 1998), is a journey through the varying and plentiful connections between old-world religions and New Age technology — connections few noticed before Erik pointed them out. As Peter Lunenfeld puts it, "Davis performs alchemy, fusing disparate strands of techno-hype, mystical speculation, and hard-nosed reporting into a Philosopher's Stone, unlocking secrets our culture doesn't even know it has."

Indeed.

ROY CHRISTOPHER: Techgnosis *analyzes the countless and largely unacknowledged connections between mysticism and cyberculture. What originally lead you to write this thesis?*

ERIK DAVIS: Sometimes I think that it just happened to be the case that I have always been interested in mysticism/religion and media/technology, so the two interests naturally fused. But the real kicker was reading Philip K. Dick in college, when I was also studying postmodernism and media theory. His interests in gnostic experience in the midst of a science-fiction world of false realities and warped signals encouraged me to start looking at my own media culture through that filter. Then I just kept noticing more and more overlaps and connections. Few people were talking about these links, so inevitably, I had no choice but to write a book!

RC: *Aside from semantic discussions on what it means to be "human," are we indeed becoming — or have we become — posthuman?*

ED: Well, unfortunately, part of the question is inevitably semantic, not just in a nitpicky linguistic way, but in the more basic sense of the term, which has to do with meaning. In other words, is the meaning (or lack thereof) of the human changing in some marked and irrevocable way? When you think that now we can blow up the earth, clone ourselves, seriously contemplate genetic eugenics, eradicate natural wildness, alter the climate, kill off millions of species, create proto-intelligence with machines, force photons to slow down, etc., etc. — the question becomes: can the being that can do and contemplate such things be seamlessly woven into the millennia that came before it? Or is there a rupture, a rupture worth talking about? The problem that I have with people who don't see a rupture, who think that we are just doing what we've always done, or are simply carrying forward the Enlightenment project, is that they don't acknowledge how much our basic context of meaning has changed. The human condition no longer means anything, because many of the limitations that once defined that condition now seem to be up for grabs.

RC: *Adapting McLuhan, you call the web, "the supreme amputation of memory." With all of this externalization of knowledge going on, from the machines of Gutenberg to the file-associations of Berners-Lee, what is the "average intelligent unit"* to do to maintain some semblance of balance?

ED: I don't know. We're all on our own! And who knows — maybe balance is overrated. My own media intake is much smaller than it once was, but that's partly because it seems like we are being lied to and manipulated at a far greater pitch these days than before 9/11. For myself, balance comes by being open to as many different kinds of media or information as possible. In other words, even if you did nothing but read news on the internet all day, you would still never catch up with the world. So why bother sticking with one media type? Instead, why not learn to navigate between the internet, musty old books, the weather, your dreams, comic books, film, your body's internal dynamics, conversation, solitude, meditation, random scraps of data, etc.

RC: *Whom do you read and respect these days?*

ED: I am never very good at these list questions. These days, I am more in the past, because my next project is about California. Right now I am reading David Dunaway's *Huxley in Hollywood* (HarperCollins, 1989), which is great; the poet Robert Duncan; Isherwood; some more Phil Dick; the novelist Kem Nunn; the pulp fantasy genius Clark Ashton Smith. When it comes to respect, I mostly respect my friends, since I've met too many people whose work I admire but whose persons make me woozy. I admire many; respect few.

RC: *Is there anything you're working on that you'd like to tell us about?*

ED: Well, I am writing a book about the spirit of California. I also have an essay in a great new book on psychedelics and Buddhism called *Zig Zag Zen* (the book, not my essay, which is called "The Paisley Gate"). It was edited by my friend Allan Hunt Badiner (whom I respect) and it includes totally amazing art (picked by the great artist Alex Grey, whom I also respect) and a wide range of opinions and styles on a most fascinating topic.

Gareth Branwyn
Media Jam
by ROY CHRISTOPHER (2001)

GARETH BRANWYN HAS BEEN MEDIA HACKING FOR NEARLY THREE decades. His book, *Jamming the Media* (Chronicle Books, 1997), is the media hacker's bible, an invaluable sourcebook of resources, how-tos and examples written with evident working-knowledge, exhaustive research, and fearless wit. He's also the "Jargon Watch" guy at *Wired*, runs the tech-review site, *Street Tech*, and has written several other books and countless articles on the web, technology, jargon, and alternative media.

ROY CHRISTOPHER: *How did you initially get involved in creative alternative media and media hacking?*

GARETH BRANWYN: I've been involved in alt.media since high school. I had a very cool media studies teacher in my senior year, a former journalist who was relentlessly passionate about the potential for media to create an informed, participatory democracy and an "active culture." At the same time, I was taking a two-year graphic arts and printing class at school. Looking back, it was amazing that our high school, in a brain-dead southern town, had such a great resource. We had a giant commercial-grade print shop and design studio. I learned everything there, from design and layout to photography, plate-making, printing, binding, etc. We could print our own student projects, so I created an underground newspaper and printed up all sorts of subversive literature to hand out to other students. The school wasn't too happy about it, but I loved it.

After high school, I went to live on a commune in the foothills of the Shenandoah Mountains. I co-ran the print shop there. We did lots of work for other alternative organizations, small business printing, 'zines, etc.

One of the great things about being so bloody old (I'm 43) is that I've had a chance to experience every flavor of fringe media from the mid-'70s on. I caught the tail end of '70s hippie media, then the punk DIY movement of the '80s, then the 'zine publishing scene of the '90s, and then web publishing in the '90s. My book *Jamming the Media* was an attempt at data-compressing what I'd learned on that journey into a book.

RC: *I contend that we all need to become media activists to some extent just as a matter of survival these days. Do you think anyone can become a media hacker?*

GB: I've always been a big proponent of "active culture," the idea that everyone in a society needs to be creative and expressive on some level and communicate themselves to others. Doing nothing but passively consuming corporate media is not good for your soul. You've got to "feed the noise back into the system," or "jam" the media. It's good for you — and it's *fun!*

As I said in *Jamming*, in the past, trying to create media was usually a daunting (and expensive) proposition. Now, nearly everyone (in the Western world, anyway) has access to astoundingly powerful media tools. Even if you're poor, you can usually access many of these tools through public libraries and the like. On the internet, there's free website hosting, free email, free discussion-group software, weblogging software, etc. On my technology review site, *Street Tech,* we use blogging software that's free, and a very powerful conferencing system that costs $95 (a free version is available, but has some limitations, like no spell check). The tools are all there in just about any medium. It's largely a question of your ingenuity in how you can access and employ them. My wife's a musician. Years ago, it cost upwards of $10,000 for her to put a record out on her own label. We'd have to beg family and friends for loans. Now, it costs less than $3,000; the recording and engineering can be done on the desktop, and we put the cost of duping onto our credit card. Thanks to a deal that our indie-friendly CD duplicator has with a distributor, she also gets free net distribution to Amazon, CD Now, Music Boulevard, and most other major "e-tailers."

It really largely comes down to the quality of what one has to say and, of course, the fact that there's an expanding glut of media (both commercial and amateur) out there competing for everyone's eyeballs. Some see this as a bad thing. I don't. The more, the merrier, I say. But we do need to start teaching people net literacy and better searching and critical evaluation skills so that they can find what they're looking for online and are able to better judge the veracity of the content they encounter. Once you know how to do your own newsgathering (and news/info/entertainment publishing), hunt down the better webzines, find the best online discussion groups, etc., you've really dynamically constructed your own media network. We all take this for granted these days, but I still think this is very exciting and powerful.

RC: *What do you see as the most powerful tool in the media activist's arsenal?*

GB: Again, since the tools for effective DIY media have become so powerful and plentiful, I think your most potent tool is the message that you're trying to get out there. The more "memetically viral" it is — the more creative and unique — the more it will cut through the sludge. Take weblogs, for example. There are now thousands of 'em. Most fade into the background noise, but those that are truly interesting, creative, well-written, rise to the top of blog portals, get repeatedly quoted on other weblogs, and spread rapidly through word of mouth.

RC: *What are you working on next?*

GB: I have several ideas for new books, one dealing with personal privacy and security in a post-Patriot Act world in which many of our civil liberties collapsed along with the World Trade Center Towers. Another is on the growing popularity of robotic combat, a la *Battlebots* and *Robot Wars.* Hey, what can I say? I have diverse interests! And, as always, I'm trying to make my website, *Street Tech* (basically my day job), a more useful resource for those seeking no-bullshit reviews and discussion on our ever-expanding world of personal technology.

Douglas Rushkoff
The Thing That I Call "Doug"
by JOHN BROCKMAN (1999)

UNTIL RECENTLY, MEDIA AND TECHNOLOGY GURU DOUGLAS Rushkoff believed that we should let technology develop at its own pace and in its own way. "I thought that this rapid acceleration of culture would allow us to achieve the kind of turbulence necessary to initiate a dynamical system," he says. "And I saw everyone who called for us to put on the brakes, or to put new governors on the development of culture, as the enemy to our evolution forward. Their vigilance would prevent us from reaching the next level of complexity."

Rushkoff abandoned his view of techno-utopianism when he began thinking that "when you eliminate fear and simply follow your bliss, you don't always get the best results. In the worst case, it can even be a recipe for fascism. Over the past few years we just let the internet go, and we've got an electronic strip mall as a result. We thought government was the enemy, and kept them out of our network. That's what gave market forces free reign.

"I started to explore whether there is a way to foster growth, new thought, cultural innovation, and even markets without getting absolutely carried away and losing all sense of purpose."

Douglas Rushkoff, a professor of media culture at New York University's Interactive Telecommunications program, is an author, lecturer, and social theorist. His books include *Free Rides* (Delta, 1991), *Cyberia: Life in the Trenches of Hyperspace* (HarperCollins, 1994), *The GenX Reader* (editor) (Ballantine, 1994), *Media Virus! Hidden Agendas in Popular Culture* (Ballantine, 1994), *Ecstasy Club: A Novel* (HarperEdge, 1997), *Playing the Future* (HarperCollins, 1996), and *Coercion: Why We Listen to What "They" Say* (Riverhead Books, 1999).

As a journalist, Rushkoff is currently writing a monthly column for *The Guardian*, *The Age*, *Silicon Alley Reporter*, *The Herald Tribune*, *Toronto Globe and Mail*, *The Fresno Bee*, and dozens of other papers around the world through the *New York Times* Syndicate. He is also a commentator for NPR's *All Things Considered*. He regularly contributes features about pop culture, media, and technology to magazines including *Time*, *Esquire*, *Details*, *The Modern Review*, *GQ*, *Paper*, and *Magical Blend*, as well as online publications from *The Site* to *Nerve*.

DOUGLAS RUSHKOFF: Lately I've been asking myself, what is media? Or, more exactly, what is not media? I've been writing for quite a while about media as a conduit, media as a way of creating communities, media as a connection from one person to another. And it occurred to me that everything is media. Everything outside my own awareness — whatever it is I call "me" — is some mediation of me. That is, until it gets to you. Everything between the thing that I'm calling Doug and the thing that you're calling John is media. Then I started to wonder, well, what is the thing that I call Doug? The best we know so far, what we call "Doug" is some distinct DNA pattern, or perhaps the vessel that's carrying out that pattern. If I'm the vessel, then I'm just a medium for a set of genes. And if I'm the DNA itself? Well, what's more media than DNA? It's a medium for a code that goes back into history and right through to the future. Has there ever been a better broadcaster than DNA?

So that's why I started wondering about what's not media? And all I've found so far is intention. Intention is not media; it's what we're using to try to drive media, what we're trying to express through our various media. As Hamlet asked, "what is a man" beyond his bestial, feeding existence? "Cause and will."

And that pretty well gets us down to the very biggest questions people in this discussion and discussions like it for centuries have been asking. What is life? What is consciousness? And I'd answer it's pure intention, and that studying media helps us distinguish between intentionality and its many manifestations.

As a child, I wrestled with this distinction by studying theatre and biology, which are both looking for answers to the same question: what is it to be alive? For biologists, it's a matter of determining what animates matter into life. For dramatists, it's the study of how to re-create life. And Aristotle arrived at the same conclusion: drama is a human will striving toward a goal. Life is the intention to maintain itself, to carry itself forward, and it does so through forms of media. Biologists define life as matter trying to sustain and replicate itself over time in some active fashion, just as a dramatist sees character as one trying to retain or even extend his sense of self — playing out his true nature.

What makes my inquiry unique, if anything, is the fact that these sorts of questions came out of the Twinkies television culture in which I was raised. It's hard for a smart kid to watch television eight, ten, twelve hours a day, without eventually having to think.

JOHN BROCKMAN: *Perhaps you're not DNA. Maybe you're television?*
DR: Maybe I am! If anything is expressing itself through me, it's TV.

JB: *Who raised you?*
DR: I suppose it was June Lockhart, Mary Tyler Moore, and Lucille Ball who raised me. I took class in Room 222 and Dr. Smith was my pediatrician! Honestly, I don't believe I was being raised or informed by these programs quite as they were intended. I wasn't watching television shows as much as watching The Television. From four or five years old I remember looking at the sets of sitcoms and wondering why almost all of them had the door into the house on the right side of the set: *All in the Family*, *I Love Lucy*, *Dick Van Dyke*, everyone came in from the right, even the *Mary Tyler Moore* show. What did this mean, especially when in the 1970s, it seemed that sitcoms about broken homes had the door on the left. *Maude*, *One Day at a Time* — shows about divorce, really, had their doors on the left. Even in the last season of *Mary Tyler Moore*, as she grew into a more desperate single woman, she moved to an apartment where the door was on the left instead of the right.

JB: *But you were always looking straight ahead.*
DR: No, I was looking at the stage set. I don't know how many other kids were watching television in this way, but I certainly credit it with launching my inquiry into how media was put together. Why is it put together the way it is? You have to take it apart to find out.

JB: *Let's talk about the so-called "human communications revolution."*
DR: I don't know that I believe in revolution as much as renaissance. So many people talk about this computer revolution where the individual user is empowered to express himself, break down obsolete institutions, or topple the corporate-industrial monoliths. It's an unnecessarily polar

and combative vision. And once it's reduced to the idea of empowering individuals, all those individuals start looking a lot more like consumers beating the "system" than autonomous human beings. It devolves quickly into "one-to-one marketing." I prefer to look at moments like the one we're living through as renaissances, as rebirths of old ideas in a new context.

JB: *Did you say "self" expression? How does a self express itself? Are you talking about "Just Do It"?*

DR: In the best light, I suppose "Just Do It" is a renaissance of a sort, isn't it? A great credo, reasserting the power of individual will. But I think "Just Do It" is a reductive and dangerous substitute for a philosophy of life. As far as Nike is concerned, "Just Do It" means just pressing the "buy" button. "No, kid, you don't have to think. For God's sake, don't think about it. Just do it!"

The most dangerous thing about the immediacy of our terrific new media communications tools is that the idea of consideration has been taken out of the equation. We're supposed to be able to have an instantaneous response. We take polls of public responses to Clinton's speeches before they're even over — as if we're supposed to know how we feel before we've had time to think. When we get an email, we tend to feel we are obligated to respond to its query right away, without having time to think about it.

The most dangerous thing about a "Just Do It "society is that it compels us to act on reflex, not intention. We are led to believe we are acting from the gut. That we are somehow connecting with our emotions and bypassing our neuroses. But this isn't true at all. We are merely moving impulsively. It's not from the gut. And the more impulsively we act, the more easily we can be led where we might not truly want to go. People who act automatically are the easiest to control — by marketers, by anyone. There's less intention and thus less life involvement.

I used to think this acceleration of human action was a great thing. I thought we'd simply bypass our restricting editorial voices, get our super-egos out of the way, and behave in that purely spontaneous, wonderful fashion that all human beings would behave in if uncorrupted by social and institutional biases.

JB: *Remind me . . . the superego?*

DR: The internalized parent, the filter, the part of us that says, "oh, wait a minute, maybe you really shouldn't do that." When I was younger, I thought the superego was a restrictive force, amplified by those who sought control us — our churches, our bosses, our schools, those who want to keep us in a state of fear and shame. Timothy Leary saw things this way.

JB: *You talk about forces trying to control us; in the same breath you use words like "fun," and "renaissance." Do you see a need to change things, or is everything just great the way it is?*

DR: Until about three years ago, I thought that we should just let 'er rip. Let technology develop at its own pace and in its own way. I thought that this rapid acceleration of culture would allow us to achieve the kind of turbulence necessary to initiate a dynamical system. And I saw everyone who called for us to put on the brakes, or to put new governors on the development of culture, as the enemy to our evolution forward. Their vigilance would prevent us from reaching the next level of complexity.

I was buying the *Wired* line of techno-utopianism. I would read stuff by John Barlow and Terence McKenna and think, let's just evolve. But something kept nagging at me. Maybe it's because I am Jewish. I couldn't help thinking that when you eliminate fear and simply follow your bliss, you don't always get the best results. In the worst case, it can even be a recipe for fascism. Over the past few years we just let the internet go, and we've got an electronic strip mall as a result. We thought government was the enemy, and kept them out of our network. That's what gave market forces free reign.

I started to explore whether there might be something in between reckless, unbridled enthusiasm and being a Marxist Jewish mother about things. There is a way to foster growth, new thought, cultural innovation, and even markets without getting absolutely carried away and losing all sense of purpose.

JB: *Let's talk about your writing.*

DR: Well, I wrote three loud books about the promise of new media. I honestly believed I was writing them for what I conceived of as the "counterculture," or at least for people who sought to use these technologies for positive, thoughtful cultural evolution. I told the story of how our tightly controlled media was giving way to a more organic, natural mediaspace. Media used to obey only the laws of Newtonian physics. It was a top-down affair where gravity ruled. People like William Randolph Hearst or Rupert Murdoch could make decisions from the tops of glass buildings, and then their messages would trickle down to the rest of us through one-way media.

But now, thanks to computers and camcorders and the internet and modems, the media has been forced to incorporate feedback and iteration. It has become a truly chaotic space — a dynamical system. Remember the famous example of chaos, the butterfly that flaps its wings in Brazil causing a hurricane in New York? To me, that butterfly was Rodney King, whose beating by LA cops, captured on a camcorder tape and iterated throughout the datasphere, led to riots in a dozen American cities. I wrote *Media Virus!* to announce that the time had come where we could launch any idea we want, whether it's as a media virus, or in a usenet group — the power is in our hands again, let's go for it. I wrote books about how young people understand media better than adults, and are already using it in new, exciting ways.

JB: *And then you found out that all the kids were filing for their IPOs. And you find out there is no counterculture. And you can't buy a real cotton shirt in Palo Alto.*

DR: Yeah, I learned all those things, and I learned them most frighteningly when I was invited to a convention sponsored by the American Association of Advertising Agencies, the 4 A's. They wanted me to talk to them about media viruses and youth culture. I was thrilled. I prepared a talk about how advertising is over, and that their tyranny over young people had come to an end. They should give up their coercive ways. When I arrived, there were signs and hand outs: "How to use Media Viruses to Capture New Audiences" — that sort of thing. People were coming up to me and congratulating me about my role in launching controversial Calvin Klein ads that I had nothing to do with. Or so I thought.

I suddenly realized that the people who had put my books on best-seller lists were not those *Mondo 2000*-era hackers and internet home-steaders I so admired, but rather the public relations and advertising industries. I had been selling "cool" to corporate America. My books were primers, required texts for young executives on how to take advantage of new media to do the same old thing they were doing before. That's when I realized that we were in an arms race, and that I was just as caught up in it as everyone else.

So I decided to write a book about the war. I spent two years taking a look at many different styles of coercion, their histories, and how these techniques have been retooled for modern times. I concluded that most of them are based on a simple phenomenon known as regression and transference. It's used in a positive way by therapists, and a dangerous way by salespeople and marketers. Basically, if people can be made to feel disoriented or helpless, they will seek out someone to act as a parent. When people are confused, they want parents who can tell them what to do, and reassure them. Once you create a situation where people feel that they can trust you, that you understand them, that you'll take care of them, or that you'll lead them, they will submit.

The other main set of techniques that are being used in coercion today are taken from neurolinguistic programming. They are really just simple hypnosis techniques, like Milton Erickson's "pacing and leading." If you're sitting in a room with someone, what you would do is subtly assume the same position as your target, and adopt some of the same breathing and speech patterns — that's pacing. Then, amazingly, you can slowly lead the person by changing your posture, breathing rate, or speech pattern. You're subject will change his posture too, to conform to yours. Then you begin to work on his thinking, as well.

This same technique plays itself out in the sales world through the sciences of demographics and target marketing. You pace your target market — listen to the language of it, "target market" — it's a war metaphor. If you're in the target market you are in the crosshairs of a marketer's rifle! To pace the target demographic, the marketer studies buying motives and propensities through focus groups, then creates messages that perfectly reflect their existing emotional states. Marketers pace our behaviors and feelings in order to lead us where they want us to go.

When this process gets automated through a technology like the World Wide Web, watch out. An e-commerce site watches and records each user's interactions with it. What screens did the user look at and in what order? Where did he click? When did he buy? Did he buy when the background was red or blue? Did he buy when the offer was in the top left or the top right? And the computer can then dynamically reconfigure itself to make a website that identifies and then paces each individual exactly. Meanwhile, the user thinks he's "just doing it."

Once the customer is properly paced, then you work on leading the person toward a greater frequency of purchases, greater allegiance. So-called "sticky" websites are really just trying to create an inexorable pull on the user toward greater and greater interaction with and loyalty to the particular brand being offered. The user is a fly, and the branded website is the flypaper.

JB: *Do you feel loyal to brands?*

DR: It's funny, I went to the Foot Locker to get sneakers a month or so ago. There was a wall of sneakers: Nikes and Adidas and Reeboks — the major brands — and then cool brands like Airwalk and Simple, the so-called counterculture brands that you're supposed to believe aren't being assembled by underage Singhalese prostitutes. I looked at that wall and I actually did have a crisis — a consumer crisis — as I thought, "What sneaker is me? Which one is the thing I call Doug? Which reflects me? How do I want to express the thing I call Doug with my purchase?"

The way kids express who they are today, and the way we are supposed to vote in a libertarian universe is with our dollars, right? But we can never really express who we are through consumption. It's a pity that it's the main option left to us. It's not empowerment at all. It's the power to be a consumer.

JB: *Do you think the self-conscious option is enough? John Cage would say that in order to change ourselves we need to forget interiority and change the world — and we'll all change with it. The inter life is over; everything is an objectification, including the names of the body — "the thing that I call Doug."*

DR: At one time I used to believe something like that. My prescription for getting more conscious was for everyone to admit that we're all flailing around in the same dynamical system and everything is arbitrary. What I call Doug, what you call Doug, what we call a word — everything is arbitrary. It's that seemingly profound insight you have in your dorm room on a little too much acid, where you can't hold onto anything. So let it all go, and realize that the reality templates are up for grabs. It's a consensual hallucination, as William Gibson would say. But I don't think that's true anymore.

JB: *I think we need a new word for this.*

DR: Maybe postontological relativism? I haven't turned into an absolutist, either, though. I don't think there's something called evil, but I do think there's a force called good. Like heat — heat is a force. Cold is not a force; cold is just the absence of heat. It doesn't exist. Ask any physicist. But there is heat, and I think there is something called good. And that implies a certain polarity, for sure. Or at least a spectrum or scale.

My problem with John Cage's reliance on the external is that it gives too much room to the libertarians or even the fascists, who will claim that we live in a downright competitive universe, so anything goes. Anything doesn't go in my book.

I started to have this realization when I was watching the Clinton/Lewinksy debacle on TV. Everyone from Dan Rather to Louis Rukeyser said, "well the economy is good, and the American public is going to support this president as long as the economy is good." As far as I'm concerned, a good economy is not good enough. The bottom line isn't the bottom line.

JB: *Then what is?*

DR: That's for us to figure out. The Bible gives a few hints. There is something to be said for a bit of Platonic idealization in all this. Growing up and saying "look, that doesn't go in my house; this will not go." Being an adult. Originally the internet made me think the only thing we have to learn is tolerance. If we can be tolerant of everything and everyone, we'll all be okay. But I'm not tolerant of everything and everyone. And I certainly see the value in realizing that we're starting to go in directions that we've been before. We should learn from those experiences rather than repeat them with new gadgets that we have even less control over.

The problem with Cage's idea is that if everything is external and there's no internal life anymore, then this is the only moment that matters. However I feel is right, and I'm going to go with that. A New Age guru might tell us this is fine. But I'm beginning to think this is not the only moment that matters. Part of growing up is realizing that my father and his father and his father, too, were working on projects that span generations, and I want to know what those projects are. And when I have children, I'm sure I'll feel this way even more.

JB: *A lot of your writing is concerned with the effects of science and technology.*

DR: I tend to think of technologies as expressions rather than things that force us into new behaviors. I'm not a technodeterminist. I believe we are in charge. When we're developing technologies like computers, networks, or nano we are designing reality, and doing it at a pace unimagined before. We are greatly enhancing our ability to exercise our intention.

What I'm asking is: What is our intention? What are we going to do with it? We better figure that out, and fast. When you look at some of the people who have been most successful at expressing their intention through technology, they aren't the scientists, but the technologists and marketers. And what are they doing with it? They're getting very rich and succumbing to what you would call toxic wealth.

JB: *Toxic wealth?*

DR: There are certain aspects of youth that are valuable to retain as an adult. And there are other aspects of youth that are dangerous to retain as an adult. When I look at our so-called adult society today, it looks to me a lot like a fetus that stayed in the womb too long and became toxic to its mother and itself. There's a great deal of thumb sucking going on in Silicon Valley. We've done the opposite of what we should have. We live in a culture that is obsessed with youth but has lost the ability to think with the elasticity of youth — so we've traded in the best and we've gotten the worst as a result. We think like grumpy old men, and act out like two-year olds.

Look at Hollywood. Who are our movie stars today? Not men, but boys. Leonardo DiCaprio or Matt Damon, who look even younger than they are. Who are the great adult men of Hollywood? Jack Nicholson, who's an adult baby. His entire show-biz image is of an overgrown child going to Lakers games in dark glasses. Or Robin Williams — however talented — still a version of the adult child. Our president is a baby. He treats the nation as his scolding parent, from whom he must hide his naughty deeds, and to whom he must occasionally apologize.

Look at what a lot of our internet heroes do with their money: they buy planes, fighter jets for that matter, or build castles they can live in as if they were wombs — it's an extension of childhood.

JB: *And how do you think we got this way?*
DR: By design. In the late '40s after World War II, we needed a way for the economy to expand, so what we did was create a consumer culture. Men returned to the factories and worked, while women returned to the home to take care of the children. Advertising and marketing catered to the needs of women and children. When they couldn't cater to a need, they created one. By the 1970s, when women went to work themselves, consumer culture became all about kids — rock music and records and toys and electronics — all items and lifestyles that appealed to either children or the child in the man or woman. We've succeeded at that. Now when a person becomes successful, what they want to do is buy into childhood and get some expensive toys in order to fulfill those same,

media-generated childhood urges. Our commercials make this explicit.

We also live in a culture where we want to be infantilized. I was recently in a state where people buy their liquor in "package stores" — from state cops. Okay, why is that? Because in America we have laws to protect us from our own vices. We feel we can be trusted to behave as adults. But what does this really accomplish? When you buy your liquor from a cop, and you have restrictions about how you're supposed to use it, then you are relieved of all responsibility for how you behave. That's why we have a nation filled with drunks. Watch *COPS* and you can see one result of infantilizing policies.

We still yearn for parents as we always have. The movie *Elizabeth*, about Queen Elizabeth, reminded me about Western civilization's transition from looking at God and Virgin Mary and Jesus and as our parent figures, to looking toward the monarchy for this same comfort. Elizabeth enacted this transition. What we did in America was to enact a new transition, which was from the monarchy, or the presidency, as our parental figure, to corporations and brands. Our transference is now projected onto brands — we look to them and to companies to provide the reassurance we want.

The strained effort by America to mourn for Kennedy in the fashion that England mourned for Diana looks like an effort to regain some of what felt like a healthier form of transference than what we have now — transference to nonpersonified entities — which I think is more frightening because we suspect that these entities don't have our best interest at heart. They don't even have hearts.

JB: *And the nonpersonified entities are treated a lot better than people.*
DR: If a corporation releases tons and tons of pollutants somewhere, killing thousands of people, no human being is going to be held accountable, and the corporation is going to pay fines that actually mean nothing to

it as an entity. Meanwhile kids are tattooing the Nike Swoosh onto their arms because it gives them a feeling of kinship and identity. It gives them such a sense of belonging.

JB: *I have never met a corporate logo I liked. The "brand" is one of the worst ideas of the twentieth century.*

DR: It's about metaphor. At every stage of the development of language we create a metaphor. When that metaphor dies — when we forget its original meaning — it becomes the component part of a new language system. Ancient people developed little symbols, glyphs — like a picture of a bull, or a picture of a house, or a picture of water — and that's the way our written languages developed. Eventually we stopped seeing glyphs as representational pictures and saw them as symbols for noises.

So the aleph, which is the picture of the bull, becomes the letter A. Or beta, which is the picture of a house, becomes a B — we use it for the sound b, and then we create new words out of it. So our new words are really collections of dead metaphors. I think our language and our symbol systems end up swallowing up the old ones so that we can conduct a denser style of communication.

Talk to teachers about the way kids are doing math now in school. Instead of doing arithmetic, they use a calculator for doing arithmetic and then, hopefully, do a more complex set of equations over it. But arithmetic as something they relate to directly disappears. Arithmetic is this thing the calculator does while they work with a larger system. Or look at the way young people watch television or listen to music. Songs become "samples" in new compositions, and scenes become "cuts" in an *MTV* video. The juxtaposition of images or sounds tells what we can call a kind of a metastory on top of the original component parts.

In today's culture, brands become iconic ways of representing an entire set of metaphors. Through its corporate communications, a company like

Nike will represent, or broadcast, an entire range of images which are then signified by that single Swoosh. And because we're looking for anchors in this relativistic haze that we were talking about before, because we're looking for symbols to represent what are now really immense thought structures, we grab onto the icons of Airwalk and Nike. That's why it's so satisfying, but it's also why it's so dangerous.

JB: *Can an individual become a brand?*
DR: John, you are a brand.

JB: *It's interesting that when AOL distributes millions of AOL floppy disks it's called "marketing"; and when Amazon runs a multimillion-dollar ad campaign it's called "branding." And Steve Case and Jeff Bezos are proclaimed geniuses. But if creative individuals take responsibility for their own work and ideas and let the world know what they've done, it's called "self-promotion." Can an individual ever enjoy the same authority and status in the culture that a brand attains?*
DR: Do individuals really want to? Human beings, for the time being anyway, exist in a different space than brands. I suppose those of us who are trying to establish a "name" for ourselves in an industry or in the media — like you or I have, to some extent, or Madonna has to a much greater extent — have franchises independent of our real-life identities. There's crossover, to be sure, but it's probably healthy to realize these are separate things. But living as a human being and a brand in the same mediaspace is a dangerous game.

As far as a strategy for becoming a person-brand, I'd suggest steering clear of any particular institution or company because the minute you go to work for Microsoft or Oracle or NBC or any company at all, you're spending your energy on someone else's brand rather than your own. The only thing you have to do to be a brand is to function as an independent —

and sign your work, taking both the credit and the blame for what you're doing. That, and make sure you've got a great sense of humor, because the inevitable attacks will feel like they're directed at you personally.

A lot of people talk about the internet as this great place to be anonymous. Why the hell do you want to be anonymous? One, if it's an idea that you had, then put your name on it — let people know it's yours. If it's worth saying, it's worth standing up for. I've never done an anonymous piece of email or BBS posting — not because I want to self-promote, but because I don't want to get in the habit of being afraid to say what I believe. That's a dangerous precedent, especially if we fear that our society might become more repressive at some point in the future.

So signing your work as an artist would is the first step. Second, it's realizing that the image that other people have of you has nothing to do with who you really are. It took me a while to get used to that one. You know, that this thing out there called Douglas Rushkoff — the thing that you call Doug — the thing that *The New York Times* calls Doug. It really hurt me for a long time that people believed reports that I make $7,500 an hour, that I'm selling out the counterculture, or I've single-handedly killed the grunge or rave movements. It really bothered me until I realized that they're not relating to me or my work at all, they're relating to the Douglas Rushkoff brand, and how it was mishandled by me or misrepresented by some journalist. And I have no right to complain because that thing called Douglas is what pays my bills.

But the bigger the person-brand gets, the more tempting the offers to surrender it to someone else. My franchise — the way it's perceived — becomes valuable to others. I'm on the Doug Rushkoff bus, and I'm going along, and the better my bus is doing, the bigger and flashier and more attractive the offers are for me to pull over, stop the bus, and get on someone else's. And I've tried that a few times for a short stint. But the minute I do that is when I feel like I'm dying. That I'm gone. And not just from a business perspective, I mean literally dying — becoming separated from my own sense of purpose.

JB: *Aren't you a bit young to have such war stories? You sound almost cynical.*

DR: I've gotten my first dose of life experience. My first run around the block. Over the past decade of new media, I've got to witness one cycle of something you've probably seen iterate three or four times by now. In 1985, '86, I watched the emergence of computer technologies, personal computers, networking, fidonet, bulletin boards, and I thought, "wow, the world is going to change." And people who had lived through the '60s were saying, "look, we've been through one of these before, and it looks bright from the beginning, but there's all these things to watch out for."

Howard Rheingold told me, essentially, "your optimism is really sweet, but we've watched this happen before, and we have to be careful and thoughtful if we want it to work out." My response was: "Nonsense! This is it! Renaissance is upon us! We're off and running!"

And then I watched the process by which those ten rules of the networked economy really function. And I watched the way the internet was turned into an electronic strip mall, and communities were turned into markets. And I watched the way the law of network externalities, which I thought was just going to get everyone online and communicating with each other, actually made things worse.

I call it the MovieFone syndrome. When MovieFone started, you could find out when movies were playing. You listened to an ad and they'd give you movie times, and then you hang up. A little later they added a feature through which you could order your tickets, for a $1.50 service charge. No one's twisting our arm, though; we don't have to buy our tickets over the phone. But once the law of network externalities comes into play and enough people are using the service, MovieFone changes from a convenience into something you have to do. If you have a date on a Thursday, Friday, or Saturday night in New York City and you're going to see a movie, you'd damn well better use MovieFone and pay that $1.50 extra per ticket, or you're not going to get into that movie. So is MovieFone still a convenience? Or is it simply a way to charge an extra $1.50 for each movie? To rein in another "externality"?

JB: *What about people that don't have the eleven dollars, or don't have the touch-tone phone?*
DR: Well, they lose out, don't they? People who want free email or ISP service have to submit to advertising. It's as if they are required to get remedial education in marketing. Only the poor must submit to the ads until they figure out how to participate in the market.

When new networking technologies become ubiquitous to the wealthy, those who aren't hooked up end up being at a disadvantage. The irony is we all end up paying more, not less, for the very same thing. Once a service like *Amazon.milk.com* is around, the milk companies will save a lot of money because they're only going to have to ship as much milk as is ordered. And maybe we'll even pay a little extra service charge to have that milk ready for us, or delivered in refrigerated kegs. It all looks like a harmless luxury until everyone's doing it. Then if you want to get your milk at the corner bodega and you haven't planned in advance, you're going to pay $4 a quart instead of $1.50. You'll pay a premium for the added convenience of simply buying milk the old fashioned way! And who's going to have to pay that premium? The people who don't have newest Microsoft Internet Explorer 7.5 and the chip that can run it.

I started looking at all these downsides. I've lived through fifteen years of one brief cycle. And the internet cycle happened faster than most. But gosh, look at the difference between *Cyberia* and *Coercion* as books. *Cyberia* announced a utopian vision. And while *Coercion* is not pessimism or conspiracy theory, it does contain a few warnings. It calls for us to employ a certain ethical restraint, and to develop our innate ability to evaluate our actions against our sense of purpose.

In the book, I propose that we all have clear moments of buyer's remorse, and sometimes they happen before we even make the purchase, or take whatever action we'll later regret. Sometimes it happens when you walk into a mall, or when you go to an online site, or when you're thinking about getting the new browser, or the new computer, or taking that job, or worse, coercing someone else. If you're an employee at the Gap, you experience that same moment of hesitation, of fear, that the customer does. Do I want to use a coercive sales technique that I learned watching the Gap's instructional videos? I'll win a bonus or a T-shirt if I can make this person buy a belt along with his jeans, and I'll get in trouble if I don't make enough three-item sales ... but I can tell he doesn't have that much money. We all experience these moments of doubt, these moments of hesitation when our true sensibility emerges. And then we all try to squash it because we want to make the extra buck, get that MIG jet, get the sale, buy the item, or promote our brand.

JB: *What do you tell companies that hire you? What do they want to know?*
DR: Well, actually, I've sworn off all consulting. I started doing it as research for my *Coercion* book, and then got a bit carried away by the income. I stopped "cold turkey" a few months ago in favor of teaching at NYU's Interactive Telecommunications program, and am lot happier as a result.

When I did consult, I tried to use my "guru" position as a leverage point to subvert the more ruthless marketing techniques. Most companies simply want to know how to sell more stuff in less time — either by selling the same goods to more people, or more goods to the people they're already selling to. I argued that customer loyalty begins with genuinely good treatment and not simply more camouflaged sales pitches. Some companies want to know how to sell online, and I usually showed them how to get out of the way. Don't try to create a sticky site that sucks people in; people don't want to be on flypaper. They don't want sticky experiences. Stickiness may be working in the short run; companies are having success with sites that you can only go in one way and that throw up windows all over the place and then send you lots of email and ask your permission to send you more email, infect you with cookies, and so on. But in the end people will react against these intrusions, and they'll react against the companies who did it to them.

I tried to give companies what I consider to be a more long-term strategy, which is give customers the most direct access to the thing they want — at the best price, with information about what it does, how much it costs, how much is it going to cost to ship it — and get out of the way. Create tools that make it easier to figure out what computer or product or upgrade is best for the individual user. Let the customer up-sell himself in good time. The best competitive advantage is going to be to offer either the best item, the best price, or the best service. Become transparent.

As far as marketing to youth culture, I tried to make companies aware of the destructive power of coercive marketing, and to see how expensive the arms race is getting for everyone. Young people eventually get wise to a company that offers nothing more than a brand strategy. Then the company has to spend millions retooling. I told them to "play nice."

I still like speaking to organizations who are nervous about the rapid development of the internet, and executives who can't understand the market valuations of all these new internet ventures. I've been telling them that the internet is really just a Ponzi scheme. It's being driven by the needs of the investment community. The money needs a place to go. That's why the only companies actually making anything resembling earnings are online trading companies. They're simply conduits for more people at lower levels of the pyramid to buy in. I mean, what other industry besides a Ponzi scheme requires businesses to demonstrate an "exit strategy"? When they ask me what the ultimate internet experience will look like, I tell them that they're already engaged in it: the frantic search for the next big internet company to invest in is the ultimate internet experience. The investors are the customers.

But the most interesting work was helping advertising agencies figure out what comes after advertising. They know their industry is almost obsolete. I think what will replace ads are sponsored media and applications. Rather than using advertisements to create brand images for products, we're going to have brands sponsoring media that is the entertainment or utility that reflects the brand attributes. I've helped an airline develop a Palm Pilot application for the global traveler, and a global phone company develop a world clock map on the web. Instead of paying for advertisements, they can give things directly to their customers.

JB: *Are you talking about things like corporate baseball parks?*
DR: Right, and if it's a Nike ballpark, and you go there, and make that one concession to corporate America, then maybe you don't have to have marketing blasting at you through the loudspeakers during every break: "This touchdown brought to you by blah blah airlines." They actually pay for the touchdowns, you know. It would make for a better game. And it would separate the emotional vulnerability we experience at a sporting event from the coercive techniques of marketers.

A sports spectacle is a great engine for generating the sort of unbridled optimism and enthusiasm we were talking about earlier. The Roman games were so good at generating support for politicians that it was illegal to have a gladiatorial contest within three months of an election. They were aware of just how much that dictator's thumb, up or down, could affect the entire crowd, and its relationship to the leader. Hitler used the spectacle, Farrakhan uses the spectacle. Promise Keepers use the spectacle; they craft their events around the tested emotional responses of their target market.

The role of any coercive technique is to suspend someone's ability to think rationally, so that they can be made to act on their emotions. It's a simple formula used by Hitler, Farrakhan, and Promise Keepers alike, as well as many multilevel marketers at their rallies. Exploit the anonymity of the mob so that everyone expresses long-repressed emotions. Label the oppressive force as a common enemy, stoke the crowd's rage and, once it's reached a peak, entreat the assembled mass to take an oath. They all must promise to sustain this righteous rage after they've left the rally. It's locked in, like a posthypnotic suggestion.

Sports spectacles today are rallies designed to promote our allegiance to corporations. I went to a Jets game where Outback steak houses handed out small signs to every fan. When the Jets sacked the opposing team's quarterback we were supposed to hold up the sign, which read "Sack Attack." On the back of the sign, however, facing each fan it read "Outback Steak House." They took the most aggressive, most carnivorous moment of a football game, where we sack the opposing quarterback, and used it as an opportunity to program us with Outback Steak House, So now we're going to associate the steakhouse with "Ah, we killed them!"

Meanwhile, everything else going on at a sports game is still based on ancient Roman techniques. The Roman games were intended to demonstrate class mobility by showing that slaves could become regular citizens. If a slave really won enough gladiatorial contests, he would be elevated to the status of citizen. What's happening in sports today is very similar, except it is an inner-city kid who gets out of the ghetto because he has talent, and has chosen to spend his energy on entertaining, rather than mugging us. Successful gladiators were permitted to commit terrible crimes, even rape, without fear of being punished — and without damaging their images among the fans. Same way here. No matter how many times a sports hero is arrested, we'll still forgive him. He has license to do these terrible things so that we can vicariously experience his outrage and pain, as well as our own safety and control.

And in the end, who's paying for it all? Look at the scoreboard. It's not the emperor anymore; it's whatever corporation has paid for that scoreboard to be there. Its name is right on top.

In a sense, nothing has changed: the same kinds of techniques that have been used for centuries by emperors, kings, popes, and priests, are now being used in service of the corporation. Where it's different is that we have technologies in place that make these coercive techniques automatic. There are machines doing this now — machines are doing the research, machines are adjusting the commercials and configuring the websites. What I'm trying to do is to insert some human control, some human thought, and some real human intention back into what we're doing.

MUSIC

MIKE LADD

AESOP ROCK

PETE MISER

YONI WOLF AND RICHARD ADAMS

DÄLEK

WEASEL WALTER

MILEMARKER

PAUL D. MILLER A.K.A. DJ SPOOKY

Mike Ladd
Rebel Without a Pause
by ROY CHRISTOPHER (2005)

SEVERAL YEARS AGO, MY FRIEND GREG SUNDIN GAVE ME MIKE
Ladd's *Welcome to the Afterfuture* (Ozone, 2000). I was instantly hooked.
Ladd's spaced-out beats and intelligent wordplay push the limits of hip-
hop until they break into noisy splinters. Genre distinctions can't hold the
man. He's been performing in every possible way since age thirteen, but
his body of work reflects the very best that hip-hop can be. After digesting
Afterfuture, I simply had to hear more.

Knowing that this would be the case, Greg explained that Ladd's first
record (*Easy Listening 4 Armageddon* [Mercury, 1997], during which a
lot of the stuff for *Afterfuture* was recorded) was difficult to find due to
record label bullshit. Finding it became a personal mission that was finally
accomplished a few years, a few states, and many record stores later (and it
was well worth it). Ladd hasn't made things much easier on me since. His
records have come out on several different labels and often under one-off
group names (e.g., the conceptual pair The Infesticons' *Gun Hill Road*
[Big Dada, 2000] and The Majesticons' *Beauty Party* [Big Dada, 2003] — I

wish I had the space here to tell you *this* story), but they're always worth the search.

His latest outings include a collaboration with pianist Vijay Iyer called *In What Language?* (Pi Recordings, 2003), *Nostalgialator* (!K7, 2004), and *Negrophilia* (Thirsty Ear, 2005). Where *In What Language?* and *Negrophilia* are collaborative avant-jazz explorations (the latter includes the Blue Series Continuum, as well as Vijay Iyer), *Nostalgialator* is more like Ladd's older stuff: straight ahead hip-hop, but twisted with his cerebral, poetic bent.

That said, all of Ladd's music runs along a spectrum from head-nodding to mind-expanding, and it often sits dead in the middle, bringing your dome the best of both. Whether it's grimy boom-bap, heady jazz, or whatever else he decides to explore next, Mike Ladd always brings it rugged and rough.

ROY CHRISTOPHER: *Tell me about* Negrophilia. *What were your aims with this record and how did it all come together?*

MIKE LADD: The concept has been with me for a long time. I think in a way, all of my records have touched on this topic, especially when you are a black artist doing stuff that doesn't make the mainstream or is esoteric, and you have to contend with a large portion of your audience being white (especially when that wasn't your primary intended audience). That said, when Petrine Archer-Straw's book came around, I had to read it, and it touched on at least some of the origins of the *Negrophilia* phenomenon, a phenomenon that has grown beyond Elvis and is as bizarre as Michael Jackson, Eminem, and Condoleezza Rice having tea and smoking stems in a drum circle in Norway.

RC: *Why is that? Why is it that when black artists create challenging black music, their audience ends up being mostly white folks?*

ML: The answer is actually pretty easy and is more of a class issue than a race issue. "Experimental music," alternative music, underground, whatever you want to call it — music that doesn't sell, sometimes on purpose — is hard to access. It's hard to find at retailers and in the media — even the internet. It takes time to find it, and it usually takes a certain amount of effort to fully enjoy it. Generally speaking the people who can afford the time to pursue music this adamantly are often middle class or richer (poor, working-class white kids don't come out in droves to see our shit either, and there is often a proportionate amount of middle-class kids of color at the shows).

For most people sitting and listening to music — especially music that takes time — is a luxury they either can't afford or choose not to. If you bust your ass all day like most of the world does (even if you're a yuppie who used to dig the occasional weird shit, but now has a job and a kid and has lost touch with his art friends), the last thing you want to do is come home and listen to some music that's gonna make your head work more. What you're making doesn't have to be that esoteric either: With so much shit out there being pushed, it's work for the average person to digest great music in an unclear package. On top of that, pop is further propagated by a culture that respects capital return over content in general. The culture that appreciates art that pushes boundaries is relegated to mostly bourgeois institutions, universities, etc.

That said, however, I would like to point out the gratifying experience of meeting someone at every show I have ever played that does not fit the demographic I just described, that is from the audience I love to access; it's just that they are in small pockets spread out all over the world. It's like a secret army.

But I don't think you can make music these days without a deep respect for pop and the people who listen to it (I don't care if you see it as understanding your adversary or knowing your global terrain). I actively ignored pop all through high school and college. I discovered absolutely amazing music in the process, but I missed out on some basic sensibilities that took me time to understand.

RC: Negrophilia *followed pretty closely on the heels of* Nostalgialator, *yet these records are very different. How did you approach these different projects?*

ML: I approached them in totally different mindsets, but I can't really explain the shit. *Nostalgialator* was mostly written on the road touring, and recorded in Brooklyn. I did a bunch of *Negrophilia* at the same time with Guillermo Brown, who is instrumental in this record — this record is as much his as it is mine. At the bidding of the record label (for reasons I still don't know), I finished *Negrophilia* alone in my apartment in Paris, which was a completely different environment than I had been used to. I think the difference can really be attributed to the great players on the record: Roy Campbell, Andrew Lamb, Bruce Grant, Vijay Iyer, and my niece, Marguerite Ladd. With Guillermo as coproducer, the collaboration helped it sound so different.

The short answer is that *Nostalgialator* is a "Pop" record, and *Negrophilia* is a "Music" record.

RC: *You've jumped around with different sounds and styles throughout your work. Do you ever wonder or worry that you make it difficult for your fans to keep up with you?*

ML: Yes, I'm broke because of it. I think I probably lose fans with every record, but hopefully gain new ones too. As long as some people stick with me, I'm going to keep exploring as many facets of myself and my interests as possible.

In 2005, I think it's pretty naive for any American to think of themselves as culturally one-dimensional. Clearly our president does, and look at how he acts. Then again, look at the skin tones of his family and it's all shifting quickly. The racial paradoxes in Bush are predictable and Machiavellian, but they still fascinate me, and I'm interested in how they will affect the world.

Okay, that's off the point of the question, but maybe another answer to the problem you are presenting. The thing is, if I am the package and everything you hear from me is a coherent part of that package, I am simply regurgitating the influence and experiences that have informed me for a very long time. Eight records in, I am deeply grateful to the fans that have stuck with me, for real.

RC: *Is there anything you're working on that you'd like to mention here?*
ML: Doing a new band called Father Divine for ROIR Records. Very happy with the way it's coming along. Shout out to Reg in Colorado and DJ Jun.

Aesop Rock
Lyrics to Go
by ROY CHRISTOPHER (2005)

IF, AS MARSHALL MCLUHAN INSISTED, PUNS AND WORDPLAY REP-resent "intersections of meaning," then Aesop Rock has a gridlock on the lyrical superhighway cloverleaf overpass steez. Every time I spin one of his records, I hear something new, some new twist of phrase, some new combination of syllables. These constant revelations are precisely why I've been a hip-hop head since up jumped the boogie, and Aesop keeps the heads ringin'. I'd quote some here, but you really just have to hear him bend them yourself.

The product of our multimedia all-at-once-ness, Aesop Rock mixes, matches, and melds references from the nonstop traffic of messages we all experience. It's a lyrical journey that expands the literature of the now and not-so-gently takes your skull for a ride, mental multicar pileup not-withstanding.

ROY CHRISTOPHER: *Your records unfold themselves over time. I'm always finding and figuring out new references and metaphors upon repeated listens.*

With all of the intricate wordplay, do you ever worry about your listeners not "getting it"?

AESOP ROCK: Nah, not really. I mean, all or most of the references I make are from shit I experienced growing up: funny random movies, TV shows, music, etc. That combined with modern references of the same sort. It's become second nature to me to write like this. I never really worried if people got it or not, 'cause it's how I tell my story. It's all part of a style that's continually developing and has been for a long time.

RC: *Your lyrics are so steeped in said wordplay, they seem to be coming from a rich literary background, yet you claim not to read much. Where does your lyrical inspiration come from?*

AR: Yeah, reading bores me. Like I said, it's mostly movies and TV, and comparing real-life situations to similar nostalgic movie situations or things like that. I like strange slang, strange wording, etc., but not based on how it reads; it only matters if you can deliver it well. So, I'll hear some weird kid's movie expression and adapt it to hip-hop slang, and end up making up my own shit. Some people get it, some don't.

RC: *Who do you like doing hip-hop these days?*

AR: I like all my friends' stuff, very genuinely. I like DOOM. Lately the rotation has been the Beanie Sigel mixtape, new Cage material for his upcoming LP. Been re-visiting Slick Rick a lot, Snoop's new one — a lot of shit.

RC: *The workaday tales of songs like "9-5ers Anthem" and "No Regrets" lay out a loose archetype for living according to one's own passions. What are you striving for? What's the ultimate outcome of your pursuits — in hip-hop or otherwise?*

AR: I'm not sure. Passions consistently change and adapt as you get older, I am finding. I still love making rap music, but I don't care about covering the same topics I did when I was a teenager, or in my early twenties for that matter. These days I just write about living my life, being a scumbag, feeling old, porn, the strength of having a crew behind you. Just boiling it all down to simple shit: friends, fun, sex, pain, violence — things like that. As I get older I get less obsessed with details and more obsessed with finding real general ways of saying a lot. Like an old man who doesn't speak much, but when he does it's some weird, clever statement that somehow sums up everything: That's what I wanna be. Easier said than done, of course.

RC: *With all of the controversy surrounding records like Danger Mouse's* Grey Album *(i.e., issues of intellectual property, copyrights, artistic freedom, etc.), the* Build Your Own Bazooka Tooth *remix contest bridges the gap. What was the impetus behind this project?*

AR: Well, Jux has a nice history of releasing instrumental versions of records, so we just built on that idea: We gave out all the instrumentals and a cappellas and said, "here, have fun." It gives the fans that are actually involved in music-making something to play with.

RC: *Tell us about the new EP,* Fast Cars, Danger, Fire and Knives *(Definitive Jux, 2005). It's coming with an extended book of all your lyrics, right?*

AR: Yeah. It's got seven new songs: three Blockhead beats, one Rob Sonic beat, and three by me. Guest rappers are El-P and Camu Tao. Cage and Metro both do choruses also. It's real family-oriented and, at this point, is my favorite stuff I've ever done. It's kinda funky. We also spent a lot of time on the packaging, which contains an eighty-eight-page book of all the lyrics from *Float* to the present. It took me fucking forever, and I almost lost my mind transcribing it all, but I had some ill designers that really pulled the book and the whole EP package together to look sick. Seems like everyone's doing DVDs or enhanced CDs, but I didn't want to do that. So, I thought this could be a cool thing, something a bit different, something that looks good and is cool for the fans to have. People lose and scratch DVDs. Hopefully the time we put into making the book and CD package look good will make people wanna hold onto it.

RC: *Are you working on anything else that you'd like to mention here?*
AR: Well, just getting ready to hit the road again. I have a few guest spots dropping soon: on the new Zion I record, the Rasco record, Cage record. Beats on the new C-Rayz record, beats and rhymes on the new S.A. Smash record. I rap on the new Prefuse 73 record too. Some mixtape shit. You'll be hearing from me a lot, hopefully. Plus, I started work on new solo material, so we'll see what happens there.

Pete Miser
Camouflage is Relative
by ROY CHRISTOPHER (2004)

"Rap is something you do. Hip-hop is something you live."
— *KRS-One*

"I'm trying to change the world before I change my mind."
— *Pete Miser, "Bring it to the Masses"*

I FIRST SAW PETE MISER ROCK THE MIC LIVE IN 1996. HE WAS THE lead mouth in a Portland, Oregon outfit called the Five Fingers of Funk, and they were opening for De La Soul at Seattle's Fenix Underground. I was intrigued because I had previously only heard Pete do the spoken word thing on a compilation of Pacific Northwestern poets and personalities, *Talking Rain* (Tim Kerr Records, 1993). His flow that night in Seattle rode atop the live, organic grooves of the Five Fingers like a true veteran lyrical navigator. I made a note in my mental.

Fast forward to 2003: My man Billy Wimsatt and I are working on a project together, and who has Billy lined up to help us but his friend and now New York resident Pete Miser.

While it maintains a positive drive in the daily existence of many, on the surface, hip-hop is full of façades. It's a hall of funhouse mirrors, stretching big personalities off into the periphery. Past all of that is where it starts to get good. And when hip-hop is good, it's the most beautifullest thing in this world.

That said, Pete Miser is the real thing. His lyrics, beats, and whole steez are straight out the truest school of hip-hop.

ROY CHRISTOPHER: *First of all, tell us about your new record. Did you try to do anything differently on* Camouflage is Relative *(Coup de Grace, 2004) that you didn't on* Radio Free Brooklyn *(Ho Made Media, 2002)?*
PETE MISER: *Camouflage Is Relative* is different from *Radio Free Brooklyn* in a number of ways. First of all, it's the first record I've made where I had a deadline to meet. I wrote and recorded the whole record in about two months. *Radio Free Brooklyn* had songs that were years old by the time it came out. *Camouflage Is Relative* is all new stuff.

A lot of people have commented on the fact that *Camouflage Is Relative* is funnier than *Radio Free Brooklyn*. My sense of humor doesn't normally show up that much in my music, but I guess it did in this record. The first single, "Scent of a Robot," is about a dude who works his day job in his cubicle at a company that makes robots. One day he realizes that he's one of the robots that the company makes! It's a pretty weird song, especially for a single, but it's in line with my sense of humor. I guess I was feeling kinda loose over the two months in which I made the record.

RC: *How's New York treating you compared to Portland?*
PM: New York treats me real nice! I mean, New York generally doesn't have time for anyone, so you can't take it personally when the city doesn't bend over backwards for you. No matter who you are, this city has seen

bigger so the train doors are still gonna close just as you try to get on the subway sometimes. On the other hand, New York speaks my language. I love Portland, Oregon, for many reasons, but hip-hop culture isn't one of them. I mean, it's there, and it's dope, but it has such a marginalized status that you have to fight just to be respected, let alone embraced. New York respects hip-hop as a legitimate cultural force. It's a nice change!

RC: *Who are you feelin' on the mic these days?*

PM: In a conversation with a musician friend of mine the other day I went off on an Andre 3000 tangent. That cat is just too ill! I mean, not only is he bananas technically, but he says so much with such simple rich imagery. On top of all that, he has the guts to abandon his rhymes for something he's really not that great at (singing.) I can't help but have tons of respect for an artist like that.

Other than A3000, these guys might be five of my top ten:

The Real Live Show (New York underground cats)

The Lifesavas

MF DOOM

Aesop Rock

Redman

RC: *When talking about our perceptions of an environment in which we are completely immersed, Marshall McLuhan compared it to fish knowing nothing of water. You've said similar things about hip-hop in the past — that people who live hip-hop don't even think about it because they're living it. With that in mind, how can we create a discourse about the culture without getting so academic and theory-oriented that we alienate ourselves from it?*

PM: What's the purpose of said discourse? What are we trying to find out? Can we find it out without participating in the culture? It seems to me that one can never fully understand a culture without participating in it. Pure study is basically tourism. Unfortunately, outside participation always taints the purity of a culture as well. But cultures are always evolving aren't they? So, what's the difference? It's like the physics principle that the act of observation changes that which is being observed.

RC: *The Heisenberg Principle . . .*

PM: Damn, talk about academic! I think it's better to go back to the Brand Nubian album title *Everything Is Everything*. If that doesn't answer your question then I give up!

RC: *Well, you and I have talked about how lame so much so-called "hip-hop journalism" is and because I get so sick of old, crusty social theorists trying to talk about some shit that they know nothing about. And me, being a hip-hop fan, participant, and a theorist, I want to talk about hip-hop, I want to talk about it seriously, I want to teach from its perspective, and I want to continue to learn from it. All of this being said, academic theory about hip-hop is going to happen — there's no stopping it — so why not do the shit right?*

PM: So, the purpose of the discourse is to talk about hip-hop in a meaningful, respectful manner, and to squash all of the misconceptions, misinformation, and misguided theory/theorists.

When I say I'm sick of wack hip-hop journalism, I guess I mean two things:

First, I'm sick of subpar writers representing hip-hop in periodicals. For the most part, if you are a hip-hop expert, it's somehow okay to sacrifice clarity, insight, and effective writing for some neato street slang style. Even worse, it's okay to be a bad writer period, style or no style. I mean, doesn't *Murder Dog* magazine understand the function of an editor? What the fuck? I'm not saying that I'm a good writer. In fact, I'm admitting that I'm not and trying not to contribute to the big ol' pile of wackness!

Secondly, I'm annoyed by journalism that covers hip-hop and, in the process, exposes its own ethnocentricity and ignorance of the culture. I guess this is mainly what you're trying to dead with your efforts.

In a discussion about this phenomenon (in this case, regarding jazz) with a musician friend of mine, he mused that it's a particularly Western tradition to pick apart a culture until it doesn't mean a goddamned thing anymore!

When I was in a science class in eighth grade our teacher told us we were going to make a snake one day. We spent the next hour putting all the ingredients of a snake into a beaker: some carbon, some water, etc. Well, at the end of the experiment, it didn't look or act like a snake. It looked like a beaker full of mud. Strange, right? You can have all the ingredients of something but still don't have a living thing? My experience leads me to believe that one can never truly know (much less explain or teach) hip-hop culture. The reason hip-hop is of any value is because it's a living, breathing culture. That means I can be the "real thing," as you say, and still have a completely different experience from DJ Kay Slay who is obviously the real thing too. Now which "real" experience do we present to the writer from the *Washington Post*? And why does he want to know? And who is he talking to? And what cultural biases are they bringing to the discussion to keep them from getting it anyway?

Hip-hoppers often complain about how they are represented in the media. They end up sounding like it's the media that validates what they do and how they live. I don't care if the media gets it because I know the media can never get it. You can't fit it into a one-page article, or even a set of encyclopedias. You can't nail it down because it's always evolving. Why bother? By trying to describe cultures, we only succeed in highlighting how limited our own experience is. To quote Nas, "Why shoot the breeze about it, when you can be about it?"

RC: *Word. Anything else coming up that you want to mention here?*

PM: Yeah, vote! Get it? V-O-T-E! And vote for John Kerry while you're at it! If for no other reason, vote for John Kerry so a freak like George Bush isn't in the position to choose the next three or four Supreme Court justices. If he does that, then his irresponsible agenda will have a legacy that will far outlast his presidency. This election matters more than any of our generation. Vote!

Yoni Wolf and Richard Adams
The Sound of a Handshake
Introduction by ROY CHRISTOPHER (2004)

UNDER THE RADAR OF MAINSTREAM CULTURE, UNSUSPECTING
genres have been quietly blending in the bedrooms of overactive imaginations. One such amalgam came in collaborative form when UK-based
indie-rock band Hood brought Why? (Yoni Wolf) and doseone (Adam
Drucker) from California-based avant hip-hop group cLOUDDEAD
(which also includes David "odd nosdam" Madson) into the studio on their
2001 album *Cold House* (Aesthetics). Having been fans of each other's work,
the two groups were destined to work together — and tour together.

Where Hood's sound jumps between "lo-fidelity avant-pop" and "pas-
toral, nearly instrumental songs," cLOUDDEAD meanders through similar
territory, but adds a skewed hip-hop vision to the mix. Though stunningly
unique on their own, the two mesh well together, play well together, and
their sounds blend into something like nothing else you've ever heard.

*What follows is an email conversation between Yoni Wolf and Richard
Adams from Hood. From the goings-on of their respective bands and their*

recent daily lives, to what kind of shoes they're wearing and the origin of the name "Hood," this conversation is much more interesting than my asking each of them questions would have been.

RICHARD ADAMS: Did you know you were mentioned by name in the lyrics to the new Hood single?

YONI WOLF: In reference to your inquiry, I indeed did not know that I was mentioned by name in the new Hood single. Is this single out? What is it regarding? Is it a song like Billy Joel's "We Didn't Start the Fire," where you mention everyone you know in an all-enveloping look at the current state of music from an historical standpoint? Or is it like a shoutout list at the end: "Micky Mantle rock rock on, Yoni Wolf rock rock on . . ."? Whazzup?

RA: It's not quite up there with the Billy Joel classic. In fact, I think you're the only "celebrity" to get a name-check. It's quite subtle, but I think you're mentioned twice. It's not quite that song by the Beloved, "Hello." (Did you get that in the States?) That name-checks a few people as well. I'll ensure you get a copy when we get some. One for the grandkids maybe.

YW: The Beloved? I don't think we got that in the States, but you have to remember I'm about twenty-five years younger than you. So I guess it's possible it came out back in the '60s or something when you were in high school and I was a first tenner in a pimp's pocket. (Whatever that means.) What are you guys working on at the moment? A new record?

RA: A new record is done — EP out in November, full-length in January.

YW: Whaddub wid sum promo? Still with Domino? New shoes: You? Chris? Who is in the band now?

RA: Yes, and with Domino USA in the States. Yes, I'm still in the band . . . just. And Chris is pretty much Mr. Everything. Steve's still behind the drum stool (or sat upon it). Gaz left last year but might return temporarily in the new year, and we have a new chap called Mark who is brimming with enthusiasm.

YW: I'm glad to hear about the new guy and Steve's continued dedication and the possible return of Gaz (the only true vegan lover of the Hood lot), but my inquiry regarding footwear was completely ignored. What do you mutherfuckers got on your feets? Currently, as of yesterday, I'm sporting these old Converse that I dug out of my closet that I got in a thrift store in London back when we were there for the Mush (cLOUDDEAD/Reaching Quiet) tour in 2002. They are white with blue trimmings, and I added a red stripe on the toe with nail polish. Pretty sharp. Oh, I'm going to a Subtle (Adam and Jeff, et al.) show tonight. It should be really cool. It's their first show (pretty much) since they finished their first full-length. Cool.

RA: Footwear. Sorry, Yoni. I missed that. I'm gonna get Chris in on this chat. They don't call him the "Imelda Marcos of Pop" for nothing, you know. The shoes on my feet are probably the same ones I was wearing on our U.S. tour. I need them replaced. At my age I seem to find myself wearing slippers more than anything. Hope your Converses went down well at the Subtle show. We were hoping to play with Subtle in London town this October, but it clashed with the one and only show we'd had planned all year.

YW: Where does the name Hood come from? I always took it to be referring to the part of the female anatomy that covers the clitoris. I always thought that particular part of a woman's private sector was pretty unnecessary. It makes it nearly impossible to discover the pleasure-inducing zone. Maybe that's the fun of it: the challenge.

I know you're a conservative, thrice-married, middle-aged barrister-turned-pop musician, so if this open talk of sexuality offends you, feel free to find your pinky finger on the delete key.

RA: I'm completely ignoring your sexually explicit theory on where the name of Hood comes from. Safe to say that we were probably thirteen or fourteen years of age when we thought of it, so such thoughts were exempt from our innocent minds.

Laurence from Domino wants us to do some shows together next year. I wonder who he's been talking to. What's in the pieline or even pipeline for you?

YW: Oh yeah!? Are you guys coming to the States? We are looking to set up a tour of America in May and then we will hopefully be doing festivals and knocking about the more civilized part of the world all summer. Let's definitely hook up.

RA: That could work; we're coming over next Spring. Should well be on the road for a chunk. Let's hope I don't go completely insane this time.

How is everything with you? The Hymie's Basement thing (Lex, 2003) was great. The first track on there was maybe my favorite (or second favorite) song of last year. In fact, I kind of went on a pilgrimage to Hymie's Basement last Christmas. I had a good scrat through their records. Funnily enough, the only thing I bought was a Donald Fagen album.

YW: I've been recording a new Why? record with the boys in the band (Josiah, Doug, and Matt — I don't think you met Matt, who we now call "Miss Ohio's"). So I guess it's Why? & Miss Ohio's. Anyway, we've been hard at work on that. It's quite pop. I've been watching these DVDs that Rhino puts out called "Classic Albums" or something like that, where they do interviews with the band now about their best album and talk about how it was made and the circumstances surrounding it. So far, I've seen Fleetwood Mac *Rumours* and Pink Floyd *Dark Side of the Moon*. I'm a sucker for that kind of shit. My dream would be to see a movie of just live studio footage of some of my favorite records being made with no commentary or anything, just a good behind-the-scenes look — all the arguments and the epiphanies.

RA: Yeah, you should see the DVD for our last album: fights, walk outs, nervous breakdowns, singers being forced to sing at near gunpoint, songs being recorded three or four times, mixes rejected, a full set of masters rejected, tears, laughter, screaming fits, complete and utter despair, the whole thing nearly being scrapped before the mixing stage. Oh yeah, it's up there. Hope your thing went more smoothly. Glad it's pop stuff. I like the pop stuff. Our next thing is pop — it's nearly into Britney territory.

YW: Oh, and my girlfriend of two years (I don't think any of you guys met Anna) and I split up last week. That leaves me feeling quite strange and aimless, but maybe it's for the best. We will still be close I'm sure.

RA: Oh, no. That is a shame. It's never easy. Keep your pecker up. Hope you feel better soon.

dälek
Gods and Griots
by ROY CHRISTOPHER (2002)

MUSIC TRANSCENDS ALL BOUNDARIES. AND WHERE MUSIC FANS
are generally open for anything engaging, the music industry is constantly
segregated by its own marketing terms. They draw lines, set up demographics, and distinguish target markets.

Caught somewhere in between these lines, dälek have been victims
of this segregation since their inception. Their first record *Negro, Necro,*
Nekros (1998) was on independent rock label Gern Blandsten Records (the
folks who brought you the brilliant, indie avant-garde act Rye Coalition),
but they do hip-hop. This put the record in a crack in the marketplace.
There's nothing normal about what dälek do but it's hip-hop to the core.
Frontman dälek's gruff vocals grind against the gritty backdrop of scraping
noise created by Oktopus and Still, the friction lending light to their dark
imagery. Lyrics spit to illuminate the spirit:

> Strange intrinsic world got me lifted.
> Skilled drunken mystic felt my earth shifted.

The most innovative people in independent music are among dälek's friends, supporters, and collaborators. They've toured with Techno Animal (Justin Broadrick and Kevin Martin's harsh hip-hop outfit), Tomahawk (one of Mike Patton's many projects, this time with guitarist Duane Denison), collaborated with the William Hooker Ensemble (the New York Jazz drummer and friends), have an upcoming tour with DJ Spooky, and Patton's Ipecac label is putting out their next record *From Filthy Tongue of Gods and Griots* (2002). Through all of this, dälek just keep rubbing their sound against the shores of others, and prove once again that innovation happens not in the fields, but between them. Feel the friction.

ROY CHRISTOPHER: *Tell me about the new record for Ipecac Recordings.*
DÄLEK: The album is *From Filthy Tongue of Gods and Griots* and is due out August 6. This album represents about four years of our work. The actual songs have been finished for a while, but the mixing and mastering aspects were recently completed. Lyrically, I continued on a very personal level, though abstract. Again, I ask the listener to find their own meaning in my personal madness. Musically this album is very aggressive; we expand on what we started on *Negro*. Perhaps a bit more focused this time around, with more of our own defined sound.

RC: *What did you guys try to do differently on this record as opposed to Negro, Necro, Nekros?*
D: *Negro, Necro, Nekros* was recorded as kind of an experiment. We had no live experience; we had no idea what we were doing. There is something amazing about that innocence. However, looking back there is a lot about us that *Negro* failed to capture. *Filthy Tongue* better represents our live sound, and has an air of confidence which can only come from four years of hardcore touring.

RC: *What's your take on why the hip-hop world, once seemingly open to so many new forms and variations, now has such high barriers to entry for new and innovative sounds?*

D: First off, what is passed off as hip-hop in the mainstream is a farce: that is *pop* music. It has its place but that's a place that hasn't been the breeding ground for acceptance of new forms and variations since perhaps the later Beatles stuff. The real problem lies in the underground, where there are really good groups. However, it seems the underground has just become an "on-deck circle" where the less-known musicians await their chance to fit molds of "real hip pop," which are dictated by the corporate world. If your ultimate goal is to make money . . . cool, I guess. But what is lost is the essence of what made hip-hop the innovative force it was in the '80s and early '90s. Hip-hop was about taking all the sounds and ideas around you, and making them into your own. It was the angst-ridden voice of minority youth. Energy and angst wise, it was the equivalent of the punk movement. I think we can safely say that the commercial music world killed both hip-hop and punk. The formulaic remnants can't afford to allow truly different music in because that would result in loss of sales.

RC: *What is it that drives dälek?*

D: I want to make music that moves me. There are sounds and words I need to get out, that I myself need to hear. We are musicians. Music is what drives us.

RC: *Your work is obviously informed by the urban milieu, but there's a lot of serious literature bubbling to the surface as well. Whom do you guys read and respect?*

D: Everything from Kerouac and Burroughs to Pablo Neruda, Jose Saramago, Burgess, Donald Goines, Poe, and Langston Hughes to keep the list short. I am also a big fan of history text and biographies in general.

RC: *Anything else you guys are working on that you would like to bring up here?*

D: We are working on a split 12" with Velma, a follow up to the Oddateee album, a split 12" with Kid606, production work on the next Jett Brando album, recordings with Faust, and the Dev-ONE solo album.

Weasel Walter
Killing Music
by ROY CHRISTOPHER (2002)

THE DECONSTRUCTION OF ORGANIZED SOUND PUT FORTH BY multi-instrumentalist composer and improviser Weasel Walter is fiercely aimed at destroying the complacency of music and musicians. This is nowhere more evident than in his rotating cast of characters known as the Flying Luttenbachers. He describes the working plan of the Luttenbachers thusly, "The nature of operations has been to utilize the most appropriate people available — pushing the resulting chemistry as far as possible — and finally to abandon the formation when creative stasis has been reached." Though he renounces all classifications of genre, the Luttenbachers are a manifestation of the attitudes inherent in free jazz, death metal, and punk rock: a sonic maelstrom of hate and disdain tempered with skills in spades. And behind all of this cacophony is a broader worldview than most drummers can shake a stick at.

Pushing the limits of music and his fellow musicians, Weasel Walter is leading the way to the noisy ends of the world.

ROY CHRISTOPHER: *Tell me more about your "against music" stance.*

WEASEL WALTER: I tend to veer toward philosophical nihilism, so this perspective is often mirrored directly in all facets of my art. There's a ton of potential dialectic beneath this simplistic sloganeering, but I generally prefer kicking asses first and taking names later. Sometimes this approach requires guerrilla tactics that certain people tend to find a bit too frank or extroverted. I don't have the time to worry about everyone else's precious tastes and social protocol. In the past I was working in a much more reactionary mental state than I am now. That is, I believed that anyone who wasn't with my program was the enemy — the usual impudence and self-righteousness of youth in full effect. I still find much contemporary music and art uninspired and uninspiring. I am seeking to offer an artistic alternative by making a conscious commitment to create music that strives to avoid and surpass the prevalent complacency I see in the contemporary rhythmic, harmonic, melodic, and timbral approaches of energy music (by this I mean music which functions primarily on a visceral level as opposed to cerebral wall-hanging "Art" or modern classical-type composition). Of course, there's still a long way for me to go, and I feel like I'm still at the tip of the iceberg. I'd like to think that the result of this struggle challenges the listener as well.

RC: *You talk of your recent music as "investigations in different systems of complexity." Do you consciously attempt to create and manipulate sonic bifurcations and bring forth new levels of complexity with sound?*

WW: Of course! I'll reiterate that there are so many possible parameters involved in organizing sound that I still feel like I'm always trying desperately to build some kind of solid foundation to base the future development of the music on. Needless to say, the dichotomy between improvisation and composition has become less pure for me through the years. I've always utilized a mixture of both methods to force moments of unexpected chaos (or entropy!). I like to keep my own band mates a bit unsure as to what is going to happen. This fights off the rigor mortis of operating in a "band" situation and getting used to a set routine. I do believe in the necessity of physical kineticism as a driving force in our modus operandi. Noisemaking has often resulted in new, instantaneous possibilities as well. Right now, I'm much more concerned with exploring unusual relationships in harmony, melody, and rhythm though. I'm less concerned with improvising and so-called chaos because I feel like I've done plenty of investigation within the possibilities of randomness/music destruction, and now I need to pursue order, as asymmetrical as that order might be. The obvious, pedestrian archetype here is the fractal and its inherent form — when what appears to be random and chaotic actually has infinite law and equilibrium behind it.

RC: *Your fans miss the fact that a lot of what drives the Luttenbachers'* *records is your worldview (the emergence of the robot as the next dominant* *species on Earth, and beyond). Care to delve into this further?*
WW: Every aspect of our art is a reflection of my personal worldview. How far people read into this is up to them. If anyone does get it on this particular level, they generally don't discuss it with me frequently.

It's not that I'm trying to create some kind of moral parable that the robot is the next dominant species on Earth. I'm not that linear! It would be a bit too obvious and predictable if the plot was: Earth bad, cosmic retribution destroy evil Earth; robot good, robot leave Earth; me = robot, me live happy ever after. This is not the case. The emergence of the robot during the apocalypse scenario on the *Gods of Chaos* (ugEX-PLODE/Skin Graft, 1997) album is symbolic indeed, but not of superiority. The albums after that document the alternate dimensions/outer space the robot encounters before its own inevitable destruction, which brings us to the present album, *Infection and Decline* (ugEXPLODE/Troubleman Unlimited, 2002). If anything, the next record will be about reformation and new systems/orders following the ultimate annihilation of everything earthly, including the robot.

RC: *With your composing, improvisation, playing, what is it that you're looking for?*

WW: Heh heh. Fulfillment, adulation, peer approval, money. You know. I'm trying to keep myself busy making things which I hope exist autonomously outside of myself and hopefully have tangible or profound depth to those few who appreciate it. My ideal scenario would be to have created something that I think is the ultimate end product of an incredible amount of effort, thought, and discipline and have it well-received, felt and understood by sympathetic people. As I've said over and over and over again, there seems to be a long way to travel before this is going to happen. I'm also searching for answers to bigger questions and this whole process is a constant exercise in research and development. I'm always looking to up the ante technically and intellectually.

RC: *Jon Skuldt gave me a great quote from you a few years ago: "Impatience is a virtue." Could you expound on what this adapted aphorism means to you?*

WW: I feel like there's a good chance I won't be here much longer and I have to see results now. I have to push things as hard as I can or I'm just wasting time like the useless drones that surround me. I can only tolerate the slovenliness of others for a short time. I don't know . . . I think you know where this is going. I try to be tolerant, but I have a hard time accepting the bread crumbs that this world has offered me.

RC: *What kind of stuff are you into text-wise?*

WW: Uh, reading has always been kind of functional to me. I usually read to further research topics I'm obsessed with and not so much for entertainment or relaxation (naturally, I rarely afford myself any real relaxation). Lots of reference books about music history, music discographies, blah blah blah. I'm interested in what really happened behind certain art and music movements in regards to personal chemistry, socio-economical conditions, etc. I'm not amenable to accepting the popular, public versions of any kind of history. What we Americans are offered as definitive history by standard media and educational sources sure smells like horseshit to me most of the time.

One of these days I'll get past page fifty-six of Harry Partch's *Genesis of A Music* (Da Capo, 1974) and past page seventeen of Iannis Xenakis' *Formalized Music* (Pendragon Press, 1992). Glenn Branca recently gave me Mark Leyner's *The Tetherballs of Bougainville* (Harmony 1997), and I laughed so hard that my teeth all fell out. I like to look at vintage bondage-type pictures of Bettie Page, but that's probably a bit more information than most people would like to know.

RC: *Anything coming up that you'd like to tell us about?*

WW: Nah. Well, actually we will be touring in July as part of a package with the Locust, Arab On Radar, Lightning Bolt, Erase Errata, and Wolf Eyes. I find this to be a significant culmination of a movement of musicians trying to investigate cultural alternatives and "kicking butt" at the same time. I think the tour will be well-documented, so that's rewarding. The Flying Luttenbachers are currently returning back to the less glamorous private rehearsal process to work on some brand new material. I'm confident that this stuff will reveal yet another distinctive side to the band. I need to give props to Orthrelm and Grand Ulena, who I see as our peers (and superiors) in the struggle to push music forward another inch. I should also acknowledge Total Shutdown, Burmese, Get Hustle, Upsilon Acrux, Kevin Drumm, Greg Kelley, Andy Ortmann, Misty Martinez, Rat Bastard, Ex-Models, XBXRX, Conqueror (RIP), Sadistik Exekution, and Glass Candy, and the Shattered Theater.

Milemarker
The Only Band That Matters
by ROY CHRISTOPHER (2001)

THE COLLECTIVE KNOWN AS MILEMARKER HAS A VAST AND PRO-
lific output that encompasses much more than the average independent
band: Dave Laney puts out a printed alternative media quarterly called
MediaReader, Al Burian self-publishes a 'zine of his travels and views
therefrom called *Burn Collector* (the first nine of which are collected into
a book) and Roby Newton does traveling puppet shows and animations.

Milemarker songs cover many sociological topics, including many
derived from living in our technology-driven culture. They liken their
early records to video-game soundtracks when compared to their live
sound at the time, but the aggression shows through. You see, in the studio,
Milemarker preferred to experiment with sounds and samples (playing
with the irony of using technology against itself), whereas live they're
more forthcoming. These two approaches finally meshed on *Frigid Forms
Sell* (Lovitt, 2000) and grew on the recently released *Anaesthetic* (Jade
Tree, 2001). The most important thing about Milemarker is that they will
force you to think about things — even if you're already thinking about

things. They stir the corporeal, the angst, the spiritual core, and the cerebrum simultaneously. As a collective, they represent the epitome of the new paradigm of artist: one with fingers that run deep in many pies.

The Clash once called themselves "The Only Band That Matters" and *Rolling Stone* once called Fugazi the same. Milemarker has earned the title through years of hard work, expansive vision, and downright challenging music.

ROY CHRISTOPHER: *As a collective of individuals with a steady, varied, and prolific output outside of the band, what is it that drives you to do so much?*

AL BURIAN: I feel like I do the band because there is this abstract entity of a band and it wants to be realized somehow — it wants to be a band. And then I feel like I do other things outside of the band because there are things I feel like expressing which don't necessarily fit into the agenda of what the band is expressing.

DAVE LANEY: I've tried to tailor my life in a fashion that allows me to spend more time on the things that I actually want to be doing. I love to play music and travel, so I play in a band. I am also horribly obsessive/compulsive, so I started a magazine which requires tons of time to be spent doing horribly mundane things. At this point, I'm actually forced to be spending my time doing these things instead of working a normal job — the mail keeps piling up and someone has to write back. Actually, I started *MediaReader* because I felt like the average DIY music magazine was ignoring a large part of the "community" that they advertised as covering. The idea with *MR* was to serve as a less specific type of magazine: not always political, not always musical, but always trying to be critical with a constructive edge to the criticism. There comes a time when you can't complain about things anymore and you just have to force yourself to pick up your own complaints and create that new thing.

RC: *Tell me about the new record,* Anaesthetic. *Is there a theme or specific issues addressed as there was with* Frigid Forms Sell?

AB: Well, it's sort of a secret theme. All of the lyrics and recording information are hidden in the packaging, so the idea is that the record initially seems to be about nothing, just a pretty object, all aesthetics. The idea is to make people pay a little more attention, sort of to involve the listener a little more actively in the process of figuring out what the record is about.

DL: The themes contained in the songs vary more, compared to *FFS*. I actually think that the new one is the most political and socially relevant album that we have released. That was part of the idea with hiding the lyrics, as well. I think that the music is more accessible on the new album, enough so that we knew we would get hell from old friends that knew the band from the get-go. To go along with what we felt would probably be the first instinct from these people, we decided to try to double their reaction and make them second guess themselves later on. That was the idea anyway: have people come up and say, "new label, new sound, lyrics about love — what gives? What are you guys doing!?" When in reality I feel like we bumped it up a notch. At least on a personal level it feels like that. Whereas the overwhelming theme of *FFS* was commodification and the dumbed-down way that we are taught to relate to others through the way that we relate to products, *Anaesthetic* contains songs about gentrification, the atrocities of textile sweat shops, modern disconnection, terminal illness, and so on. I feel like throwing yourself into the mix is a big part of relating to other people, and of being able to step past sheer social commentary from the position of an untouchable critic.

RC: *There seems to be a lot of Michel Foucault's influence on* Frigid Forms.

AB: You are making some pretty grand assumptions there, young man. In fact, I have never read Michel Foucault. I was assigned some of his writing in college but I did not do the reading that day. My housemate claims that her entire college cultural studies major was essentially majoring in Michel Foucault, but I only remember her doing various video projects which involved wrapping herself in tin-foil. And considering that, perhaps I should investigate this Foucault fellow.

DL: Ha ha. I, myself, years ago, had read some short thesis of Mr. Foucault, but to be honest, I can not even begin to tell you what it was about. Maybe I should, as well, do some investigating.

RC: *Richard Metzger once said that the most subversive thing one can do is to become popular. In the spirit of this quote, I have often argued in defense of bands like Rage Against the Machine, stating that — in spite of the fact that they create revenue for evil companies such as Epic/Sony — they reach and influence more kids than any activist-minded indie band (and probably lead kids to those bands eventually anyway) can. What do you (as an activist-minded indie band) think of the "mainstream vs. underground" debate and said point of view.*

AB: I assure you that neither Rage Against the Machine, our band, nor any other band that has ever or will ever exist has subversion in mind when seeking popularity. The pursuit of popularity has to do with deep-seated feelings of personal inadequacy, usually left over from traumatic experiences such as being chosen last for the kickball team in grade school or something like that. Now me, personally, I don't have any quibbles with the political platform of Rage Against the Machine, the Foo Fighters, the post-Buddhist Beastie Boys, or any of that type of music. My main concern is, when you examine the average mosh pit at one of these events, sure, those guys are all wearing Zapatista T-shirts, they all signed the Mumia petition, but take a closer look: aren't those pretty much the same guys who were picking you last for kickball back in the olden days? Everyone has a right to enjoy music, and if Rage Against the Machine is willing to handle this demographic, so be it, but the point is that I don't want to be around those people. I'm not into hanging out with those guys, they weren't nice to me in grade school, I'm still bitter about the whole thing. That is the difference between "mainstream" and "underground" to me: do you want to convert the maximum number of people to cause X or T-shirt slogan Y, or do you want to help build a culture where people who feel alienated can find some commonality.

DL: That's a difficult, ongoing debate. I do mostly agree with what Al said, but also think that there is some break point to the oversimplification. A lot of what I spend time doing is trying to build and support the community that I consider myself part of. There are limitations and compromises to everything, and I think it's important to distinguish between the differences of building a community and solely maintaining a community. In order to build something, you have to broaden awareness about things and reach people that already don't have the exact same political platform or ethics as yourself. This is the argument that I assume RATM would use as justification to touring with the Wu-Tang Clan and going the route that they did. RATM is really a weird phenomenon case study in the history of this argument, which is another reason why people use them all the time. There is also Fugazi, who went a completely different route, built what they have by themselves, and still hit an enormous audience. Even they have to deal with a huge contingency of football player jock types at their shows, buying their records, misinterpreting their lyrics, etc., but I do believe that when you look at the greater picture of the examples that both bands have set, it comes into focus very quickly that Fugazi did all this stuff with much more integrity in tact than RATM. Both of these bands are seemingly flukes of the modern rock industry, and both are hard to compare to the average indie rock band.

The overbearingly truth is that major label ethics can be very, very sleazy. From the little bit that I've seen from friends of mine that have signed on to the major game, everything changes completely. Even in a strict financial sense, history has proven that it works out for very few bands, and even when it does, I'm not into an economy that (to quote from Steve Albini's article in the ages-old *Maximum RocknRoll* issue on major labels) makes the label $710,000, the producer $90,000, the manager $51,000, and, finally, the band $16,000. The real atrocity here is that the label made forty-five times more than the band, and the guys getting the kickbacks off the band probably know little to nothing about the band. There have been countless articles written on this, and there have been major-label bands that superceded the law, bands like Beck. But still, and keep in mind that this paragraph is only in reference to the finances and not the "artist shall have all control over her art" type thing, to go into one of these deals is a gamble that is usually lost by the band. It has, sadly, been proven over time. Which is to say that to encourage someone to be the next RATM is to encourage someone to shoot themselves in both feet.

Lately I've been almost obsessing over the idea of other people making money off of me working. I quit my job and got a job at a nonprofit, where there are no kickbacks to dudes in suits or higher-up positions. Of course, I recently got fired when I left for three months of touring, but I liked the place. There was no attitude, barely any superiors, and I felt good about what I was doing. In response to your question "do you think that getting famous is the ultimate act of subversion?" I say, no: getting famous on your own terms is the ultimate act of subversion.

RC: *Whom do you read and respect?*
AB: Milan Kundera's *Unbearable Lightness of Being* (Harper & Row, 1984) is a good book; I also like Don DeLillo a lot, particularly *White Noise* (Viking, 1985). Jerry Mander's *Four Arguments for the Elimination of Television* (William Morrow, 1978) is a good nonfiction choice. Orwell, Camus, Kafka, Salinger are good classics. Recently I've been getting really into the author John Fante.

DL: I've always been into the old Russian writers. Dostoevsky is my favorite. Tolstoy and the like, Camus (though French), Mark Twain. I know, I know, all this stuff is as old as rocks, but fantastic nonetheless.

RC: *What made technology such a major theme in Milemarker songs?*

AB: People occasionally misinterpret our band as very sci-fi and future-obsessive, when this is actually not the case at all. For instance, the opening line of *Frigid Forms Sell*:

> We keep waiting for the robots to crush us from the sky
> They sneak in through our fingertips and bleed our fingers dry.

Sounds like the press kit to *The Matrix*, but the giant robot has been a popular allegorical symbol since World War II, particularly in Japanese cartoons and movies, I would say clearly representing anxiety over nuclear war. So the point there is that we're all looking for the big, instantaneous Armageddon ending (witness people's susceptibility to Y2K panic), while the actual dangers are right under our fingers, in the small and mundane encroachments technology makes into our daily lives. An example: I was talking to my co-worker the other day and she mentioned how she has to get a stronger prescription for her glasses. She said that the eye doctor had told her that her eyesight would continue to deteriorate unless she stopped working with computers. "But in this day and age I don't really see how I can do that," she said. It struck me as really crazy that this person was literally making the choice to give up her eyesight so as not to go against the status quo of technological advancement. That's a totally fucked-up world to be living in, and this is the sort of thing that people deal with right now on a daily basis. So I think the root of any technological obsession or phobia you might pick up on just comes from being freaked out about the contemporary state of things.

DL: Al is the real technology freak. He has written most of the songs that are about such things. I've always thought that his best subjects come from observing the world around him, figuring out what makes him feel uncomfortable or alienated, and writing about that discomfort.

RC: *Anything else you guys are working on that you would like to bring up here?*

AB: Dave and I are always working on some printed matter or other; the new *MediaReader* should be out soon enough, and my 'zine *Burn Collector* should have a new issue out, oh, who knows when, probably not for a while. You can contact PO Box 641544, Chicago, IL 60644 for more info about these publications. Roby continues to make things at such a furious pace that anything I could mention would be outdated before I even finished typing. She's been contemplating putting together a video compilation of her puppet shows, which I wish she would do some day, as the world would be a kinder and more palatable place if such an object existed.

DL: The new issue of *MediaReader*, issue #5, should be completed by mid-January and set to go on tour with MM (U.S. tour Jan/Feb). Should be pretty exciting this time around. A bit bigger, a lot fancier, and still free.

Paul D. Miller aka DJ Spooky
Subliminal Minded
by ROY CHRISTOPHER (2001)

IF EVER THERE WERE A POSTMODERN-DAY RENAISSANCE MAN, he is Paul D. Miller. Painter, philosopher, social scientist, DJ, author, and producer (among others) are all hats that fit snugly on his head. He is probably best known as "DJ Spooky aka That Subliminal Kid," but this is only one of many roles he has taken on and made a success of in a process he calls "social sculpture." He's also the only DJ I've ever seen cut up a Marshall McLuhan record, closing the loop in more ways than one.

With his records, lectures, installations, writings, and a new magazine in the works, Paul D. Miller is always on the cultural futurestep.

ROY CHRISTOPHER: *The worlds of academia and pop culture are oft found at odds with one another, yet your work resides — and prospers — decidedly in the crossfire between the two. From your unique vantage point, how do you perceive the two worlds and their interaction?*

PAUL D. MILLER: Well, the basic idea for me is to somehow convey a sense of how conceptual art, language art, and an engagement with some kind of idealism can function in this day and age. Basically, as an artist, my work is an investigation into how culture gets made. I guess you could say it's process oriented. That doesn't mean I'm going to sit down everyday and write "cultural crit" stuff. Folks who I like to call "low-level cultural bureaucrats" do that; it's a false and ultimately sterile way to try to beat culture into some kind of formula that they then try to stamp their name on to make some kind of "career," and it's a modus operandi that disgusts me.

A weird hero of mine is a Victorian age biologist, Paul Kammerer, who in the late nineteenth century was the first person to really explore ideas of "synchronicity" — how things converge in patterns. He would walk around and collect examples of simultaneity - coincidences would be marked and registered with exact mathematical precision, and he searched long and hard for an equation that would describe how things manifested in urban reality. He'd call this kind of stuff "the law of sequences" or a "law of series" — "Das Gesetz der Serie" in German (that's also parallel to how we name the elements of a music track these days: "a sequence"). He was looking for algorithms of everyday life, how patterns appear — stuff like what the biochemist Rupert Sheldrake would call "morphic fields," or how morphology of structure can affect all aspects of the creative. In other words, patterns ain't just about bein' digital, they are global, they are universal. They are rhythms that hold everything we know and can understand together.

But anyway, Kammerer's idea of sequential reality and process-oriented events — it's one of the first systematic attempts at figuring out a rhythm of everyday life in an industrial context. It ended badly — he committed suicide. I'm more concerned with praxis: how to foster a milieu where dialog about culture becomes a way to move into the pictures we describe with words, text, sounds — you name it. Like I always enjoy saying, it's a method that becomes "actionary" rather than "re-actionary" — you end up with a culture that is healthier and more dynamic.

What Kammerer would call a series, someone like Henry Louis Gates would call "signifyin'" — it's all about how we play with perception of events, and this is the link that I make between DJ culture, techno-science, and the art of everyday creativity in a digital environment. I'm not really concerned with the "academy" per se — it's one reflection of the illusions of class structure and hierarchy that have clouded any real progressive contexts of criticism and think have been an absolute bane to any kind of creativity in American culture for the last decade or so. When theory gets too in the way of culture, it's dead. Period. No comma, no colon, no semi-colon — it's the end of the sentence, and it's time for a new paragraph. Turn the page, close the book, check a different website, 'cause that's when things get really, really boring. I think that youth culture reflexively understands this.

Part of my goal was to bypass the notion of the "critic" as an "authority" who controls narrative, and to create a new role that's a lot more concurrent with web culture: you become the cultural producer and content provider at the same time. It's a role consolidation. Especially when you're in a situation where the pop culture mags are terrible, and the art/theory stuff is so out of touch with what's going on; it's time for a new situation. End the mix tape, stop the CD player, press cancel on that file that was downloading, whatever. I started DJing as a conceptual art project that critiqued a lot of the absolutely terrible things I see in American media, and the end result was to create my own platform: social sculpture — self as shareware or generative syntax for a new language of creativity, or something like that. Heraclitus of Ephesus said way back in the day:

The soul is undiscovered, though explored forever to a depth beyond report (Fragment 73)

The critics that I respect in an arts/culture/theory kind of context — Erik

Davis, Simon Reynolds, Beth Coleman, Alondra Nelson, Kodwo Eshun, Margo Jefferson, Ron Eglash, Manuel De Landa, N. Katherine Hayles, Neil Strauss, Peter Lunenfeld, Douglas Kahn, Friedrich Kittler, and a host of others — these are progressive voices in the world of cultural criticism, and I think that they'd be interesting people whether they were writing, or doing music or art, or whatever. Life is interesting. The writing that gives meaning and some kind of hope to life in this world should be interesting as well.

The DJ "mix" is another form of text and its involutions, elliptical recursive qualities, and repetitions are helping transform an "analog" literature that is increasingly becoming digitized. The "mix" mirrors that kind of web of text that you can find anywhere from hypertext missives from altx.com to the cesium clocks at the Naval Observatory in Washington, D.C., that keep the time for the whole country. I guess I sit at that crossroads like the old blues singers, thinking of better ways to make rhythms of information. Only there's no devil to sell my soul to — I have a different muse. Kind of like Giambattista Vico's book from way back in the day, *The New Science* (Cornell University Press, 1984).

RC: *Realizing that the aforementioned juxtaposition of mental territory could be the least of your obstacles or concerns, what do you find most challenging in your various areas of work?*

PDM: What I find challenging is the basic sense of mental inertia that carries our culture along. People really don't think about the absolute wonders that surround us and make this life livable and our way of thinking sustainable. DJing for me, like science fiction, points us to a place where everything doesn't have to be the same. The same track? The same beat? Day after day, night after night — it would be like some kind of living death if that were to happen in DJ culture. And, yeah, that's how a lot of the culture works. There's an old phrase from Olaf Stapledon's classic, old-school science fiction (where a being from the edge of the universe comes into contact with humanity through mental waves — kind of reminds me of voodoo):

> First he conceived from the depth of his being a something, nei-
> ther mind nor matter, but rich in potentiality . . . it was a medium in
> which the one and the many demanded to be more subtly dependent
> upon one another; in which all parts and all other parts and all char-
> acters must pervade and be pervaded by all other parts and all other
> characters; in which each thing must seemingly be but an influence in
> all other things; and yet the whole must be no other than the sum of
> its parts, and each part an all pervading determination of the whole. It
> was a cosmical substance in which any individual spirit must be, mys-
> teriously, at once an absolute self and a mere figment of the whole.

But on another realm, in another zone, I wonder what he would have said of something like New York's Soundlab, a digital art happening where all elements of the mix are shared by everyone who participates in the event. Soundlab is cool, and I like stuff like that where the formalized considerations of art and digital media are live and direct — living, breath-ing material to play with as the rhythms speak their codes to all present at the event. I like the Jamaican and Silicon Valley approach to what Amiri Baraka called "the changing same": versions and versions of everything, all change all the time. But the main essence of the culture's most progressive stuff is unconscious, and that might be the most healthy thing going on.

Anyway, that's just my basic response. Inertia — it's not just boring, it's against the basic principles of physics! I wake up almost every day with this on my mind: if everybody knows things are completely fucked up and bound to get worse, do they just want to forget about things? The answer is pretty much a resounding "yes!" And as with *1984* or *Brave New World*, and most of the fictions that make up the fabric of everyday life today, the game is: how do you remember? How can we make sense of the loops if there is no space outside them? This is the most interesting thing I try to convey in my art projects — life at the edge of language; my mixes are a kind of post-literary "aphasia," but still within the loops that hold reality together these days. I want to break those chains and see what else there is. It's like hearing a time stretched sound at the end of a loop cycle on an Akai S-3000 sampler and knowing where the closure points are, but somehow it always just sounds right to close the loop, repeat the phrase ad infinitum.

The Situationists had their concept of the "derive" or "psychogeographie," but these days that kind of sense of wandering through an indeterminate maze of intentionality is what makes up the creative act — selection and detection, morphology of structure. Those are what make the new kind of art go round. My challenge to myself is to always try to create new worlds, new scenarios at almost every moment of thought. It makes me feel like floating in an ocean of possibility. The challenge is to narrow the focus to convey that state of mind; there's a lot of translation issues involved, but anyway, that's how I see it. There's an intense moment in Andre Breton's Second Manifesto of Surrealism where he writes, "the simplest Surrealist act consists of dashing down into the street, pistol in hand, and firing blindly as fast as you can, as fast as you can pull the trigger, into the crowd. Anyone who at least once in his life, has not dreamed of thus putting an end to the petty system of debasement and cretinization in effect has a well-defined place in that crowd, with his belly at barrel level." Your average kid in high school can relate to that at this point. For me the idea is to show where art can take new directions and become a total form to inhabit.

RC: *What's your take on why the hip-hop world, once open to so many new forms and variations, now has such high barriers to entry for new and innovative sounds?*

PDM: I think that hip-hop has really given us such a powerful tool to create some kind of cross-cultural dialog, and it's given a whole generation of African Americans a sense of self that's profound, while at the same time, it's been a window into America at large for most of the rest of the world. Paradoxically, it's re-enforced so many clichés about what "Blackness" can be, and that's an intense paradox in a world that is truly hybrid (far more so than anyone wants to admit).

There's a great scene in Samuel Delaney's *Dhalgren* (Gregg Press, 1977) where the main character, "The Kid," focuses on the ruins of the city that the story takes place in and it reflects his own sense of psychological dispersion. I feel like that sometimes. Samuel Delaney is such a powerful voice in describing these kinds of issues and so is Ishmael Reed, but, again, they are a different generation, and I can only imagine what it was like to be African American and creative and have to deal with all the total bullshit that critics, art-world people, and the assorted people who make up the "cultural discourse" of each time period create. It took someone like August Wilson something like thirty years to "break through" the "pink ceiling" (it's not transparent, and it's certainly not glass — race in cyberspace can play all sorts of tricks on your mind), and it's definitely a racially coded world in terms of cultural discourse.

Again, the idea is how to, like Napster, create milieu where people can exchange culture and information at will and create new forms, new styles, new ways of thinking. Think of my style of DJing as a kind of memetic contagion, a thought storm brought about by my annoyance and frustration with almost all the conventional forms of race, culture, and class hierarchies. Hip-hop is a vehicle for that, and so are almost all forms of electronic music. Again, it's all about morphology of structure — how things can shift from one medium to another. Culture in this milieu acts kind of like what Derrida describes in his infamous essay "Plato's Pharmacy": "science and magic, the passage between life and death, the supplement to evil and to lack . . . the difference between signifier and signified is no doubt the governing pattern. . . . In being inaugurated in this manner, philosophy and dialectics are determined in the act of determining their OTHER." Dialectical triangulation — language becomes its own form of digital code. Check the theater of the rhyme as it unfolds in time.

I can only wonder what James Baldwin would have said if he had been at the Detroit Electronic Music festival last year (I was one of the headliners). There were over 1.5 million people at that festival — it was bigger than Woodstock (where I also played in 1994). No fights, no weird sense of alienation, just folks from almost every race, color, and creed hanging out. It was the first twenty-first century carnival of the north. Hip-hop is always innovative and it can absorb almost anything. The music itself is far more dynamic than many of the people who make it. There's so much more to be done. We're just beginning — and even after twenty years of hip-hop, I think that the amount of permutations it can handle has just scratched the surface. Stuff like Q*Bert's *Wave Twisters*, artists like Daze, DZINE, Soundlab, Saul Williams, Anti-Pop Consortium, Talvin Singh, Kodwo Eshun — all are pushing the envelope and making more room for new sounds and thoughts. The amount of new stuff happening is almost giddy in sheer volume.

I think I'd have to disagree with the statement that there are boundaries about how new sounds can be spread. When people are faced with conditions where "conservatives" control the zone, they have to innovate to get their message out. Innovation leads to constant elevation. And that's not "Social Darwinism"; it's more like a cooperative model of how information spreads in the hothouse environment of net culture, where "newness" is celebrated with how many people check in on the information. And if stuff like "All Your Base Are Belong to Us" or the "I love You" virus are any indication, this kind of "social engineering" — as hackers call it — can happen with an ease far and above almost any word-of-mouth situation in human history. I'm just happy to be around to see if it can change even more.

RC: *Brian Eno once said that music was the center of our lives for such a long time because it was a way of allowing Africa in. He even went on to say, "A nerd is a human being without enough Africa in him or her." Do you feel that the current American musical milieu is lacking in Africa-ness?*

PDM: I think that the whole Brian Eno thing about black culture and Africa is just simply a miscategorization. I respect and enjoy Eno's work, but the whole "Africa is not computer oriented" thing just doesn't fly. Yes, there is a "digital divide," but if you look at the precedents — cultural and metaphysical — the systems Africa developed have influenced net culture at a deep structural level. Word-of-mouth culture, rhythm structure, the routing of information in a networked environment — all of these have African and world precedents, and to ignore that is to be almost solipsistic. The current American music milieu is totally African! From Britney Spears (yes!) on over to David Bowie and U2 and, of course, Hip-hop like Eminem and DJ culture at large; techno, rock, hip-hop, jazz — you name it, it's almost all part of an African recontextualization.

What Paul Gilroy called the "Black Atlantic" is just a small pond in the world that I portray here. You have to think of all the issues involved with aliases, multiple narrative threading, social engineering environments, identity as a social cipher. All of these are tropes brought to the forefront of immigrant culture in America. Afro-Diasporic culture was the first Generation X, and the current multivalent entity we call the U.S. is enthralled with the unconscious implications of Africa in the New World. It's just that it's beneath the radar screen. William Gibson took the "loa" concept of his book *Neuromancer* (Ace, 1984) as a sampled fragment from John Shirley's *City Come a Walkin*'s (Four Walls Eight Windows, 2000) "city avatars," and if that isn't a kind of transmigration of context and form,

I don't know what is. The best thing that happened in the 1990s was the explosion in youth culture's engagement with electronic media. The best is yet to come. Close the circuit, flip the switch, upload the file — it's time to beta test the new wetware, or something like that. Anyway, it's more exciting than going to the mall maybe. Africa beats that any day of the week. Hands down.

Eno was wrong. McLuhan was right. He said a long time ago that the forces of language in an electronic context would release the "Africa Within." Maybe Eno doesn't use computers enough.

RC: *Do you have any upcoming projects you'd like to mention?*
PDM: Yeah, I'm in the middle of setting up a new magazine called *21C* that's a re-invention of the *21C* of the mid 1990s — only a lot more multicultural oriented. Also, I'm almost finished with my book projects, and there's a whole bunch of art projects and installations — I have some work in "Bitstreams" at the Whitney Museum, a piece in the show at the Museum of Contemporary Art in Sydney, Australia, and an installation at an alternative arts space in Houston, Texas, called "Project Rowhouses." It's a very busy time. The easiest way to check out that stuff is my website; it has funky beats.

But anyway, yeah, the whole literary/arts angle in America is so fucked up and conflicted, the only way to maintain a "stay of execution" on your artwork and cultural production if you are a progressive African American in this day and age is to constantly innovate and change your mode of production. If you don't, it's kind of like that "unique circumstance" in Philip K. Dick's classic short story "The Minority Report" (a story where people are put in jail or sent into exile because of crimes they might commit) — stuff that would make the "normal" critics scream with joy in my case. Psychological involution becomes psychological profiling (kind of like driving down New Jersey drive if you're black); racial profiling becomes emblematic of the way people can even think about literature, art and culture. "Better keep your eyes open," the main character says to someone asking for advice on how to avoid the thought police. "It might happen to you at any time."

CULTURE

BRIAN COLEMAN

HAL BRINDLEY

DOUG STANHOPE

PAUL ROBERTS

TOD SWANK

SHEPARD FAIREY

STEVEN SHAVIRO

MARK DERY

Brian Coleman
Nostalgia is Def
by ROY CHRISTOPHER (2005)

"WHY THE HELL DIDN'T HIP-HOP ALBUMS EVER HAVE LINER notes?!!??" quoth journalist Brian Coleman, "Hip-hop fans have been robbed of context and background when buying and enjoying classic albums from the Golden Age: the 1980s." With his self-published book, *Rakim Told Me* (Waxfacts, 2005), Coleman set out to fix that problem and to fill a void in the written history of hip-hop. That, and where a lot of writers who acknowledge the influence and importance of hip-hop tend to focus on its sociological implications, Coleman stays with the music, how it was made, and where these artists were in the process. He brings a breath of fresh air to the study of hip-hop, just by dint of focusing on the music itself.

ROY CHRISTOPHER: *For the uninitiated, tell us about the premise behind* Rakim Told Me.
BRIAN COLEMAN: Well, the book is twenty-one chapters, each one explores one classic hip-hop album from the '80s. The premise itself is

something I call "invisible liner notes." It's the stories behind all these albums (e.g., Public Enemy, Run-DMC, Boogie Down Productions, Eric B & Rakim, etc.) — the history of the groups, from back when they first started. And, most importantly, it's about talking to the artists themselves about their work as musicians, as creators. It seems to me that when you talk about music a lot of times, people tend to view the image of a group or at least the end product of their art, an album, as the most important thing. I think that the process of making them what they are as a group is as, if not more, important.

If you want to check out background on the book, or even sample chapters (and find out how to buy it), check out my website: *www.waxfacts .com.* It's more interesting than me telling you about it.

RC: *Where most writers discuss the anger, misogyny, or politics of hip-hop,* Rakim Told Me *focuses on how these classic records were made, down to the minutiae of drum machine models and the subtle nuances of early samplers. Do you think that hip-hop's relevance and influence strictly as music has taken a backseat to its relevance as a sociological topic?*

BC: That's a great question. And the short answer would be "yes." I'm not sure why, but in hip-hop, maybe more than any other musical genre, the journalists and authors who write about it can be (or at least seem to be) so detached from it. I understand the allure of an academic discussing why and maybe how Tupac is so influential, but I really wish that more fans would start writing about hip-hop. Because sometimes you get the feeling that some of these writers aren't true fans of the music — they just like it well enough and find it interesting but are really just using it as a springboard to extrapolate on other extramusical things.

When I sit down and chop it up with my friends about what hip-hop albums I love, I'm not like: "Wow, isn't it weird how many white people like hip-hop? Why do you think that is?" I'm more like: "Holy shit, how did Schoolly D get 'PSK' to sound like that? Did he do that drum program himself? And that story about his mom tearing apart his room in 'Saturday Night' is fucking hilarious." If writers are really fans of the music and the art form, personally I just wish they would put the energy into describing why it's such a dynamic music and stop trying to describe and translate it to their unhip academic peers. That's why I think that David Toop's *Rap Attack* (first edition came out in 1984) is the best book ever written about hip-hop. Because it describes the music and the culture in a fully comprehensive way, but it also captures the energy of the people who make it, and also the excitement that fans get listening to hip-hop. In the end, the highest goal of any hip-hop writer, in my opinion, should be to want to make people throw down the magazine or book they're reading and go right to their stereo and put on the song or album you're talking about. That's what Toop did for me, and if I can do that for even a small percentage of my readers, then I've accomplished something.

RC: *What prompted you to self-publish a book as opposed to going through a publisher?*

BC: I've been in touch with various publishers, directly and through an agent, over the past year or so. And although I had some interest and some good conversations with people, it wasn't enough to make me think that anyone was really that interested in what I was doing. But I guess I was convinced enough of the importance of this book. And I took cues from some of the artists in this book, who didn't really care what other people thought about their work, and went for self — Schoolly D and Luke from 2 Live Crew, for example. Not that I'm on their level in terms of chutzpah or in terms of artistic merit, but I know people with "real" book deals and they aren't happy with them (same with artists I know who have "real" record deals). So I was like: "If I'm going to get fucked putting out a book, I'd at least like to be the main one to blame." Putting out a book isn't easy, but it's certainly not as hard as people might think. If you know how to use computers well enough or, even better, know a friend who can use Quark or InDesign (I was the latter, of course — props to Matt Nicholas, my designer!), then why the hell not? I've been pretty happy with what's gone on thus far. I'm almost breaking even and it's only been out about four months.

RC: *Based on your experiences, would you recommend self-publishing to aspiring book writers out there?*

BC: I'd say yes. But it depends on what kind of person you are. If you're unorganized and unmotivated then it's probably not for you. But then again, if you're unorganized and unmotivated then you're probably not going to put a whole book together on your own. As long as you think it through before you start and don't set your sights too high at first, then it's not a bad idea. I always had it in my mind that this would be a slow build, and it has been.

The way people react to, and then purchase or not purchase, your book is a whole other thing. I mean, if your book isn't very good or very interesting to the masses, then hundreds or thousands of people probably won't want to read it, so get ready to look into the "bucket of truth" (*Upright Citizens Brigade* reference). If it doesn't sell, be prepared for the financial and emotional consequences (which would, in certain instances, be much more harsh and embarrassing if you were on a "real" publisher). But if you can be a little bit objective and step back and say, "I dig this book and I think people like me will dig it," then you should do fine. I'm writing about albums that millions of people own, so it's not like it's really that obscure. If you were going to do some kind of fiction or a philosophy book, I wouldn't know. But let me say this, go to *www.loompanics.com* (one of my favorite sites ever) and tell me that just because a book is weird or obscure that it doesn't deserve to be out there.

RC: *You've kind of set this book up as the first in a series. Are you planning to do a similar book about the '90s?*

BC: Well, I didn't tell anyone, even friends of mine, that I was even writing this book until I got the copies back from the printer (I'm secretive like that, because music writers and bloggers gossip like old ladies). But to answer your question in a vague way, it's not out of the realm of possibility.

RC: *Who do you like doing hip-hop right now?*

BC: I like a lot of people doing hip-hop right now. Mostly people on the indie scene, since I think major labels have no real regard for people making music or especially hip-hop as art. But even on the majors there are people like Common who still sounds great to me. I love that Dead Prez are signed to Columbia (although who knows how long that will last — maybe they already got the boot). I think Timbaland deserves and doesn't get much props for doing his own thang and going against the grain (even though sometimes what he does isn't original, it's just different and retro) within the corporate rap thing. And on the indie tip, I mean, where do I start? I'd say that Madlib is probably at the top of my list, 'cause his mind is always working and it's full of energy and invention. I like most everything MF DOOM does. On the Boston tip, my boys Edan, Insight, Mr. Lif, Akrobatik, and 7L & Esoteric consistently make forward-looking music and spit serious wisdom. I could go on and on and it would be boring, but I still love listening to hip-hop these days. In the new issue of *Scratch Magazine* I reviewed twenty-five albums and I probably liked at least two-thirds of them. That's a good sign.

But here's an important point that I always like to make, when given the chance: It's almost impossible to really say "Yeah, I listen to hip-hop" when you meet someone, and have them understand what you're talking about (and vice versa, for you to understand what they mean when they say something like that). I mean, does that mean you think 50 Cent is a great rapper, or does that mean you know about Ultramagnetic MCs, KRS-One and the first Wu-Tang album (if you know the latter then you'd never make the former judgment)? I'm cautious saying I like hip-hop overarchingly, because there's a lot of hip-hop in 2005 that I think straight-up sucks. Ten years ago only some of it sucked, so you could get away with the blanket statement. But I think a lot of MCs and producers out there bring shame to the term hip-hop, in the classic sense, if that's what they think they are. By "classic," I'm talking exactly about the artists in the twenty-one chapters in my book. But I mean, Lil Jon? He's not hip-hop. He's the antithesis of hip-hop. He'll destroy hip-hop if kids keep buying his records. I think Jay-Z has done a lot of damage, too, so let's hope he's retired for good (although that's just wishful thinking). A lot of popular rappers get free passes for making mediocre music and that upsets me. But I get over it once I put on the Perceptionists' *Black Dialogue* (Definitive Jux, 2005) album.

In the end, I just wish fans were more critical and vigilant and had higher expectations. And yes, by vigilant, I mean that they should accost rappers on the street and beat them with sticks for making shitty music.

Hal Brindley
Wild Boy
by ROY CHRISTOPHER (2005)

REMEMBER WHEN THOUGHTS AND THEORIES ABOUT SO-CALLED "Generation X" were on the tip of everyone's tongue? We were called "slackers," and older people said we lacked motivation and passion. I've always taken issue with these characterizations because I've constantly seen people my age pursuing paths and interests that had no prior archetype — and working very hard at them. Now that the focus has shifted to the next generation, and now that we've been pushing for a while, our generation is emerging in new careers and pursuits quite different from our forebears — and in many that didn't exist before.

Hal Brindley has been steadily following his own beat. From behind the bars of a BMX bike to behind the shutter of a camera in the wilderness, his drummer has lead him all over the world. I traded mail with Hal during the late-'80s BMX 'zine heyday, so having watched him sell his previous BMX company and then having seen it disappear completely, I wanted to find out how his path had shifted so dramatically. As with many of our generation's pursuits, it makes much more sense when you see the passion behind it. Naysayers be damned.

ROY CHRISTOPHER: *Well, I guess the obvious first question is how'd you go from BMX entrepreneur to wildlife photographer?*

HAL BRINDLEY: I was getting burned out on the business (Play Clothes). It had become too successful and became full-time hard work. I named it "Play" because I didn't want to work. I never wanted a real job and that's what it had become. I've always loved animals and nature, and I wanted to do something with my life that would make a difference, something that mattered to me. One day I decided to sell the business and become a wildlife photographer 'cause it sounded cool. I knew nothing about it. I just bought a camera and started taking pictures. I wanted to be able to travel the world and write it off as a business expense. I found someone to buy the company (Rex Shupe). He paid roughly $60K for it and ran it into the ground within half a year. He's a good guy, just not terribly self-motivated, as the self-employed need to be.

From my perspective it was perfect. I didn't really want to sell it because my business was so personal to me. Play *was* me, but having a wad of cash is pretty cool too. So, I ended up with both (sorry, Rex). I've been kind of a slacker ever since, except for a few periods of intense house remodeling. That's how I've been surviving — bought, remodeled, and sold two houses. I spend about half the year traveling. Now I'm finally starting to make some effort on the business end of wildlife photography. I don't expect to get rich at it. Just have a pleasant, adventurous life.

RC: *I still have some old 2B Home Cooked stickers. How'd you get into the business side of BMX in the first place?*

HB: I wish I still had some 2B stickers! It's funny, I have nothing from the old days; it's almost like it never happened. I have a Play sweatshirt and a couple tees and that's it. Oh yeah, I still have a 2B bowling shirt from 1990 that's practically brand new. How I got into it: My good buddy Steve Buddendeck came up with the name 2B, which originally stood for Buddendeck and Buddendeck. (Him and his mom! Ha! How uncool is that!) They were going to make shorts. Meanwhile, I was a freshman in college making a 'zine called *Stop Zine* and I learned how to screen print so I could make some shirts for it. My first designs I made under the name "20 Inch Garb." Then Steve and I decided 2B should be Brindley and Buddendeck. I think we were snowboarding in West Virginia at the time, probably 1989. I started printing the tees and I worked for a summer as a waiter to place the first three ads in *Go Magazine*. (Being a waiter sucks ass and it was the last job I ever had). Most of our marketing was through 'zines. We played the super-cool, underground hardcore angle 'cause I guess we really were. No one else was doing it at the time (except maybe Club Homeboy), and it took off. Steve and I were really just in it so we could put ourselves in ads.

RC: *What are you shooting other than wildlife?*

HB: Nothing! That's all I shoot! Animals are an endless fascination to me. There are so many unbelievable and crazy creatures out there that most people have never heard of. I get excited every time I learn about an animal for the first time, and I get super excited when I see a creature for the first time in the wild. You can't beat it: finding a tapir in the middle of a rain forest, or seeing a polar bear in the tundra, or crawling after a wombat in a field in Australia, or swimming with a manatee, or seeing a leopard attack a crocodile at a waterhole in Africa. It's just the best. These creatures are all getting crowded out by humans and many will be gone soon. It's nice to be able to see them before they disappear, and it's even nicer to think that maybe I'm helping to keep them from disappearing.

RC: *Do you still follow BMX or ride the little bike at all?*

HB: I had a spell of several years where it gathered dust. Then I got divorced four months ago (you may remember Abigail from the "Oldest Guy at the Prom" Play ad many years ago), and my world flipped upside down. I moved into my dad's spare room and started living like a kid again (I'm thirty-four, by the way). There's a free skatepark here in Charlottesville, and something inside me really wanted to ride some more. So, I go out there every now and then — mostly right when it opens when there's no one there because I'm embarrassed at how rusty I am. I skate there about as much as I ride. It felt good to do a few barspins, a couple big transfers — getting up the nerve to do a 360 was even a challenge. It's funny to be on the other side now: to be a wash-up. To be the guy kids are reading about and thinking, "That will never happen to me. I'm hardcore, and I'm gonna ride forever!" Well, we all know you're not, but I hope you can find something you love just as much to do afterward. I don't follow BMX at all now (I did just watch the Kink video last week to relive the pudding wrestling scene that I helped Chris Hargrave shoot). That's not so weird 'cause I never really followed it when I was in it. We always just did our own thing.

RC: *What have you been working on and what's coming up?*

HB: I decided to get into underwater photography this year so I've got four different diving-related trips planned in the next few months. I'm gonna try to open a gallery/bar 'cause it sounds like a good way to pick up chicks (just kidding, of course, if my new girlfriend happens to be reading this) and try to accomplish as many things as possible on my "things to do before I die" list. My words of wisdom: There's no time like the present.

You can check out my latest trip on *halbrindley.com.* Sign up for the email list if you want to be notified when I put up new stories.

Rock on, honkies.

Doug Stanhope
Deadbeat Hero
by ROY CHRISTOPHER (2004)

IF YOU RECOGNIZE DOUG STANHOPE, YOU PROBABLY KNOW HIM from the later seasons of *The Man Show*, where he played Coy Duke to Joe Rogan's Vance. But that, my dear people, was hardly a glance into the world of Stanhope. His stand-up finds him teetering on the brink among several forms of utter oblivion. He stares down the evils of narrow-mindedness wherever they may lurk, attacking any and everything you might hold sacred, find wholesome, or think is just plain good.

In spite of his ubiquitous vulgarity, his profane humor, and his relentless vendetta against your favorite traditions, Doug is a good guy. Not only that, but he's damn smart, too. His comedy is laced with serious commentary, astute observations, and blistering critique. His penchant for the perverse often hides this side of his work, but trust me, you'd have to get up pretty early in the morning...

In the midst of all of this obscenity, intellect, and outright venom, though, you get the feeling that Doug is on your side, fighting the big, ugly system right along with you. As he says, "To err is not only human, it's revolutionary."

ROY CHRISTOPHER: *Well, this being my first postelection interview, I figure we ought to get into that. I know you're pissed, but what can we do?*

DOUG STANHOPE: Oh, I'm not pissed anymore. You see, I won $800 at roulette in Shreveport this week. And I just booked a gig at a women's prison. Then I go to Costa Rica for a couple weeks. I only really get pissed when I'm doing nothing — or nothing that I enjoy — and start living vicariously through CNN. Powermongers will always rise to the top so long as people have a desire to be lead, and the world will always turn its back to all that is unfair, so long as the majority are unaffected.

The illusion that we have any more than a lottery ticket-holder's part in changing the big picture simply by voting distracts from all the difference we can make on a personal level, even by just cutting a sucker an even break.

RC: *Okay, let's not mess around here, Doug, you're a smart guy. Do you ever think that your association with* The Man Show *or* Girls Gone Wild *betrays the intelligence of your comedy?*

DS: Yep. But I didn't do it for the comedy. I did it for the experience. Sure, the money was good, but I've done equally dubious things for nothing but the story. I did Jerry Springer in its heyday — a completely invented story — just because it was amusing. I did comedy on a tour bus to an Indian casino as a goof. I made out with Brett Erickson in a bar in Louisiana this week — deep, plunging tongue kisses — just to annoy dangerous military rednecks that didn't like *The Man Show*.

Selling out includes not doing something you'd enjoy, on whatever level, just because of what someone else might think. Maybe you've betrayed yourself for thinking I was intelligent.

RC: *Maybe I have. How'd you get into doing stand-up anyway?*

DS: I was living in Vegas and thought I was funny. I wrote five minutes of jack-off jokes and went to a local bar that had an open mic. Now — fourteen years later — I have a world of jack-off jokes. Only in America.

RC: *Who do you like doing stand-up these days?*

DS: Guys you wouldn't know — Dave Attell, Mitch Hedberg, and, of course, Joe Rogan you probably know, but there's also a whole world of unknowns who never get heard: Andy Andrist, Sean Rouse, Brendon Walsh, Brett Erickson, Brian Holtzman, Lonnie Bruhn are all guys who are brilliant but who knows if they'll ever be known beyond XM Radio — and only then if they get their shit on CD.

RC: *What are you reading lately? Any recommendations?*

DS: *The Lucifer Principle* by Howard Bloom (Atlantic Monthly Press, 1995): Helps you get past the whole Red State/Blue State thing and look at the whole nature of the beast.

RC: *What's coming up for Doug Stanhope?*

DS: I'm debating between defecting to Costa Rica or running in 2008. In the meantime, there's always smoke being blown up your ass here in LA about some television project or another. The road pays the bills but too much of it just makes me hate comedy and humanity equally. If I could keep focus for more than two minutes, I'd write a book. Or maybe do a show on satellite radio. I'd really like to go to Massachusetts and gay-marry Gary Coleman, although I don't actually know him. It'd really be funny, though.

Paul Roberts
Peak Oil Recoil
by MC PAUL BARMAN (2004)

COUNTRY BY COUNTRY, OIL EXTRACTION IS PEAKING, LEADING to dry wells, sky bells, and land grabs. How much will the final barrel cost? Infinity dollars? *The End of Oil: On the Edge of a Perilous New World*, the first book by Seattle-based journalist Paul Roberts, is a profound look at the science, politics, and personalities involved in one of Earth's most cataclysmic issues. I based my smash hit, "Yesterday Is History" on the galley copy and spoke with Roberts on March 31, 2004. Houghton Mifflin put out the paperback edition of his book in April 2005.

MC PAUL BARMAN: *You wrote "The Federal Chain-Saw Massacre" about forestry, "The Sweet Hereafter" about sugar, and "Bad Sports" about SUVs. What do these topics have in common?*

PAUL ROBERTS: They're all commodities produced en masse and distributed around the world. They're all subject to high demand. They have been cheap in the past and they're becoming more expensive. It's no longer okay to just go cut a forest, because you'll run into all sorts of obstacles. People will criticize you. You'll run afoul of regulations. It's the same thing with oil.

Oil is way more problematic in the sense that it's not just environmentally difficult but there is also political considerations. Most oil is in unstable regions: Saudi Arabia, Russia, the Caspian, West Africa. All these places are politically prone to volatility. It wouldn't be out of the realm of possibility for a country like Angola or Venezuela, or even Russia, to have a civil unrest that would, among other things, cut production. It would cut exports and that would leave countries like us, that depend on imports, in the lurch.

Lastly, we've got to ask, what are we doing to the climate? The way we burn fossil fuels is just not sustainable. Whether we're talking about coal or oil or natural gas, we produce a lot of carbon, and I'm sure you know the suggested link between carbon dioxide and climate change.

The final endpoint is: oil is a finite substance.

MCPB: *Why do you care to share the fact that things need to change?*
PR: I wish I could say that I have been an impassioned advocate for humanity all my life. I care a great deal about my neighbors and I would like to see the human race continue. I find that I am deeply bothered by all kinds of injustice. I'm curious. I'm kind of the classic storyteller.

Doing a book, as opposed to a magazine article, you get to spend more time on a topic. You get a larger canvas, which means that you look at the whole pattern. You bring in all these different elements. You set them there till the big picture becomes in focus. You start to see these larger trends. And that's when you really start going, "Wow, I've got to get this down, and I've got to share this with people."

MCPB: *Let's assume, and correct me if you think this is an unlikely assumption, that we don't address the problems you raise in your book for ten years. What is the situation?*

PR: By then you'd see, if you hadn't already, signs that "easy oil" (that I refer to in the book) was running out. We will be forced to search for oil in increasingly obscure locations that are environmentally sensitive or politically dangerous — things that make getting oil out more expensive. So the price of oil gets even higher than it is today.

You are going to see a lot more evidence that climate change is not just real, but really serious. We will know the extent of the increased melting of the ice caps. We'll see how far disease is spreading. As tropical areas expand, as temperature rises, these diseases are going to spread. We'll see heavy rains and the kind of things they predict will be catastrophic in the event of a warming climate. More floods, more hurricanes, and those kinds of things.

I don't know that we'll be invading more countries for oil, but I suspect that countries that have oil will struggle to maintain stability. We are going to see repeated cases of unrest, civil war, disruption in places like West Africa. Venezuela is going to remain unstable. Who knows what happens with Russia? It's moving back toward an autocratic regime that doesn't promote stability. People get angry and they tend to rise up.

Then you have Saudi Arabia, what happens there? That country is on the edge of collapse. It has this raging young population boom of young people who are poor. They already realize they're not going to be as well-off as their parents. There's just not enough jobs for them. They're angry at the pro-Western tendencies they see in this oil elite. They are very susceptible to fundamentalism. The Islamic faith, like any other faith, has got some really powerful and important ideas in it and it can be misused as easily as Christianity or Judaism, or any other religion. It is particularly powerful among people who are poor and angry. It's misusage has been terrible there. We're going to see more of that without question.

If America continues to use more and more oil, and we have to rely on and lean on Middle Eastern countries, why would people who are already angry at the U.S. be any less angry?

MCPB: *What do you think it would take for the American two-party system to be replaced?*
PR: Something huge because I don't think Americans want the two-party system replaced. I think they want it to work better. They want it to change fundamentally, but I don't know that most Americans pay enough attention to politics to really know what they want.

There's an American fundamentalism that's rising up, a desire for a simple view of how the world works. The less and less educated we are, the less aware we are about energy or politics or foreign policy, the more we want this simple view. Us vs. them, black vs. white, the more that desire comes to mark the American character. The greater the desire for an easy-to-understand world — good guys and bad guys — then the harder it is for any sort of change to happen and the easier it is for politicians of all stripes to sell total garbage. To claim that if those darn Saudis just produced more oil, then we wouldn't have these high oil prices, that's five percent of the problem. The big problem is that we're using too much oil. You don't have to be a leftist to suggest that. It's more like good business sense. No one is willing to commit themselves to a bright clean future that is free of oil until, a) they're forced or, b) it's clear that they can make money on it.

MCPB: *You said things like, "This is the most serious crisis of the industrial age" and "The Depression is going to look like a birthday party if we don't plan ahead." So what can the individual do?*
PR: People must begin to educate themselves. Push to understand what's going on. Break through this energy fundamentalism that we have. I call it "energy prudery." Say, "Where does my oil come from, how much do I

use, and what are the impacts of using all that oil? How much electricity am I using? Where does it come from?" All over the country people think their electricity comes from hydropower. They have this nice image of a dam churning away in the Tennessee Valley or up in the Northwest. The fact is most people get their energy from where? Coal and nuclear.

People need to invest some time in understanding it. That doesn't just mean buying my book, although that should be an important first step. People should get to the point where they hear statements on the newspaper, on the radio, and can go, "Okay, I buy that," or, "I don't buy that." They can fit what they hear into a larger picture.

They should understand that gasoline prices going up in the summer and down in the winter, isn't always going to be that way. They should understand why oil prices will be trending up. They should understand what the costs are of having this tight relationship with the Saudis and what it has allowed the Saudis and Americans to get away with.

If one of your friends showed up to your house and said, "I want to build this system globally that's gonna run on oil. It's gonna suck oil from all these unstable places and you're gonna run your car on it. It's the one fuel that you'll need. The entire economy will depend on it, but at any minute it could collapse. By the way, gasoline is highly toxic, volatile, and flammable, so it could blow up at any minute. Let's build the system." You would slap him.

We have to look at it as if we just dropped in from another planet. People have to step back and go, "Whoa, it's nuts," at least once a month.

People have to start making decisions about what kind of car they're going to buy. That's the most important thing people can do. There are people who would never buy a big car. There are people who would always buy a big car and they're lost. They're not going to change their minds. They don't believe there's an energy problem. They don't care anyway. But there are people on the fence. They say, "Well, I like the big car because it feels safer. I've got all these kids. I'm a little afraid, but worried about how much fuel it's using." Those people have to be talked to and do the thinking themselves. They're the ones that can change. There's a lot of potential there.

Tod Swank
Foundation's Edge
by ROY CHRISTOPHER (2004)

TOD SWANK STARTED FOUNDATION SKATEBOARD COMPANY (THE name comes from the Isaac Asimov sci-fi series of the same name) fifteen years ago. That's no small feat in the cutthroat skateboard industry. Skateboard brands come and go as often as the tides of the Pacific lap the shores of San Diego. He's since built a small empire, launching such brands as Pig, Toy Machine, Zero, Dekline, and Deathbox, among many others.

The name Tod Swank has been a part of skateboarding history since the early '80s. Aside from being an industry mogul and organizer, he's also been a professional skateboarder, a photographer for *Transworld Skateboarding Magazine*, and an avid 'zine-maker. I clearly remember the first time I saw a *Swank 'Zine*. A friend of mine in Alabama got one in the mail, and we all rushed over to his house to see it. They were so rare. To us, it was a photocopied piece of gold.

Swank's house sits on a cliff in San Diego that overlooks Mission Valley and the intersection of Interstate 8 and Highway 163. I rode my bike over there through the sculpted neighborhoods and wide streets one

Sunday evening in March. "This is what I do every Sunday," he said as we settled in to chat. "I usually do yard work, then come out in the garage, have a beer, watch the sun set."

ROY CHRISTOPHER: *How did Foundation originally come about?*
TOD SWANK: In 1989, I was riding for Skull Skates, Steve Rocco started World Industries in late '88, and I went to him because I wanted to ride for World Industries, but he wouldn't let me.He said he'd help me start a company, but he wouldn't let me ride for the team. So, I thought about it for a few days and decided to do it even though it wasn't really what I wanted to do. Stayed with him for two years, until 1991, after we did one video — one last effort to see if it would go with [World Industries]. Nothing really happened, and theywere getting busy with their other brands, so I told Rocco I was going to do it on my own. He was like, "No problem. Here's the shop list. You can have whatever inventory's out there. Gimme a call if you need anything." There wasn't much inventory, so it wasn't a big deal, and he's always been really supportive. No paperwork: just a handshake deal. So, from 1991, I just ran it. And 2004 is our fifteen-year anniversary because I count those first two years with Steve, because that was the start of the brand.

RC: *What's it take to create a brand?*
TS: It's a team of people really. I mean, Foundation's been floundering for years financially, but I believe in it. Ed [Templeton, pro skateboarder] came to me and wanted to do something; I got Josh [Beagle] to start Pig, and we did that together. We work on that together and we work on Foundation together. Ed pretty much does Toy Machine, and Jamie [Thomas] did Zero. Basically we're the financial resource and the infrastructure support team, so that these guys can make their ideas happen.

RC: *But you obviously haven't said "yes" to every idea, right?*

TS: I've said "no" to a lot of ideas, and we've done ideas that didn't work out. Poot, our girls clothing company, which was, I think, a little bit ahead of its time, and we didn't know what we were doing. Landspeed was a big failure.

RC: *How did* Skateboard.com *get started?*

TS: Actually, that was one of the failures too. I got it in 1996, along with *Snowboard.com* and *Surfboard.com*. At one point, we had like six people working fulltime: two tech guys, this one girl working on editorial, Miki Vuckovich. We were trying to do a bigger version of what *Skateboard.com* is today: multi-sport, putting companies on the web for them, putting all their products on the web for them, basically doing web development. That didn't work. Nobody jumped on that one. So, flash-forward to 2000, I just sat on *Skateboard.com* and let *Snowboard.com* and *Surfboard.com* lapse, which was a stupid thing to do. Then I met Chris Mullins and Lloyd Jobe. They came to me. They met up in Seattle trying to think of a new business to do, and Chris had the idea for an e-commerce site. They called me because Chris knew my history. That's what I was waiting for. I was just sitting and waiting for the right time to come around again to do something with it. Tum Yeto [Swank's distribution company for all of the brands he's helped found] sells to all of the mail orders, but they just buy so little. It's so hard to get your product out there on the market. So, I just thought of *Skateboard.com* as an avenue — not just for Tum Yeto, but for all companies — to be able to have a better, wider presentation of their products. We do it through technology that lets us buy thin and wide; instead of buying just a couple of items and buying deep, we're buying a lot of items of a wide variety so that companies have the opportunity to get stuff out there — stuff that might not get out there when dealing with a shop owner or a buyer. The technology that we use just takes it off the website when it hits zero in the quantity field. It just disappears, so people don't see stuff that's not available. [We started this] coming up on the beginning of the dot-com crash. So we got a little bit of money to get it going and then the ground fell out from under it. We've just been trying to build it, doing everything we can without spending a ton of money.

Just to clarify, *Skateboard.com* is not a part of Tum Yeto. It's a totally separate business with a totally separate group of owners. Skateboard.com pays its bills to Tum Yeto just like it does to any other company. I'm officially chairman and mainly VP of industry relations. And that's really just me trying to keep it on scope with the best interests of the industry. I think *Skateboard.com* can lend itself to being beneficial not only to manufacturers, but even to retailers. We have different strategies where retailers could use *Skateboard.com* to bring in additional income because of its wide breadth of products that it has. For the consumer, it's about getting the right product information, having the best selection, and quality customer service.

RC: *Do you ever think of all of this brand-building and doing skate companies as creating culture?*

TS: I probably never thought of it until realizing that we're at our fifteen-year anniversary for Foundation. Foundation's not the most successful brand out there. I mean, it's had its heydays, and it's doing well right now; it's got an awesome team, and we just did an awesome video — probably our best ever. We couldn't even reach the point we're at right now without going through all the trials and tribulations. So, realizing that it's our fifteen-year anniversary and realizing that there is somewhat of a culture surrounding it. — I never intended that. I just wanted to be a part of the skateboarding culture, but at the same time you end up building loyalty and people who are really into it because it's done something different. So, that's pretty awesome to think about.

It's always been a really independent, fragmented, and almost selfish industry. I get torn thinking about the purity of skateboarding and the culture of skateboarding, and selling out skateboarding to bigger things. But the way I see it, skateboarding will always have its purists, and people who want to skate however they want to, and they'll always do that no matter what else happens. Potential future benefits are only going to happen if we take the reigns. It sickens me sometimes looking at payroll checks to riders. These kids are out there killing themselves and I wish there was a way that we could calculate it out so that they would reap the benefits of what they're doing.

Skateboarding is just too small. Here we are in its third downturn and it's been around forty years. It sucks how small it can get. I recently met with my CPA, who works with all kinds of other industries, and I asked him about the change in the climate of our industry compared to other industries. He said, "This is gnarly. I don't see this anywhere else. You're going through a huge, huge change in such a short period of time." And it's not just Tum Yeto; it's the whole industry. I think that if we had our shit together as an industry, this kind of down cycle wouldn't be as significant. And it goes back to the riders and what they're getting out of it. People don't realize that if we're not making money, nothing's going to happen, no one's going to get paid, everyone'll just skate on their own because they love it. But wouldn't it be better if we could go skate, love it, and get paid? That's the dream job!

RC: *Where did all of the previous era's infighting come from?*
TS: I think the crux of it was when Rocco started and busted up the Big Five of the '80s: Powell, NHS, NorCal, Tracker, and Vision. Those guys didn't talk to each other. They were at war with each other. There was no working together for the benefit of the industry. I wasn't there. I didn't sit next to these guys and hear what they had to talk about or anything, so I don't

really know, but because we haven't had an association this whole time, just makes me think "okay, well, they didn't do shit" basically. So, when Rocco started World Industries, what he really did was liberate skateboarding so that it could move forward. He helped a lot of people start companies, not just me. He lent money and gave advice to a lot of other skateboarders who wanted to start companies. He wanted to see the industry run by skateboarders. The funny thing is, here we are ten years later or whatever, and all of the guys that are running the companies, are guys that I skateboarded with or knew before any of us even fathomed that we were going to be working in the industry. So that's a pretty cool bond, and there's been pretty good communication between all of these guys, and we talk about how to make things better overall. If the industry's strong, it's going to be better for everybody. And then it comes down to having that competitive edge of doing a better job than the next guy. But if the industry overall is doing shitty, it's not going to do anybody any good.

I've been watching hip-hop culture, and I'm pretty amazed by it. The music is so different, the videos are awesome, and the movement is just full of good, creative energy, and the industry around it is just amazing. They maintain their fan base even though they're selling everywhere and they all have clothing companies that sell in all the major department stores. I think, "God, I wish skateboarding could do that!" And someone might say that that would suck and it would mean skateboarding sold out, but how can they do it and still do cool things and still be edgy and still make a ton of money? When everybody's making more money, the pie just gets huge and everybody's doing better. That's what I'd like to see. Then I wonder if it's the right thing for skateboarding. I wonder if it's supposed to be organized. But then I always come back to the team riders and what they're getting, all these guys who are doing such amazing things on their skateboards, and what they're getting out of it, and it's shit. It's a joke. It's a shame. That's one thing that keeps pushing me to try and see skateboarding do something different. The industry has to evolve. If we're working together, we can dictate what is presented out there. And then we can reap the benefits of it. If we don't organize as a group and be unified, then someone else is going to do it and they're not going to do something that's in the best interest of skateboarding. They're going to do something that's in the best interest of what they're doing right now. Fuck those guys. We can do it. There's no reason why we shouldn't be able to do it.

RC: *Any final thoughts?*

TS: Skateboarding has always amazed me, because the couple of times that I thought it had reached its limit, it always moved on. I totally gave up that way of thinking. Skateboarding right now is at a point that it's never been before — ever — so we should really be stoked about that and keep pushing for what's in its best interest overall. It does amazing things. It turns out amazing people who are creative and interesting and have great ideas. It's amazing when you watch TV or look at magazines for other sports and see the sweating-out of skateboarding. It's all over the place. I'm not saying that skateboarding should be on TV, or maybe I am. Maybe part of it should, because if that part of it is, it'll help the rest of it. All of those pool guys, and all of those guys who don't care about any of that shit would have more resources. If the companies could afford to have their few guys that go to contests, their few guys that are their style guys because kids look up to them, and then they have their core group out there that deserves to be backed up, but doesn't really get backed up. These guys are purists, and they do it on their own, and they work their jobs. I'd love to have a team that was just that group of guys who just love skateboarding and go out and skateboard. Maybe if skateboarding was bigger, I could fund that more.

I can't imagine doing anything else. I'd like to get to a point where I could sit back and relax and enjoy it, because I get so wrapped up in working and whatever's going on. It would be nice to be able to enjoy it more, go out and ride more.

Shepard Fairey
Giant Steps
by ROY CHRISTOPHER (2002)

YOU'VE SEEN THEM: "ANDRE THE GIANT HAS A POSSE" STICKERS, "Obey Giant" posters, Andre's face covering entire sides of buildings. You've seen them and you've wondered what it was all about. And once you found out, perhaps you wondered why.

Nearly the entire world has unknowingly fallen prey to Shepard Fairey's phenomenological street-media experiment. Long-time friend Paul D. Miller recently described Shepard's postering activities as "obsessive."

Using an image of the late, large (7'4" 520 lbs.) wrestler-cum-actor Andre the Giant's face, Fairey has slowly spawned an underground cult sensation. As he wrote in 1990, "The first aim of phenomenology is to reawaken a sense of wonder about one's environment. The Giant sticker attempts to stimulate curiosity and bring people to question both the sticker and their relationship with their surroundings. Because people are not used to seeing advertisements or propaganda for which the product or motive is not obvious, frequent and novel encounters with the sticker provoke thought and possible frustration, nevertheless revitalizing the viewer's perception and attention to detail." Adopting and adapting philosophy from Martin Heidegger, Marshall McLuhan, Guy Debord, and Hakim Bey, Shepard Fairey has caused many a reawakening, and established himself as one of the leading designers of visual identity working today.

Teaming up with fellow street artist Dave Kinsey, Fairey formed Black Market, (BLK/MRKT). Here they bring their often edgy, experimental design attitudes to the corporate world, stating "Rather than bringing the underground to the surface, Black Market, a visual communication agency, works to blur the distinctions, to attack everything with the same." And they do. Their client list includes heavies like Mountain Dew, Earthlink, Levi's, Sprite, Netscape's Mozilla project and Madonna's Maverick Street imprint, among others, as well as smaller firms like Ezekiel Clothing, DC Shoes (who actually made a Fairey-designed line of Giant shoes for a while), *Strength Skateboard Magazine*, logos for the DJ documentary *Scratch*, and countless others.

A colleague of mine recently commented that he regards the Giant sensation as a "well-managed fluke." As pejorative as that might sound — with his Giant clothes, snowboards, skateboards, a forthcoming book project, and a CD project on the way, not to mention his posters and the ubiquitous "Andre the Giant has a Posse" stickers — I doubt Fairey would disagree.

ROY CHRISTOPHER: *On the surface your Giant campaign is seemingly intentionally pointless, but under the absurdity, what is the point?*

SHEPARD FAIREY: The campaign started off as a joke and I purely by accident noticed, after putting stickers around as a meaningless joke, that when something exists for reasons that are not obvious, application and context become the meaning and, therefore, how it relates to the things around it. Bringing these surrounding elements into question, purely by contextual association — sort of like, "well, it's next to a bunch of band stickers, so it must be a band." In this process, band stickers as a medium for communication to a greater or lesser degree, will be examined simultaneously with my sticker.

The sticker did not start as anything profound, but as I observed peoples reactions to it, I saw the potential to use it as a devise to stimulate a Rorschach test-like response from people and ultimately create a dialog about the process of imagery absorption. Plus, I was just trying to get something out there that signified my existence, even anonymously.

RC: *One of the most profound and politically powerful aspects of street art (graffiti, postering, stickering, etc.) is the reclamation of public space. Do you see yourself as a proponent of this movement?*

SF: Absolutely. Another facet of the project is to call into question the control of public space. As taxpayers, we own the public space and we pay the politicians salaries. We are their bosses, not the other way around; however, the politicians favor the powerful businesses who would obviously prefer that there were no other visual noise distracting from their paid advertising and signage. We basically live in a spectator democracy and one of the few ways to actually be heard is through street art. I don't just mean a political agenda, in the traditional sense. Street art itself is political, in that it is a "medium is the message" act of defiance. I'm not an anarchist, so I feel that street art should be integrated in a way that is respectful of private property. Not that paid advertising has any kind of ethics; they get away with whatever they can, and billboards encroach on the whole visual horizon. My feeling is that it's all or nothing. Either no billboards and no street art, or there's advertising and some tolerance for street art and other low budget grassroots promotions. That's the only way to be democratic.

RC: *You've been arrested and even beaten up by police for simply engaging in your art form. How do you justify what you do in the face of this oppression?*

SF: I probably wouldn't be doing what I am doing if there weren't an element of oppression. I guess I feel like I can't be belted into submission when I feel that my project helps initiate a dialog about the use of public space and possibly drags some of the silent majority out of the woodwork to voice their opinion on the subject. If you make it past one arrest and still have it in you, you'll probably be doing it no matter what. I'm diabetic and have gotten in trouble in jail when the cops wouldn't give me my insulin, so I recently got a "diabetic" tattoo, as a precautionary measure, in case I ever passed out in jail. I don't consider myself a symbol or a martyr, I just don't want to give in to the system.

RC: *The Obey Giant campaign has raised awareness to our society's overwhelming brand consciousness. As memetic devices, the stickers and posters have been wildly successful in spreading this metamessage based primarily on absurdity. Was this your original intent, or did it all just get out of hand? Or both?*

SF: It started off innocently enough, but I quickly became obsessed with the idea of producing art that competed with and distracted from heavily funded advertising campaigns on a shoestring budget. As a creative person, I was excited by all the different methods I could use to virally spread my campaign. After many years of hard work and grassroots proliferation it had a life of its own and became its own juggernaut that I was avidly fueling but not solely propelling.

RC: *You move seamlessly from wheat-paste street campaigns to creating corporate identities and back. What do you say to the detractors who claim that when you cross that line, you undermine the legitimacy of your work?*

SF: I tell them, if they'd send me some nice donations to pay for all of my stickers and posters, then I would never have to do corporate work. I also tell them if they still live at home or have never had their own business or a project as ambitious as mine, then they are really in no position to be judgmental. Seriously though, the point of my campaign is not to point the finger at corporations and accuse them of being evil. We live in a capitalist society, companies exist to try to profit. The point of my campaign is to encourage consumers to be more discriminating and not let themselves be easily manipulated by companies and their advertising. The money that I make from doing corporate work allows me the freedom to do other things that I want to do, such as, travel around to different cities to put my stuff up and to make more posters, stickers, and stencils all the time. There is stuff for sale on my website, but there is also a network of people that I send stuff out to free. This is very expensive. The other thing is that I'd like to make corporate or mainstream companies not suck as hard, by doing some artwork for them that doesn't insult the consumer. I look at it like "wouldn't it be great if you could turn on the radio and hear great songs even on the Top-40 station?" I know this philosophy won't appeal to the elitist who thinks it's cool to be marginalized and special and into the hip things that no one else knows about, but I'm a populist, and I think that attitude is very immature.

RC: *Who do you find challenging in the design world these days? Who's pushing the limits? Who's work do you like?*
SF: I like people who blur the line between fine art and graphic design. People like Stash and Futura, Evan Hecox, Dave Kinsey (my partner), WK Interact, Haze, Rick Klotz from Fresh Jive, Ro Starr, Ryan McGinness, Kaws, Twist (he is more of a painter/graffiti artist), ESPO — too many to name. There are a lot of people who have grown up with a lot of advertising and sensory over-stimulation from video games and MTV, who are making very smart and engaging art and graphics. I don't know what to call this movement, but *Tokion Magazine*'s next issue is focusing on it. I really think the changing of the guard in the art and design world is beginning.

RC: *What's coming up for you and BLK/MRKT?*

SF: I have a book of my street art installations coming out through Gingko Press and Kill Your Idols (the guys who made the *FuckedUp + Photocopied* punk rock flyer book). I also have a CD compilation called *The Giant Rock 'n' Roll Swindle* (Fork In Hand, 2002), coming out with special packaging, featuring songs by Modest Mouse, the Hives, Jello Biafra, the International Noise Conspiracy, the Bouncing Souls, etc. It also, has an enhanced CD ROM segment with my poster images, video, and stencil instructions. I'm really excited about that because punk rock really stimulated my interest in art and politics. Besides that, we just moved to Los Angeles and opened a gallery in our new space. We are doing shows with a lot of the artists that I mentioned above. I'm also constantly working on poster designs and stuff for the clothing line. Not enough hours in the day, I tell ya. I got married too, and my wife *rules*, so I'm trying not to take her for granted.

Steven Shaviro
Stranded in the Jungle
by ROY CHRISTOPHER (2002)

STEVEN SHAVIRO IS A POSTMODERN SEER DISGUISED AS AN English professor at the University of Washington. His books and various other writings slice through the layers of our mediated reality and show what factors are at work underneath. He cuts open the tenuous sutures between academic fields and dissects contemporary culture like the slimy animal that it is. His book *Doom Patrols: A Theoretical Fiction About Postmodernism* (Serpents Tail, 1997) roams the land between the lines of traditional fiction and cultural commentary and comes back with dead-on insight and understanding.

Shaviro is currently working on a book about cyberculture and how its rampant connectivity is changing our lives.

ROY CHRISTOPHER: *No one field of study seems able to contain your work. In what fields do you see yourself sowing seeds in the scientific/literary landscape?*

STEVEN SHAVIRO: I am trying to write in between different fields of study. "In between" seems to me to be a good place to be, indeed a necessary place, if you are trying to figure out things about contemporary culture. Because contemporary culture itself is not a unified field, but involves all sorts of encounters and transformations between different things. Everything is hybrid today.

So, as a critic, I am trying to write in between the fields in which I have been specialized as an academic (literature and film) and other areas (which include science studies, media and communications studies, etc.), as well as in between standard academic writing and journalism. I call myself a critic, but I am not making value judgments from on high, rather, I am involved, or implicated, in the things I am writing about: the mutations of contemporary culture, its responses to new technologies and to political and social changes, and so on.

RC: Doom Patrols *is one of the most interesting book projects I've come across in my reading. Where did you come up with the idea to do a "theoretical fiction"?*

SS: I was writing that book in a way that obviously came from my studies in poststructuralist theory, which means the writings of Foucault, Deleuze and Guattari, and so on, but also thinkers like Marshall McLuhan and even Andy Warhol. I was trying to confront all this theory with a lot of other stuff going on in contemporary (or at least recent) culture: comics and slasher films and Microsoft and even Dean Martin. Now, one of the dangers with a theoretical approach to culture is that the theory becomes the measure of all things, and the stuff you are looking at turns into just illustrations of what is already being stated in the theory. This is what I was trying to avoid by making my work into a "fiction." What I meant was, that I was trying to write this examination of culture and cultural theory in the way a novelist might write. I was using abstract ideas rather than characters in the literary sense, but I was trying to dramatize the ideas and bring out their inner life, in the same way a novelist might do with his/her characters.

RC: *You've written extensively about film theory and I'm finding this more and more the focus of culture critics and theorists. Do you believe the image has taken/is taking over? Have we reached "the twilight of the word," as Harlan Ellison calls it?*

SS: I don't think words are disappearing. The World Wide Web, for instance, is still very much a textual/writerly medium, despite all the graphics and Flash animations and so on. I am not one of those who worries about good words giving way to evil images.

But I do think that the new technologies and new media we are experiencing today are changing the relationship between words and images. One of McLuhan's most useful ideas is that every new medium changes "the ratio of the senses," the balance between vision and sound, or words and music and images — the hierarchies they make with one another. So, yes, I think that the word isn't as supreme today (and will not be as supreme tomorrow) as it was in what McLuhan called the "Gutenberg Galaxy," or the age of print.

I'd also say that literary writing today has become a very conservative medium. Except for certain types of science fiction, and experimental writing (from Burroughs to Acker to Doug Rice), literature seems to have retreated into the past. Most of the novels that get celebrated in *The New York Times Book Review*, or other places like that, are almost acting as if nothing had changed over the course of the past century. Whereas things like music and film and video are much more involved in what it means to be alive today, in a postmodern, multimedia age. I learn much more, and get much more of an emotional effect from Björk or Outkast or the Basement Jaxx, or from David Lynch or Wong Kar-Wai or Claire Denis, than I do from Don DeLillo or Nicholson Baker or Martin Amis (and I am choosing writers here who are at least trying to get a pulse on the present). I am myself a writer — because that is what I am good at, I am not much of a musician or visual artist. But I am trying to make my writing wrap itself around musical and visual forms, because they are where the most interesting things are happening today.

RC: *Tell me about* Stranded in the Jungle. *What is your aim with this book?*
SS: The book is composed of a series of short takes (approximately 800 words each) of a variety of contemporary, or near-contemporary, cultural phenomena — ranging from pop music and SF novels and films, to reality television and alien abductions. The main aim of the book is, a) to write in a more accessible style than I employ elsewhere and, b) to try to focus on how these various phenomena feel (as opposed to what they might mean, which is what my other writing tries to do). It's a series of impressions, in a very precise sense. Moments frozen and unpacked. The book is conceived for publication on the web, and I post new chapters as I write them. There are thirty-seven so far, out of a hoped-for total of eighty or so. I don't know when I will be finished. I have not written any new chapters recently, because I have been busy with other stuff. But I hope to return to *Stranded in the Jungle* soon. (The title comes from a doo-wop song that was a minor hit for the Cadets in the 1950s, and then was covered by the New York Dolls in the 1970s).

RC: *Is there anything else you're working on that you'd like to mention here?*
SS: I am also working on another book called *Connected: Computer Networks, Virtual Reality, and Science Fiction* (University of Minnesota Press, 2003). This is an extended, book-length single essay on cyberculture and how it is changing us. I move back and forth between things that are actually happening now, technologically and socially, on the net, and

things that are only happening (for now) in science-fiction novels, but that resonate strongly with those actual events. I cover a variety of subjects, from Napster and digital copyright, to webcams, to the stock market, to artificial intelligence. I hope to finish the book by the end of this year (2002). I probably will hold back from putting it online, at least at first, because I would like to get a conventional publisher to accept it.

Mark Dery
PostFuture Shock
by ROY CHRISTOPHER (2000)

MARK DERY SYNTHESIZES THE NEWEST FRINGES OF OUR CUL-
ture into a united media interrogation of postmodernity. His books and
countless articles place cyberculture, posthumanism, artificial intelligence,
underground music, science fiction, etc. under a shrewd lens of inquiry
and he returns adept insights and new ideas.

Overlooked and underrated, Mark Dery should be added to the short
list of valid modern visionaries.

ROY CHRISTOPHER: *Many of the subjects in your analyses of cyberculture
tend to have a "pro" or "con" view of the exponential progress of technology.
What's your personal take on our current overdrive technological progress?*
MARK DERY: Well, if by "overdrive" you mean the runaway speedup of
techno-evolution, I think we need to learn to philosophize in a wind tun-
nel. We tend to mime our speed culture rather than make sense of it. The
smeared graphics and train wreck typography of designers like David
Carson, formerly of *RayGun* magazine, are one example of this mimesis;

"blipcore" techno that buzzes by at heart-attack tempos is another. We live in the age of blur; to understand who we are and where we're going as a wired society, we need to be able to sketch an exploded view of the cultural bullet train as it streaks past at full throttle. The dug-in, hunkered-down stance of cyberpundits like David Shenk, who fulminates against "life at hyper-speed" and keeps his TV in his closet, is a bunker mentality. No one's going to stop the world so we can get off. The info-vertigo we're suffering from, the unrelieved sense of personal disorientation and social disloca-tion, is going to be a fact of life from now on — deal with it. Obviously, I'm not saying that we should throw out our moral compasses just because there's no one true magnetic north, culturally speaking, anymore. My per-sonal take on the breathless hyperacceleration of technological change and the social upheaval it's causing is that, rather than consign unfashionably "humanist" notions of social justice and political change to the recycle bin of history, we have to learn how to be moral animals in a world where all the old, comforting bedtime stories about God and progress and the providential hand of the free market are deforming and disintegrating as our culture, our increasingly posthuman technology, accelerates away from our nature — human psychology, which is still bounded and shaped by those evolutionary artifacts we call bodies. That's what a lot of my writ-ing and thinking is about.

RC: *With the enthusiasm for externalization and "leaving the flesh behind" that has come along with advances in technology, do you foresee a renais-sance of the "Human Factor" coming as the next wave?*

MD: We have to ask what "The Human" is? That's the vexed question. When I interviewed David Cronenberg (in my parallel-dimension life as a jour-nalist), he professed bafflement about the very notion that we're becom-ing posthuman. To him, the media's colonization of our inner landscapes and the cyborgian offloading — into ever-smarter, increasingly lively machines — of more and more of our mental and physical functions is all too human. Humans are tool-using apes — signifying monkeys — and technology is part of us, at this late date. Even so, there's a spontaneous recoil from the suggestion that the alien in the mirror is us. That's the parable of the Unabomber, who inveighed against technology while hacking together nasty little pieces of exploding hardware and writing apocalyptic manifestos on a rattletrap typewriter. Where does nature (what you call the "Human Factor") end and culture (technology) begin? The Unabomber didn't include the typewriter in his technological demonology, which is a curious sin of omission. According to the SF novelist J.G. Ballard, the typewriter is a cyborg incubator: it encodes us, stamping the linear bias of the assembly line, and all of industrial modernity, across our imaginations. The distinction between ourselves and our tools is becoming increasingly arbitrary — more and more of a reassuring fiction — and the anxiety provoked by the blurring of this once clear-cut distinction manifests itself in the fetishizing of the "Human Factor." The "renaissance" you're talking about is already upon us. Mail-order catalogues from Smith & Hawken and Pottery Barn and other merchandisers of gracious living abound in "distressed" faux antiques and pseudo-Shaker furniture and ersatz Arts & Crafts housewares — mass-produced talismans of a time before mass production, when the human touch left its traces on everyday objects. To be sure, these sorts of commodities are partly about shoring up one's social standing with icons of timeless good taste, but they're also about the veneration of the handmade, i.e., the human touch, and of objects "humanized" by the passage of time, transformed from generic things into weathered, worn, one-of-a-kind treasures with pedigrees and personalities.

RC: *What are some of the newer areas of technological advancement and the sociological ramifications thereof (that you haven't already researched) that have sparked your interest?*

MD: The new plastics that have enabled the current renaissance in industrial design, emblematized by the soft, biomorphic, translucent "blobjects" spawned by the iMac. Quantum computing. Xenotransplantation and the engineering of transgenic animals. The far fringes of comparative ethology, where researchers are exploring the no man's land between human and animal intelligence.

RC: *For those who haven't yet read it, what can you tell our readers about your newest book,* The Pyrotechnic Insanitarium *(Grove Press, 1999)?*

MD: Like many, I feel as if contemporary America is an infernal carnival, equal parts funhouse and madhouse — a "pyrotechnic insanitarium," to borrow a turn-of-the-century nickname for Coney Island. In *The Pyrotechnic Insanitarium: American Culture on the Brink*, I wonder: Are social forces such as the yawning chasm between rich and poor tearing the fabric of American society to shreds? Or are our premonitions of cultural chaos just a toxic cocktail of turn-of-the-millennium fever and media-fueled hysteria? I find the answers in Oklahoma bomber Timothy McVeigh's visions of black helicopters and the Heaven's Gate cultists' fantasies of alien saviors; in Disney's planned town, Celebration; and Nike's dreams of global domination. Along the way, I puzzle over the popularity of blow-up dolls of Edvard Munch's The Scream and wonder what, exactly, Jim Carrey's talking butt is trying to tell us. *The Pyrotechnic Insanitarium* is a theme-park "dark ride" through contemporary America, a culture torn between angels and aliens, the smiley face and The Scream. Keep your hands inside the moving vehicle at all times!

RC: *Who do you admire doing science right now? Who do you consider to be truly forging new paths? And who do you like that's reporting these paths?*

MD: Truth to tell, I'm not much of a disciple of science. I read social histories and cultural critiques of science; my "hard" scientific reading is strictly

Homer Simpson fare — magazines like *The Sciences* and *Smithsonian*, the science page of *The New York Times* (despite the unabashedly pro-business flackery of *Times* science reporter Gina Kolata, recently exposed in an excoriating cover story in *The Nation*). I'm a great fan of Stephen Jay Gould, a luminous scientific mind who has the political virtue of being on the side of the angels — that is, whatever side the unreconstructed sociobiologist Richard Dawkins isn't on. And he's ferociously funny — a vanishingly rare trait among popularizers of science. Also, the popular science writer Timothy Ferris is always enlightening and entertaining. But my favorite writer on science and technology remains J.G. Ballard, the SF visionary and postmodern philosopher par excellence, whose ruminations on our over-lit media landscape, stalked by "the specters of sinister technologies," are an inexhaustible mother lode of brilliant insights and mordant *bon mots*.

RC: *Do you have any projects in the works you'd like to mention?*
MD: I just signed on as editor of *ArtByte*, a magazine of digital culture — formerly a magazine of digital art, as its name suggests — whose roll call of contributing writers includes Bruce Sterling, Erik Davis, and other SF/cybercrit writers familiar to your readers. I've been charged with radically reconceptualizing the magazine as a smart, snarky meme-splice of *I.D.* (the American design magazine, not the British youthstyle mag), *The Baffler*, and the late, much-lamented Australian cyberzine, *21C*, with a dash of *Suck.com* at its best. It will feature coverage and criticism of e-culture, targeting the terminally wired, and the incurably informed: readers who feel at home in what Alvin Toffler called "blip culture," readers with rapacious media appetites who thrive on information overload but want to engage critically with the ever more mediated world around them. I'm frantically brainstorming a plan for global domination.

At the same time, I'm juggling several book ideas, one about the insect as cultural icon, another a social history of irony. Then, too, there's "My Dinner With Hannibal," the mash note to Hannibal Lecter I've always wanted to write — a literary dissection of the haute-couture cannibal in the age of Martha Stewart. With the return of '80s-style greed-is-good meanness and conspicuous consumption (symbolized by the grotesque hypertrophy of the American car into the gargantuan SUV), it seems like an idea whose time has come.

LITERATURE

STEVE AYLETT

PHILIP K. DICK

ADAM VOITH

DAVID X. COHEN

SEAN GULLETTE

BRUCE STERLING

Steve Aylett
Rogue Volts of Satire
by ROY CHRISTOPHER (2004)

"It is superfluous to be humble on one's own behalf;
so many people are willing to do it for one."
— *Celia Green*

"All I ever wanted was to pick apart the day
Swallow up the pieces
Spit 'em at your species"
—*Aesop Rock, "Night Light"*

READING A STEVE AYLETT BOOK IS LIKE READING AN OLD PUBLIC
Enemy Bomb Squad track: layers and layers of frenetic clips and blips fly
by at light speed. His epigrammatic style packs so much into each line that
the pace and energy are relentlessly held at a fever pitch. The characters are
adapted to their environs — some albeit with more success than others.

Aylett coined the concept "fractal litigation" whereby, "the flapping of a
butterfly's wings on one side of the world results in a massive compensation

claim on the other." He was born in England and regrets the whole thing. He hopes there's no afterlife because that would mean "more shit to deal with." His stories take place in decidedly alternate realities: He breaks down the myriad structures of the day, rearranges them into heretofore unseen configurations, and then describes the action along all-new interstices. In these parallel worlds, no juxtaposition of power is safe from Aylett's blistering satire.

His latest book, *Tao Te Jinx* (Scar Garden, 2004), is a collection of quotations from twelve of his previous works, as well as interviews and other stories. It's a pocket manual for blowing minds. "Break your own heart — I'm busy," "A machine is an office for dying," and "The great thing about being ignored is that you can speak the truth with impunity" are only a few of the classic Aylett epigrams collected here.

Another one, "My interviews are often spiked because I give the wrong answers," could render the following exchange completely pointless, but I tried it anyway.

ROY CHRISTOPHER: *From this angle, your work is very slippery. Actually from every angle. What is it that you are you trying to do?*

STEVE AYLETT: Most of my writing is satire, and most of that satire talks about manipulations, lies, and evasions, mainly in regard to power manipulations. But I go on about other stuff as well — if you want to be specific about particular stuff you could choose a particular book passage or story and I could walk you through it, but you'd probably find it to be very straightforward when it comes down to it. An exception to the satire stuff is *The Inflatable Volunteer* (Orion, 2000), which is basically a nonsense book.

RC: *This satirical "slipperiness" extends into the ontologies of your stories: cars that run on attitudes, racist guns, etc. The structures of consensus reality*

are broken down and recombined in utterly new ways. Do ever wonder — or
care — how many people really "get it"?
SA: I'd like at least a few people to get it, and at least a few people do.

RC: *Even with the blown-apart realities in your books, you have a real beef*
with postmodernism. Can you tell us a bit about this?
SA: I'm not so much bothered by the matter of literary postmodernism,
than by postmodernist notions as they're used in real life — where people
carry those ideas over into the world, thinking that the words are the
same thing as the object they label (that the map is the territory, contrary
to Robert Anton Wilson's urging), and that the objects and facts can be
shuffled and reorganized in the same way that their labels can be, including actual people. A lot of times this is harmless: if you give a muddy brick
to a student of postmodernism and tell him it's the beer you just bought
him, he should accept it with thanks. But human beings have a tendency
to turn just about any philosophy into a justification for the manipulation
of others, usually by relabelling people as objects or lower-order creatures,
which can then be furnaced or disposed of in any old way. But postmodernism doesn't even have to be subverted to those ends — it's the archphi-
losophy of relabelling and can be used to smooth the way for any atrocity
or neglect, any sort of evasion of the real results of your actions. Look at
the news and see hundreds of examples of this.

I do old-time satire in the Voltaire/Swift tradition. Real satire, by
taking people's arguments (or evasions or justifications) to their logical
extremes, snaps people back to the reality of the situation — i.e., that their
evasions and justifications are cowardly bullshit. Of course it only works if
there's a scrap of honesty in the reader to begin with, so it doesn't always
work, and the way things are going socially, it'll work less and less. There'll
be no honesty to appeal to, and no concept of that. There'll be no admission
that there are facts and nobody will even remember the original motive for

that evasion — that to deny that there's such a thing as a fact, means you can do anything to anyone without feeling bad about it. If you tell yourself they didn't feel what you did to them, they didn't feel it. To deny you did it means you didn't do it. Welcome to the swamp.

Depending on which way things go, my stuff will later on be completely baffling (because honesty is one of the main anchor points for the satirical mechanism to work), or be seen as a simple and obvious statement of stuff that was being frantically avoided by almost everyone at the time of writing. This is assuming it's read at all or if anyone exists to read it. I suspect the baffled reaction will be the one to occur, if anyone's around. Hypocrisy won't exist in the future because hypocrisy requires an understanding of honesty as at least a concept. So satire will be a sort of inert, inoperative device which won't hook into anything.

I'm on a hiding to nothing, is what I mean.

RC: *How'd you get started writing anyway?*
SA: I started when I couldn't find the sort of books I wanted to read, so I had to write them myself. Beyond a certain point, or after a certain number of books read (a few thousand, or in fact quite a while before that) it became clear that no new ideas were being related, only repetitions, and even the most obscure searching didn't turn up any, so, as I said, I had to do it myself.

RC: *What's coming up next?*
SA: The next thing to come out is a book called *Lint*, which I think is the best thing I've done. It's out from Thunders Mouth (Avalon in the U.S.) around April/May 2005.

Philip K. Dick
Speaking with the Dead
by ERIK DAVIS (2003)

AFTER SPENDING THE BULK OF HIS LIFE CRANKING OUT PULP paperbacks for peanuts, the science-fiction writer Philip K. Dick is now finally recognized as one of the most visionary authors the genre has ever produced. While masterminds like Arthur C. Clarke anticipated techno-logical breakthroughs, Dick, whose speed-ravaged heart called it quits in 1982 when the man was only 53, foresaw the psychological turmoil of our posthuman lives, as we enter a world where machines talk back, virtual reality rules, and God is a product in the checkout line.

Dick's fractured and darkly funny novels have left their mark on video games and rock bands, avant-garde theater and electronic opera. But his influence has been particularly profound in Hollywood. Ridley Scott turned Dick's novel *Do Androids Dream of Electric Sheep?* (Doubleday, 1968) into *Blade Runner*, one of the most powerful SF films of all time. A 1966 short story formed the basis of the Schwarzenegger hit *Total Recall*, and Steven Spielberg turned Dick's tale "Minority Report" into his dark-est flick yet. The reality slips and cartoon metaphysics of *The Matrix* are thoroughly indebted to Dick, and his spirit hangs heavy over Richard Linklater's astounding *Waking Life*.

In the course of my current researches into techgnostic religious phenomena, I was experimenting with electronic voice phenomena. I was recording the analog noise between tracks on a scratchy old copy of Karl Muck conducting Parzifal with the Bayreuth Festival Chorus onto a cassette tape. Then I would cut, splice, and process the tape in various ways, and then listen to the results. On the third attempt I heard a voice that I recognized, from a tape once available through the Philip K. Dick Society, as belonging to the late science-fiction writer. More incredible was my discovery that, by recording my own questions on the same cassette tape, I was able to initiate a genuine dialog with this mysterious voice. Subsequent research proved, however, that all of the quotations have already made an appearance somewhere in Dick's fiction, letters, or essays. Nonetheless, the conversation seems worth presenting:

ERIK DAVIS: *Mr. Dick, the world has only been getting stranger since you left us. We are surrounded with clones, identity theft, patented genes, faster-than-light particles, AIBO, and obsessive virtual gaming. Some scientist in England promises to build a chip called a "soul catcher" that will sit behind your eyeballs and record your life. Doesn't all this sound strangely familiar?*

PHILIP K. DICK: Over the years it seems to me that by subtle but real degrees the world has come to resemble a PKD novel. Several freaks have even accused me of bringing on the modern world by my novels.

ED: *How exactly would you characterize those novels?*

PKD: My writing deals with hallucinated worlds, intoxicating and deluding drugs, and psychosis. But my writing acts as an antidote, a detoxifying, not intoxicating, antidote.

ED: *After years of neglect, most of your books are back in print. Even so, you remain best known as the guy who wrote the book they based* Blade Runner *on.*

PKD: I've been calling it "Road Runner."

ED: *Heh. What did you think when you first saw that rainy, claustrophobic cityscape?*

PKD: I thought, by God, these guys have figured out what life is going to be like forty years from now. My God! It's like everything you hate about urban life now, escalated to the level of *Dante's Inferno.* You can't even run in the future, there's so many people milling around, doing nothing.

ED: *Today it seems as if your work will live on through the movies. How was your own experience working with Hollywood?*

PKD: They buy and sell human beings. It's like it says in the Bible about Babylon, they sell pearl, ivory, and the souls of men. And that is exactly what is going on in Hollywood, they deal with the souls of human beings.

ED: *Steven Spielberg and Tom Cruise made the movie* Minority Report *out of one of your stories. Spielberg calls it a "gourmet popcorn" movie. Does this mean you wrote gourmet-popcorn fiction?*

PKD: I do seem attracted to trash, as if the clue lies there.

ED: *What do mean, "the clue"?*

PKD: The symbols of the divine show up in our world initially at the trash stratum.

ED: *That's one of the strongest messages in your fiction, that religious and mystical forces keep breaking into our mundane, technological world. What*

questions can we ask ourselves to keep us tuned into to these higher forces?
PKD: The two basic topics that fascinate me are "What is reality?" and "What constitutes the authentic human being?"

ED: *But people have been hashing out these puzzles for millennia. Isn't the shifting nature of reality just good fodder for science fiction?*
PKD: The problem is a real one, not merely an intellectual game.

ED: *How so?*
PKD: Because today we live in a society in which spurious realities are manufactured by the media, by governments, by big corporations, by religious groups, political groups. We are bombarded with pseudorealities manufactured by very sophisticated people using very sophisticated electronic mechanisms.

ED: *Most of these people aren't trying to rule the world, though. I don't buy that big conspiracy view. People just want to make a buck.*
PKD: I do not distrust their motives; I distrust their power.

ED: *But if people's motives aren't so bad, what's wrong with them using virtual technologies to spread their messages?*
PKD: The bombardment of pseudorealities begins to produce inauthentic humans very quickly. Fake realities will create fake humans. It is just a very large version of Disneyland. You can have the Pirate Ride or the Lincoln Simulacrum or Mr. Toad's Wild Ride — you can have all of them, but none is true.

ED: *Some people believe that conscious machines are just around the corner. What happens when the President Lincoln robot at Disneyland wakes up? Will he believe he's real?*

PKD: I once wrote a story about a man who was injured and taken to a hospital. When they began surgery on him, they discovered that he was an android, not a human, but that he did not know it. They had to break the news to him. Almost at once, Mr. Garson Poole discovered that his reality consisted of punched tape passing from reel to reel in his chest. Fascinated, he began to fill in some of the punched holes and add new ones. Immediately his world changed. A flock of ducks flew through the room when he punched one new hole in the tape. Finally he cut the tape entirely, whereupon the world disappeared.

ED: *If I remember correctly, the world also disappeared for the other characters in the story.*

PKD: Which makes no sense, if you think about it. Unless the other characters were figments in his punched-tape fantasy. Which I guess is what they were.

ED: *So what's the message?*

PKD: If I control my reality tape, I control reality. At least so far as I am concerned.

ED: *Philosophically, that sort of solipsism has always been an irrefutable option. But as we learn how to manipulate the biological wiring of the brain, those philosophical issues become practical problems.*

PKD: I wonder if you recall the "brain mapping" developed by Wilder Penfield. He was able to locate the exact centers of the brain from which each sensation, emotion, and response came. By stimulating one minute area with an electrode, a laboratory rat was transfigured into a state of perpetual bliss.

ED: *Recently Michael Persinger has found similar results for religious ecstasy.*

Maybe that's how we finally bring spirituality back into our technoscientific society. The funny thing is that when people hear about these discoveries, they can't help imagining all sorts of fiendish forms of mind control. What's stopping, say, the government from using this kind of technology?

PKD: Well, the government would have to let out a contract for the manufacture of a billion sets of electrodes, and in their customary way, they would award the contract to the lowest bidder, who would build substandard electrodes out of secondhand parts. The technicians implanting the electrodes in the brains of millions upon millions of people would become bored and careless, and, when the switch would be pressed for the total population to feel profound grief at the death of some government official, it would all get folded up, and the population, like that laboratory rat, would go into collective seizures of merriment.

ED: *Heh heh. For someone reputed to be paranoid, you seem remarkably unplussed.*

PKD: Paranoia, I think, is a modern day development of an ancient, archaic sense that animals still have that they're being watched. Imagine you're a mole, walking across the field. You gotta have a sixth sense that something's overhead cruising, like a hawk.

ED: *Or like a satellite. Today the "hawks" that watch us are not other people so much as recording and surveillance devices. What do you say?*

PKD: The ultimate in paranoia is not when everyone is against you but when everything is against you. Instead of "My boss is plotting against me," it would be "My boss's phone is plotting against me."

ED: *So as machines become more interactive and intelligent, we become more archaic and animistic.*

PKD: A native of Africa is said to view his surroundings as pulsing with a purpose, a life, that is actually within himself. Within the past decade, our environment — and I mean our man-made world of machines — is beginning to possess what the primitive sees in his environment: animation. In a very real sense our environment is becoming alive, or at least quasi-alive, and in ways specifically and fundamentally analogous to ourselves.

ED: *You could say that while humans once saw themselves reflected in the natural world, we now find ourselves reflected in machines. Is this a new development?*

PKD: What could a man living in 1750 have learned about himself by observing the behavior of a donkey steam engine? Could he have watched it huffing and puffing and then extrapolated from its labor an insight into why he himself continually fell in love with one certain type of pretty young girl? This would not have been primitive thinking on his part; it would have been pathological. But now we find ourselves immersed in a world of our own making so intricate, so mysterious, that as Stanislaw Lem, the eminent Polish science-fiction writer, theorizes, the time may come when, for example, a man may have to be restrained from attempting to rape a sewing machine.

ED: *It doesn't even seem possible to separate the organic from the technological any more.*

PKD: This is going to be our paradigm: my character Hoppy, in *Dr. Bloodmoney*, who is a sort of human football within a maze of servo-assists. Part of that entity is organic, but all of it is alive; part came from a womb, all lives. One day we will have millions of hybrid entities that have a foot in both worlds at once. To define them as "man" versus "machine" will give us verbal puzzle games to play with. What is and will be a real concern is: Does the composite entity, does he behave in a human way?

ED: *I don't follow you here. Give me an example.*

PKD: Many of my stories contain purely mechanical systems that display kindness—taxicabs, for instance, or the little rolling carts at the end of *Now Wait For Last Year* that that poor defective human builds. "Man" or "human being" are terms that we must understand correctly and apply, but they apply to a way of being in the world. If a mechanical construct halts in its customary operation to lend you assistance, then you will posit to it, gratefully, a humanity that no analysis of its transistors and relay systems can elucidate.

ED: *But if machines become more human, what happens to our ideas of human agency?*
PKD: As the external world becomes more animate, we may find that we — the so-called humans — are becoming, and may to a great extent always have been, inanimate in the sense that *we* are led, directly by built-in tropisms, rather than leading. So we and our elaborately evolving computers may meet each other halfway.

ED: *And what happens then? How would you tell that story?*
PKD: Someday a human being, perhaps named Fred White, may shoot a robot named Pete Something-or-Other, which has come out of a General Electric factory, and, to his surprise, see it weep and bleed. And the dying robot may shoot back and, to its surprise, see a wisp of grey smoke arise from the electric pump that it supposed was Mr. White's beating heart. It would be a rather great moment of truth for both of them.

ED: *If the future had a slogan, what would it be?*
PKD: "God promises eternal life. We can deliver it."

ED: *What worries you most about our deepening embrace of technology?*
PKD: The reduction of humans to mere use — men made into machines.

I think of Tom Paine's comment about one or another party of the Europe of his time, "They admired the feathers and forgot about the dying bird." And it is the "dying bird" that I am concerned with. The dying bird of authentic humanness.

ED: *So what is an "authentic human"?*
PKD: The viable, elastic organism that can bounce back, absorb, and deal with the new.

ED: *Some people believe that our machines may soon prove themselves even more capable of elasticity and novelty than ourselves.*
PKD: We are perhaps the true machines. And those objective constructs, the natural objects around us and, especially the electronic hardware we build, they may be cloaks for authentic living reality inasmuch as they may participate more fully in the ultimate Mind.

ED: *So technology may actually be staging the emergence of a higher state of consciousness. Why is this happening now?*
PKD: Information has become alive, with a collective mind of its own independent of our brains.

ED: *I see. Many people argue that memes are already a form of living infor-mation, but they draw none of the religious or metaphysical conclusions you do. How do you respond?*
PKD: What does this mean, to say that an idea or a thought is literally alive? And that it seizes on men here and there and makes use of them to actualize itself into the stream of human history? Perhaps the pre-Socratic philosophers were correct: the cosmos is one vast entity that thinks. It may in fact do nothing but think.

ED: *So the building blocks of the cosmos are not matter or energy, but information.*

PKD: The universe is information and we are stationary in it, not three-dimensional and not in space or time. We ourselves are information-rich; information enters us, is processed and is then projected outward once more, now in an altered form. Since the universe is actually composed of information, then it can be said that information will save us. This is the saving gnosis which the Gnostics sought.

ED: *Yowza. But the world is so terribly screwed up. How do you explain that?*

PKD: We appear to be memory coils, DNA carriers capable of experience, in a computer-like thinking system. Although we have correctly recorded and stored thousands of years of experiential information, there is a malfunction of memory retrieval. There lies the trouble.

ED: *At the same time, you suggest that information can save us. But I don't understand how information wins in a world defined by entropy and decay.*

PKD: Here is an example. A new ambulance is filled with gasoline and parked. The next day it is examined. The finding is that its fuel is virtually gone and its moving parts are slightly worn. This appears to be an instance of entropy, of loss of energy and form. However, if one understands that the ambulance was used to take a dying person to a hospital where his life was saved, then one can see that through hierarchical outranking there was not only no loss but in fact a net gain. The net gain, however, can only be measured outside the closed system of the new ambulance. Each victory by God as intelligence and will is obtained by this escalation of levels of subsumation, and in no other way.

ED: *You're talking about emergent phenomena, the "holons" that Arthur Koestler and Ken Wilber describe. Does this nested process help explain* *what's happening with technology and globalization? It seems to me that nobody really understands what's been unleashed.*

PKD: I think we're getting a restricted view of actual patterns. And the restricted view says that people do things deliberately, in concert, where in truth there are patterns that emanate from beyond people. What we don't realize is that the billions of discrete and entirely ego-oriented left-hemisphere brains have far less to say about the ultimate disposition of the world than does the collective Mind in which each of us shares. It will decide.

ED: *So what do we do in the meantime? How do we embrace the change without losing ourselves?*

PKD: Do not believe — and I am dead serious when I say this — do not assume that order and stability are always good, in a society or in a universe. Before the new things can be born, the old must perish. And that hurts. But that is part of the script of life. Unless we can psychologically accommodate change, we ourselves will begin to die, inwardly.

ED: *So you don't hold out much hope for business as usual.*

PKD: I can't seriously believe that much of our cultural pattern or physical assets will survive the next fifty years.

ED: *That sounds pretty pessimistic.*

PKD: You have to consider that we're only made out of dust. That's admittedly not much to go on and we shouldn't forget that. But even considering — I mean it's a sort of bad beginning — we're not doing too bad.

ED: *Finally, you've had twenty years to contemplate the universe from the afterlife. Do you have an answer yet? Do you know what reality is?*

PKD: Reality is that which, when you stop believing in it, doesn't go away.

Adam Voith
Missives from the Downtimes
by ROY CHRISTOPHER (2002)

WHILE I STRUGGLE TO KEEP A FEW WEBSITES UPDATED AND maybe put out a 'zine a year, Adam Voith publishes books. Not only that, but he does it differently. TNI Books (Adam's imprint) puts out a biannual magazine/book thing called *Little Engines* (crammed with short stories by the leaders of the new literature underground, sandwiched between a few pages of ads), excellent novels (some of which he also writes), and random other printed matter. He also maintains engaging blogs and the TNI web empire.

ROY CHRISTOPHER: *What was your original goal for TNI? Has it changed any since you started?*

ADAM VOITH: I suppose the original goal was to get my own book out there for folks to buy and read. Inside that were probably some mini-goals like "avoid a bunch of rejection letters from publishers who have never heard of me," or "learn everything you can about getting a book made as fast as possible because it will help you down the road," and even "kill

313

time: you're out of college and where has that gotten you?"

So I got some of my writing out there and quickly discovered that making a book sell goes far beyond getting some pages printed up and bound together, but I also started to figure out that both writing and publishing might suit me. I think maybe (if I could make a gross general statement with no actual research and no claim as to the validity of the statement) that's somewhat rare. You see this more in companies working with art on an independent level, but once you step into the world of "big" publishing, I'm not sure the guys upstairs are spending much time on their own creative energies.

So from there, the idea of stepping outside of self-publishing my own stuff began to kick around in my head. Once the decision was made to work with some other people's books and projects, the goals started changing to that order. So currently, for example, when I'm looking for ways to distribute the books, I'm a bit more hyperaware of what's at stake. There are other artists trusting this company to treat their work in the way it deserves to be treated, and so it makes the goals focus more on general success for the company rather than just my own books and writing.

RC: *What the hell made you think you could just go off and publish your own books anyway?*

AV: Honestly, because I saw people doing it with music and, in lots of cases, it was working for them. I'd been involved with 'zines in the past, and knew that there were ways to get printed material around to small groups of people, but mostly I was inspired and encouraged by particular record labels making their way.

RC: *Good point. Having just started Camden Joy's new book,* Lost Joy, *(TNI Books, 2002), I thought maybe you could give some insight on TNI's connection to the underground world of music.*

AV: Well I learned about art (making art, enjoying art, buying art) first and foremost through independent music and some form of punk rock. While the whole idea of ethics being more involved in punk than, say, a software company might be a bunch of bullshit, there were certain ideas and attitudes that I took and try my best to continue to take from that scene. In terms of the connection the company has to a music world: I put ads and send review copies to rock magazines as much as I do to literary outlets. There are a fair number of record stores that sell the books. Many of the folks involved in *Little Engines* lead double lives in the world of rock. There are all of those literal connections to independent rock, but I like to hope that some of that connection folks see is found in the spirit of the company itself.

RC: *Do you ever think of going the Jim Munroe route (the "sell-out secret") and publishing something through someone else bigger in order to fund your own stuff?*

AV: I'd consider working with a larger publisher if the timing was right, and if the things I find important are addressed in a way that satisfies what I'm trying to do with my writing and my books. I hinted at this above when I said I was trying to learn all about book making because it would help me down the road. While I take great pride in the independence of TNI Books, and while making art in an independent arena is, in my own opinion, crucial to the survival of those arts, I'm not working in complete opposition to larger publishing houses. For sure, there are great books coming out of some of the bigger publishing outlets. My main concern, though, is to build up an audience on my own before looking into those other options. If the time comes when some larger publisher is interested in what I'm doing, I'd certainly see what the nature of their interest was, but for now I'm not sending my work anywhere on that level. The only other place I've been sending/publishing stuff outside of TNI Books releases is a small broadside publisher in Chicago called *THE2NDHAND*. Amazing stuff they're doing, and all on one sheet of paper!

RC: *You bring up a point here that I've been debating with many people on both sides of this issue: is "independent" work more authentic than work backed by corporate money? Is something automatically suspect when it comes from a corporate source?*

AV: The question you pose is totally interesting. There are urges in me that push to say *yes*, independent is better, but there are calmer parts of me that know there are plenty of totally authentic pieces brought to you by corporate money. I think the bottom line is that in our economic model, there's no way to fully tiptoe around corporations. And the fact is that some folks making art probably do indeed need to reach that larger audience the big dogs are able to hit.

RC: *The origin of my take on this debate was a quote by Richard Metzger: "The most subversive thing anyone can do is become popular." I've used this quote to analyze and spark debate about the position of a band like Rage Against the Machine versus a band like Fugazi. Most people tend to be easing up on the staunchly independent stance, but tempers often still flare. The question for someone in your position is how some influx of money from another source would affect your business, your goals, and — most of all — your product.*

AV: Well, first of all I should probably point out that subversion isn't necessarily a goal of mine. I can fully understand how that can become a goal for some artists, but for me the more important factor (in light of this discussion) is the honesty of the artwork, and whether the way that work finds its way into consumers hands tarnishes that honesty. I'm not sure if folks are tending to ease up on the staunchly independent stance or not, but if they are, I don't see any evidence that says they should. I suspect (and am often convinced) that going the "major" route, be it in publishing or music, is probably a worse choice now than it was ten or so years ago.

It's not like things in the realm of gigantic corporations are getting more artist friendly! However, I also see plenty of nasty stuff in the world of independent art. I'm often frustrated with this topic as a debate because I can point to numerous records or books that were presented to me through some large corporate situation and say "these are quality pieces of art."

However, I can also look at a Fugazi record (like you cited) and say that there's not much of a way that record would make sense or carry the weight it does were it to be released by a major record label. So clearly the situation isn't black and white. The issue for me has to focus on the actual piece of artwork (or the "product," if that isn't offensive to you). If the artwork makes it into the hands of the public with minimal assholeness, money stealing, dishonest promotions, etc., then someone's doing okay. For me, so far I've found that doing things independently makes the most sense right now, but in general any stance like this certainly requires a skeptical eye every now and again.

RC: *In your fiction, you often write about personal issues. Do you have a process for fictionalizing your experiences, or do you switch stuff around or just make stuff up?*

AV: It's a combination of all of these things, for sure. Often the personal issues I write about center around internal conflicts I have. I think I tend to put these conflicts/contradictions into a format that can be laughed at or is amusing to lighten what is actually at stake. I don't have a particular process, but lately I've been working more and more with stories that are more fiction than fact, which hasn't always been the case.

RC: *I know in my own forays into fiction, I've tried to recount events that I think are story-worthy without making it completely obvious when and where these stories happened, or what events inspired them. Using actual events has been crucial to me, because I know exactly how these stories unfolded and how they made me feel. But you hear the horror stories from writers who have written about actual events in their lives and then ended up hated by their friends.*

AV: Well, maybe those folks should seek new friends! I'd be bummed out if a friend of mine hated me because I found something about them or some situation we both encountered worthy of writing about. There is a fine line though — a line that I've crossed a few times myself. Obviously everyone's writing from experience in some regard. And I tend to agree with your point that this allows a writer to get at some very true feelings and emotions. I've been reading a lot of nonfiction lately, and it's been very inspiring! True events are so often more interesting, enlightening, sad, funny, etc. than made up stuff!

RC: *Is there anything you're working on that you'd like to bring up here?*

AV: I've got a new novel called *Stand Up Ernie Baxter: You're Dead*. It should be out sometime early next year. It's about a dead stand-up comedian and his old high school sweetheart. I'm both excited and nervous about the book. The format is odd, some of the chapters are done as comics, and the humor is done in a very rough way in this book, but I feel like I've written something I can be proud of. It's not a super heavy book, but there are certain themes that I really had a good time brushing up against. It's taken me far too long for how short the book is, but finishing it has been really fantastic. It's quite a rewarding process wrapping up a book.

David X. Cohen
Futurama's Head (in a Jar)
by TOM GEORGOULIAS (2002)

DAVID X. COHEN IS THE EXECUTIVE PRODUCER AND HEAD writer of *Futurama*, my favorite TV show. In case you haven't watched the show, it's about a pizza delivery boy named Fry who is accidentally frozen in a cryogenics lab and revived 1,000 years in the future. Instead of getting a chance to reinvent his life, Fry's career implant chip predetermines that he, again, is destined to be a delivery boy. After a futile attempt to resist his future, Fry joins the Planet Express delivery company and works alongside several other misfit characters in similar circumstances.

David, whose middle name does not begin with an X, and his crack team of high-tech comedians and CG wizards are responsible for this super-smart, animated comedy that Fox works so hard to keep you from seeing. Even with a difficult 7 PM EST Sunday time slot and constantly shifting air dates for new episodes, those folks who make the effort to watch or tape the show are always treated to a hilarious excursion into the year 3000. Sassy comments from Bender, the surly robot who drinks, steals, and smokes; guest appearances by Gary Gygax and Deep Blue; and a bar where designated device drivers drink for free — three tiny bits of the intricate *Futurama* universe and comedic gold for hackers and geeks alike. In fact, there are so many inside jokes hidden in the background scenery that you often have to watch portions of an episode in slow motion to catch them all. No doubt about it, devotion to the show is always rewarded.

TOM GEORGOULIAS: *You have degrees in both computer science and physics, yet you are the executive producer of a satirical, science-fiction cartoon. How did this happen?*

DAVID X. COHEN: Ah, the same question my parents asked in reference to certain piles of tuition money that went out the window.

I always planned to be a scientist. Both of my parents are biologists and my favorite subjects in school were math and physics. (Go math team!) At the same time, I liked to draw cartoons (which I would force my sister to buy for a penny — the beginning of my professional writing career), and I wrote the humor column for my high school newspaper, and later was a writer for the *Harvard Lampoon Magazine*. At some point, I had a sudden panic when I realized that there was the option of trying to write professionally, and that I had to make a choice. But I didn't — instead I took a year off and worked at the Harvard Robotics Laboratory.

Finally, I decided I should go to graduate school before I forgot everything I knew, with the idea that I could try writing later if I wasn't sure I had made the right choice. After three years of graduate school, I felt I wasn't enjoying it as much as I should, and that there was no end in sight, so I took a leave of absence and began writing sample ("spec") TV scripts. After a year or so of unemployment, this got me a job writing a couple early episodes of *Beavis and Butt-Head*. Later I got hired at *The Simpsons*, and about five years after that, Matt Groening asked me if I wanted to work on *Futurama* with him. Which I did, of course.

TG: *Have you ever considered leaving the creative business for a job in the technology field?*

DXC: Once in a while, when I'm fed up with the illogic of the TV business. And also briefly a couple of years ago, when I lived in fear that all of the computer scientists I knew were about to become billionaires in the internet IPO boom, leaving me behind.

But in truth, I've now forgotten a good percentage of whatever I once knew, so I'd have a mountain of catching up to do. I have expertise programming the Apple II, if that's still in big demand.

I still like hacking around on the computer. Maybe I'll crank out some shareware some day. A cheesy videogame of some kind.

TG: *What influences do you draw upon in creating both the stories and the science & technology for each episode?*

DXC: One of the first rules that Matt Groening and I agreed upon for writing *Futurama* was, "Science shall not outweigh comedy." Still, we wanted to get in as much science as possible where it didn't clog up the gears of the story. Obviously, a lot of our technology is drawn from ideas in science fiction rather than actual science. For me, *Star Trek*, Arthur C. Clarke, and author Stanislaw Lem are some sci-fi inspirations. We had fun early on trying to decide which standard ideas we would use (e.g., faster-than-light-travel, without which the show would be impossible), and which ideas we would dismiss as ridiculous (the transporter — since our ship can land anywhere, we didn't need it!). Actually, as far as faster-than-light travel is concerned, I wanted to make at least a nod to the problem, so in one episode we mentioned that they actually could not go faster than light, but that the speed of light had been increased.

Now and then, we throw in some pretty obscure science references when and where we think they won't distract the casual viewer. For example, my friend David Schiminovich, an astrophysicist at Caltech, has provided comedy particle physics diagrams for a chalkboard seen in the background of one episode. We've also referred to the P =? NP question and the Heisenberg Uncertainty Principle. In fact, we may have broadcast the only dialog about the Uncertainty Principle in network sitcom history. The Professor loses at the horse track when his horse is narrowly beat out in a "quantum finish." He complains, "No fair! You changed the outcome by measuring it!"

Our hope is that, although such material will fly by most people unnoticed, it might make die-hard fans of the people who do appreciate it.

I should also mention that we have several genuine ex-scientists on our writing staff: Ken Keeler has a Ph.D. in applied math and a masters in electrical engineering; Bill Odenkirk has a Ph.D. in inorganic chemistry; and Jeff Westbrook has a Ph.D. in computer science. I'm actually somewhere in the middle of the pack educationally!

It's really a privilege working with such knowledgeable and interesting people. I think it helps me keep my sanity, since outside of our writing room there isn't such a high concentration of scientists in the TV industry. And I do still consider myself a scientist by nature.

TG: *What standards do you measure an episode against before you consider it a finished product?*
DXC: We've found that *Futurama* episodes seem to work best when there is a compelling dramatic story underlying the comedy. For that reason, we try to take seriously both the epic nature of science fiction and the human emotions of the characters (even if they're not technically human). Interestingly, perhaps, these are things that need to be worked out very carefully at the beginning of the process, yet are the most important to the finished product. If you derail early on with the story and emotions, it's very hard to patch things up later.

So, for us to be fully satisfied with an episode, it needs to be funny and dramatic at the same time. A tall order!

Of course, the animation, voices, music, and sound effects are critical as well, but the artists, actors, and engineers who work on those aspects of the show are so brilliant that I don't personally need to direct the bulk of my concern toward those things.

TG: *Do you feel any pressure from higher-ups at Fox to throttle back the content?*

DXC: Matt Groening has always insisted on a high level of autonomy for the show, since that's how he's used to doing things at *The Simpsons*. We rarely get into arguments over the content of the show, though there was one notable exception — our Christmas special from 2000 was taken off the schedule at the last minute, having been deemed "inappropriate" for broadcast. It was not shown until a year later, in a later time slot. However, the content was not altered. At most, we get rid of a "hell" or "damn" or "ass" from a script once in a while.

TG: *What is the general feeling among the* Futurama *crew concerning the way Fox treats this show? After all, it's already January 2002 and we've only seen three episodes for season four, two of which were originally scheduled to air in season three.*

DXC: Frustrated, bitter . . . you can guess. Obviously our time slot is a terrible handicap, yet the ratings have not been bad when we are not bumped off by football. My opinion is that the only thing *Futurama* really needs to be a big success is for Fox to promote it and tell people that it's good. But evidently, they aren't interesting in doing that. Why, I'm not sure. It seems like it would be very much in their interest as well as ours. But, as I mentioned earlier, television is not the most logical business.

TG: *Outside of your* Futurama *duties, what other interests do you have?*

DXC: Outside of my *Futurama* duties? Whuh? I've spent almost all my waking hours working on *Futurama* for the past few years, so sometimes I get confused when I hear the phrase "outside interests." However, some things I seem to remember liking are: bridge (the card game, not the structure — no offense to the structure), fossils, computer programming, and tennis.

TG: *You mentioned in a* Science Fiction Weekly *interview that you were considering reducing your role at* Futurama *and working on other projects. Can you elaborate on this?*

DXC: If *Futurama* is renewed for a 5th season (as of now, January 2002, we haven't heard one way or the other), it is true that I'd like to take a partial step back. I don't think I could leave completely, since I love the show so much, but at the same time I don't think I can take another year of working until midnight night after night. One idea I had is to stay involved in the stage of the process where we work out the stories. That way, I could retain some of the satisfaction that comes from helping plan the evolution of a universe!

Sean Gullette
Faith in Chaos
by TOM GEORGOULIAS (1999)

SEAN GULLETTE IS A VERY BUSY MAN. WITH SEEMINGLY CONTRA-
dictory roles as both a webmaster for KGB Media and a computer skeptic,
he splits his time between graphic design work and acting. Gullette has
been in ten independent films, including the leading role as Maximillian
Cohen in *Pi*, the winner of the 1998 Sundance Film Festival Award for Best
Directing. *Pi* is a film about a brilliant, paranoid mathematician who tee-
ters on the brink of insanity as he searches for the numeric order behind
the stock market.

TOM GEORGOULIAS: *The film is certainly one of the most intense science
fiction thrillers because of the way mathematical concepts are intertwined
with flashing black & white images and an electronic soundtrack. You share
the credit for writing* Pi *with director Darren Aronofsky — what prompted
the two of you to create this film?*

SEAN GULLETTE: A New York character of our acquaintance had written
a shelf's worth of conspiracy theory books, which all hinged on highly

improbable (and, in fact, clinically insane) numerical "coincidences": e.g., J. Edgar Hoover's day of birth and the license plate number of the limousine JFK was riding in. Quickly we realized that a character who sees a (persecuting) numerical order behind the visible, everywhere in the world, could be dramatically interesting, but that if he was merely insane it would be difficult for an audience to sympathize with him. Who is a real number paranoid? A mathematician. We built a back story for Max, and a character from that story, and then sort of let Max and the writer's journey dictate what would happen next.

Darren is a very hardworking gifted guy, and I hope and believe he'll be making challenging films for a long time to come. Our director of photography, Matthew Libatique is on his way to being one of the most interesting young DPs out there. Clint Mansell, who used to front the group Pop Will Eat Itself, did his first film score for us, and it gave an emotional dimensionality to the film that makes a huge difference. Eric Watson, the producer, has a great gift for bringing creative people together and getting one guy's chocolate in the other guy's peanut butter. All three of them worked on Darren's second feature, *Requiem for a Dream*, which just wrapped. I'm in there too.

TG: Pi *is essentially about fundamental questions of the nature of the universe and our understanding of it. Max Cohen is searching for order behind the chaotic systems, and he blurs the thin line between genius and madness. What intrigued you to take on the role of Max?*

SG: We just sort of built him from the ground up like a garage robot, using whatever parts and know-how we had available. And I knew this would be an interesting process and I wanted to work with Darren again, 'cause we were friends and we had done a film in school called *Supermarket Sweep,* and it was a lot of fun.

TG: *Throughout the film, there existed a gap between the organic and the inorganic, most notably Max's isolation and nonstop work on his theory. However, after Euclid crashes and the number is in Max's head, he ends this separation and accepts the world around him. In discussions with others who have seen the film, some feel that he reached a pseudo goal while others think he simply gave up. You played Max, what do you think?*

SG: At the risk of sounding prissy: I did my job. Interpretation is yours. Not only are there no right answers to the questions fiction poses, but mine would be even less "right" than yours.

TG: *Aronofsky stated in his DVD commentary that you were a literature guy and one of your first assignments was to sit down and write long streams of digits in order to become intimate with numbers. What other research or steps did you take to prepare yourself for the role of Max Cohen?*

SG: In those days I was really kinda "method acting" in my unschooled way — wearing Max's clothes around, walking the walk, ordering Max's favorite foods, having filthy fingernails, being a dick to my girlfriend. Other mental devices. It's a good way to get into a far out character and find details about him, but it's a lot of work to keep up and I think now there are other ways to get a good performance.

TG: *Max Cohen pushes his limits of understanding by pursuing truth through mathematics, while Lenny Meyer and Rabbi Cohen seek to understand through Kabbalism. Both approaches border on extreme fanaticism, yet the underlying principle that drives them and the larger philosophical questions* Pi *asks are the same. How has playing the role of Max Cohen affected your own beliefs?*

SG: To me the film sort of reduces to this: At the beginning, Max looks at a tree blowing in the wind and he sees chaos, and feels a terrible fear and loneliness at the whole organic world he can't understand and colonize and control with his reason. At the end, he just sees a tree, blowing in the wind, and it's okay.

Bruce Sterling
Future Tense
by PAUL D. MILLER (1999)

"For if the Jazz Age is year for year the Essences and
Symptoms of the times, then Jes Grew is the germ making it
rise yeast-like across the American plain. . . . The letters after
their names are their tommy guns and those universities
where they pour over syllables their Big House."
— *Ishmael Reed,* Mumbo Jumbo

"The city no longer exists, except as a cultural ghost for tourists."
— *Marshall McLuhan, "The Alchemy of Social Change"
from* Verbi-Voco-Visual Explanations, *1967*

FIRST THINGS FIRST: IT TOOK ME A ZILLION YEARS (SUMMER TO
winter 1999) to write this 'cause I didn't know where to start. I think about
Bruce Sterling's writing and see a precedent that runs throughout a lot
of American science fiction. It's a tradition of writing where the future is
far more of a barometer to measure the present than the past, and it's the

fracture points in the lines of thought holding it all together that his work explores. He, like J.G. Ballard, is one of those people who can peer deep inside the structures holding together contemporary society and weave together stories that somehow make past, present, and future blend in a way that is incredibly well researched and astute, not to mention excellent fiction as well. A difficult task indeed. Sterling has been on the writing scene for ages, and with his peers Neal Stephenson, William Gibson, and in a more remote "hard science" fashion, Greg Egan, has sparked the imagination of people within both the arts and technological communities for the last two decades with science fiction created from stories and situations that would only be remotely possible in our world. A tape recorder, a geographically dispersed conversation that took place over several months, a chain of email corrections and file exchanges, and the article was done. The stories, like the conversation, are fractured and full of a strange humor — fluid but crisp, openly flaunting the kind of hypertext narrative drift that drives editors bonkers, but kept tantalizing close to the "reality" we inhabit. The thing that differentiates Sterling from many of his compatriots in science fiction is that he focuses on the everyday and uses his explorations (take that one literally because he travels more than almost anyone I know), as a platform from which to write about America and the world it finds itself in. Sterling strikes a fine-tuned balance between shear impossibility and "the real" to create milieu that are all too hauntingly familiar. Heimlich versus unheimlich, the familiar and its distortions and permutations, remote possibility and unerringly "scientifically possible" renditions of future worlds — what could be more relevant to today's uncanny world of contemporary hyperreality?

To me Sterling is a writer working within a strain of American fiction at least as old as Edward Bellamy's classic *Looking Backward* (Signet, 1960) — a story that predicted credit cards, politics based on pop culture, and an American Utopia based on technology and individual choice taken to societal extremes. But where Bellamy would write a "passion" that created an almost "palpable barrier" between citizens and the culture they constructed out of America's dreams, Sterling explores the outer fringes of a culture that Bellamy could only dream of. "This passion for losing ourselves in others or for absorbing them into ourselves," he wrote back at the turn of the nineteenth century, "is the greatest law of solidarity." And indeed, Sterling's latest fictions are an exploration of that theme inverted and remixed into an America fraught with technological disruptions of the human condition most previous writers — even in speculative fiction — would have barely conceived.

In his most recent novel, *Distraction* (Spectra, 1999), Sterling sets the scene in a mid-twenty-first-century America being torn apart by various economic, social, and political issues. I look out my window and think of the present moment as I write. My laptop monitor flickers to life as I, with the push of the "spacebar," banish the looping images of Bart Simpson scrolling across the now blank screen surface of my computer. The word "cyberpunk" at 5 AM draws a relative blank for me, and my computer has responded by going into screensaver mode. I look out the window and see a swimming pool several stories below me, and wistfully gaze out over the parking lots and swamp trees surrounding the hotel I'm staying in. A series of convergences, open texts, and a hot summer night flash across my mind, the mental equivalent of the process my computer is going through. Tallahassee, Florida, and I'm on tour with a hip-hop MC named Kool Keith playing around the country to promote his album called *Black Elvis* to large crowds of kids dressed in all manner of costumes and from all manner of ethnic backgrounds. Basically it feels like the future is here now — but I realize it was never gone, it too was just another screensaver banished with the push of a button.

It's the summer of 1999 and strange things have been happening. Reality as a Spike Jonze commercial. Reality as a Hype Williams video. Wars with small-time European dictators are covered relentlessly by the press while far more devastating situations in Asia and Africa are rendered into filler between "jungle" soundtracked automobile commercials (or even Macintosh's "Think Different" celebrity branding campaign of the dead and the living). Switch channels, look at a different billboard and you might see a Chihuahua singing the praises of Taco Bell while hip-hop beats play in the background. Get the wrong email and you might even receive a worm virus that selectively deletes your entire address book by propagating itself through your friends and colleagues. Record-level droughts, an iceberg the size of the state of Rhode Island — twenty-four miles wide by forty-eight miles long — breaking off of Antarctica, antibiotic-resistant bacteria, genetically engineered crops, presidential politics as celebrity sports, etc., etc. I think you get the picture. There's even stuff like the Black hardcore hip-hop MC DMX raising his hands at Woodstock in the symbol of an "X" above his head and yelling at the ocean of white people in front of him, "How many of y'all niggas don't give a fuck? Put your hands up!" and the crowd putting itself into a sea of symbols — X marking the spot of their ethnic meltdown at a festival meant to celebrate the dying values of '60s counterculture that ended in a rainbow riot of smashed cash machines and burning concession stands. A strange telemetry seemed to be the driving force of the summer's events — the list goes on: presidents, prime ministers, the continuing break-down of the former super power known as the Soviet Union into all sorts of strange polities, white males going bonkers and shooting up kindergartens, high schools, and day-trading stock companies, etc. I could stop there, or I could mention the stunning popularity of movies like *The Matrix* and *The Blair Witch Project* that pointed to the psychological implosion of one of the prime

American directives of the last two centuries — expansion at all costs — but that would be giving away the idea. Outer space in 1999 took a back seat to our own inner turmoil and fears and, in a sense, has created the backdrop to the kind of narrative milieu that Bruce Sterling inhabits and describes with ease. The signs are all there, but of course, they're in real time, and quite, perhaps all too much, contemporary. I guess you could call it "Summer of Bruce."

A long time ago J.G. Ballard, a writer that I feel is Sterling's predecessor in many ways, wrote a simple statement that seems to drift over me like some sort of over-lit neon expanse, a Times Square icon hanging on my screen as I write: "above all, science fiction is likely to be the only form of literature which will cross the gap between the dying narrative fictions of the present day, and the cassette and video tape fictions of the near future." In a world where Garth Brooks can create new recording personalities on a whim, and where during a flight to Japan earlier this summer, I realized that I was flying Air Nippon's Pokemon jet — a vehicle done over to completely mirror the environment of the video game of the same name, I realized, yes, it's definitely been a Bruce Sterling summer. Science fiction is a kind of psychological exploration of a fascination between science and technology, and in remarkable feats of prestidigitation, writers like Sterling, William Gibson, Pat Cadigan, and Neal Stephenson (with bows to Octavia Butler, Thomas Disch, and Samuel Delaney) have always focused on the mutuality of science and the desires that it evokes and obeys. This century began with books like Olaf Stapledon's classic *Star Maker* (1937), George Schuyler's *Black No More* (1931), and H.G. Wells' classics, and went from there to pulp fiction and Hollywood, only to close the circuit and arrive at the footsteps of people like Ursula K. Le Guin and Michael Moorcock — introverts who live through the multiple (for lack of a better word) "operatic" agency of the serial-oriented stories they write, as an almost mandarin-like reflection/inversion of pulp culture. But where this crowd focused on the far future, or far past, the brand of sci-fi Sterling and Gibson pioneered was much closer to home. The loops holding the past, present, and future, were getting smaller, and their telemetry was beginning to go into narrow focus mode: Then this year we get Stephenson writing *Cryptonomicon* (Avon, 1999) from the contemporary past, Sterling writing *Distraction* (like he almost always seems to do these days) about a closer cycle of near future narratives, and Gibson remaining relatively mute while he still thrashes out the more Hollywood-oriented nuances of the genre in his *All Tomorrow's Parties* (Putnam, 1999).

But time waits for no man, and indeed all these different permutations of the American dream fade away when we see the huge sweeps of cautionary and speculative fiction in the form of videos and music albums laid out before us like some virtual feast that we can never leave, unsatisfied until the end of the cycle — you know, the "ctrl+alt+delete" for a forced quit/shutdown of your computer. But the screen will somehow, someway turn on again. Strange loops take us into the mix of literary elements, some have more force than others and, in a sense, you could say Sterling is probably, metaphorically speaking, about as strong as a black hole in this department. Like Pollack used to say, "it's all in the process." To describe Sterling's work I really would like to use words like "autoreferentiality," "metasignifier," "narrative catalyst," and stuff like that, but that would destroy the poetry of the words he uses. One of my favorite theorists of the kind of cultural and economic flux that Sterling describes, Gayatri Chakravorty Spivak, wrote in her recent book *Critique of Post-Colonial Reason* (Routledge, 1990) that "simply put, culture alive is always on the run, always changeful . . . it is an absurd denial of history simply to ask for its prohibition." In other words, shit happens, and like Harlan Ellison said at the height of the disco era back in 1977 about Sterling's first novel: "Go. Rush inside and marvel at this kid named Sterling, 0.995 fine, who writes like a cynical angel." We owe it not so much to Sterling, but to ourselves, to make sure nothing gets in this man's way as he tells us his stories. He enriches us. "Who am I to stand in the way?"

PAUL D. MILLER: *Your work has everything utterly fragmented and involuted. Characters are extensions of a social reality where almost everything can be changed and attained. I think of the origins of sci-fi this century as opposed to the fictions of the past: unitary governments, reflections of imperial realities held together by the firm reigns of some centralized narrative, and basically at the end of the century, with your work, all of that has been thrown out the metaphorical window. What's up?*

BRUCE STERLING: Well, you know, that's a very interesting question, but it all went into the ether, because I couldn't possibly repeat all of that. Let me see if I can rephrase it. Unless you wrote it down that piece of genius is lost to mankind. I think essentially what you were saying is how come my stuff is broken up into little pieces and is decentered and polyvalent, when if you read an H.G. Wells novel, it's all about socialism is going to unify the world. Is this what you are saying basically? Okay, well my problem is I am a postmodernist, okay? I don't believe in single, dominant narratives that have all the answers. I don't believe in any kind of totalizing intellectual framework that offers an unchallengeable center to human affairs — corners and holes in the wall and fractal structure and places where things are seeming to obey and going their own way.

PDM: *I think that your "zone" of sci-fi is far more open to how hybrid the world really is. It seems like America has been so frightened of truly realizing how intertwined it really is, that we've created fictions to hold out anything that couldn't be assimilated. And that's what, for me at least, makes your work have such a strong resonance with what's actually going on. In* Distraction *the groups that create the fabric of the story have an almost* *cybernetic role — homeostasis, reflexivity — all of these issues are what Weiner and Claude Shannon would have described as parts of info theory. But for you they become narrative structure. Smart. Cool.*

BS: "Mixed cultures, mixed codes," he repeated helpfully. How do I see that as a narrative tool in my book? Moderators, regulators. Well, I've hung out with government people, military people, and cop people and other sort of subcultures. And I think that every time; I mean they all present a kind of front as if they had all the answers and were in complete command and control. This is the impression that a soldier or a cop is very anxious to present to you. It's part of what they call the atmosphere of deterrence. If you see a cop, all cops are like doctors or something. They are all in the state of total brotherhood and solidarity and they want to present a unified front to the outside world of Marx and criminals and dumb civilians and so forth. But once you are actually under the skin of an enterprise like this, you soon find that the stuff that cops are really upset about is rivalry with other cops. Like the Federal Bureau of Investigation hates and fears the United States Secret Service. Everybody despises the Internal Revenue Service. There are tremendous interservice rivalries. Then even if you get below that, you'll soon find that there is stiff, internal competition among cliques within the FBI. Or, you know, there's the Mormon Mafia within the FBI for instance, who were despised and feared by all other FBI agents.

PDM: *Well, yeah, if you're out in the world, you'd just think, well they have it all under control, and the situation is crazy ill. But then again, America's ability to transform any culture is amazing. Politics and industry seem to get displaced in your work by biotech and America's other main exports: entertainment and arms sales. But the internal policing of the U.S. is a whole different ballgame. I sometimes think of what J. Edgar Hoover must have been like — extreme fracture points there. But religion is such a wildcard* *these days. It's really remixed America in ways we can't even ascertain yet.*

BS: Yeah, the Mormon Mafia; there are a buttload of Mormons in the FBI — for some reason the Bureau attracts Mormons. It's not a politically correct thing to say, I'm sure, without trying to make any religious allegations here. I can just say that it's a matter of common knowledge in the FBI that the thing's full of Mormons.

PDM: *Wow. Well, that's in tune with a lot of your critique of ethnicity in the U.S., and it's not a negative. It's difficult to get a grip on how that affects law enforcement, but I would think in one way or another it does. It would make an incredible story, but it's not something you would check out unless you were another law agency or a science-fiction writer, eh?*

BS: Yeah, well, why would you? Why should you have to? It's not like you can exploit that knowledge to help yourself in any way. But within the FBI, this is just something that looms large, right? So I just don't believe in the central thing. I mean, there is no quote government unquote. I mean, there's an image of a government, but once you're behind the image of the government you see it's really all about bureaucratic in-fighting and interservice rivalries, and so forth and so on.

PDM: *Polyphrenia, eh?*

BS: Yeah, that's right. I mean, I think it is just more accurate to describe it in that way.

PDM: *Fact and fiction blur in such a weird way these days. That's what I love about your work. It looks at different cultural trajectories and extrapolates them in such a way that we arrive at some pretty wild places. But then again, who would have thought we would be able to land on the moon a hundred years ago, eh?*

BS: I suppose it just reflects reality in a somewhat more exaggerated way. Yeah.

PDM: *Is that what made you intrigued by the science-fiction medium?*
BS: What made me become a science-fiction writer? Well, you know, I couldn't think of anything better to do. Really, that is pretty much the answer there. I mean I thought of . . . I got a degree in journalism, just writing. I mean there are things you can do to earn a living, science fiction isn't high among them, generally. Like other forms of creative endeavors, a few people on the top are making millions, and then there are tons of people who are, you know, just trying to scrape the rent together, or they have day jobs. But, you know, I looked at other ways of earning a living, and I just didn't care for any of them very much and, I don't know, I just think it suits me pretty well. It really is kind of my métier.

PDM: *Coming out of journalism gives you a way to explain things in a concrete way, and it gives your work a resonance with events that happened historically and create new situations out of totally different situations. You just have a great frame to bounce the events off of. That whole 1960s "New Journalism" thing gets a serious reworking, eh?*
BS: I guess so, but I just think that my own personality is well-suited to this line of work. I couldn't really make it into sciences, per se, because I can't concentrate long enough. I can write journalism, but I don't really have that kind of nose for news that a top-flight journalist has to have. A real journalist is a kind of guy who can go over to your house when your child has died in a car wreck and ask you for a photo. You know? And that's really what's required. There's a toughness of mind there that a top-flight journalist has to have. You know it's like being in the army or something. You just can't flinch when there's blood all over the floor, and I don't really

have that. As journalists go, I'm like an art critic, just one of these kind of epistolary-style, essay-writer guys.

PDM: *I think that's what makes travel so amazing in a lot of your stories. The reader is really given an "overview" of the situations and geographic contexts they live and move through. I think it's cool.*

BS: Yes. Some critic pointed out, I think it was Paul DeFillipo but it might have been this other guy, he said that I was obsessed with mass evacuations. And that hadn't occurred to me. Somebody wrote that like five years ago, and I thought, yeah, I am obsessed with mass evacuations, and *Distraction* is full of places that have been evacuated. There are sort of postdisaster zones, or places that were wiped out by giant tornadoes, or places where everybody picked up and left. And another obsession of mine, which somebody else pointed out, that bugged the hell out of me, 'cause I hadn't been aware of it, was my early obsession with submarines. It's like almost every book I wrote up till 1990, had a submarine in it at one point or another. And if it didn't have a submarine, it had a hot-air balloon, which when you think about, is kind of the functional equivalent of a submarine, right?

PDM: *Depth psychology or something like that. But again, it really works and conveys a whole sense of culture on the move, and that's what I see as being the "core" issue of "cyberpunk," a term I think you coined, eh? But is there a narrative strategy? Could there be another layer of meaning? Networks, displaced peoples, and nation states on the verge of being consumed within larger trading structures are also a recurring motif.*

BS: Why? I can't tell you. It's like why is J.G. Ballard obsessed with empty swimming pools? I do travel a lot. When I was a teenager I was an oil-company kid; we were on and off of aircraft all the time. I went around the globe, I don't know, it must have been six or eight times before I turned twenty. And I think that world travel had a very formative influence on me. And even now I log a lot of mileage. Like in the past three weeks, I have been in Turkey, Cyprus, Georgia, New York City.

PDM: *Post-Soviet/Russian federation Georgia?*
BS: No, Georgia, USA, Atlanta. Yeah. Almost as exotic a place as Georgia, Russia, really. And I'm not even on tour or anything. This is just something I was doing in order to, I don't know, amuse myself, or pick up some loose change.

PDM: *I think that's what makes a lot of your work have such a gravitational pull, they're almost like an extended dialog about how stories arise out of conflict. Dialog as dialectics or something like that, but done with great flair and the highest attention paid to detail. Hey, even the word jazz comes to mind sometimes, and it's derived from the French verb "jazzer" which means to "have a dialog." Definitely a central motif in* Distraction.
BS: Yeah. Well, it's talkier than a lot of other books, because politicians talk a lot. They are always on tour and giving speeches, and there is always a message, and you're on message for the day, right? I see this book as part of . . . it's a linked series of books. It's like *Heavy Weather* (Bantam, 1994), *Holy Fire* (Bantam, 1996), and *Distraction* are three books which are written with a very similar technique. They are very different from one another because they examine different aspects of human life. Like *Heavy Weather* is an ecodisaster novel in which everybody is dealing with the consequences of some terrible catastrophe, or expecting one, or, you know, trying to come to terms with it. And *Holy Fire* is about things like life-extension and cosmetics. And *Distraction* is about politics and science. But they each have starring characters who personify the problem at hand, and then sort of go on a tour of fields of data, where they are behaving as

our binoculars to examine the problem. So they are very different books and have very different settings, and are not formally linked in any way; they're certainly not a trilogy, or any of that nonsense. They are related works. I am using the same techniques in each one. So I haven't done these three books in fairly short order, plus the short story collection. I wanted to get a lot done in the '90s. I really felt that I had a pretty good hold of how I was working these things out. I was pretty well up on the mountainside there and I wanted to drive a big set of pitons in there. But, now I think I am going to write some nonfiction here.

PDM: *You've also written nonfiction, again, with that hyper well-researched flair you always bring to bear on whatever topic you choose. Your new stuff is on historical computer stuff, eh?*

BS: It's been ten years since I had a nonfiction book out. So every once in a while I like to sort of take a breather, go back, refresh myself, brush up my chops, and then come back. Yes, that's right. I'm trying to sell my *Dead Media* book now. I am doing a book on obsolescence in media. And I want to talk about media that are no longer used. You know, it's a very hot thing in the DJ line of work. You see all these guys who are into analog synths, and there's like this weird black market in like thermeotic valves and vacuum tubes, right? Because they are "spankier sounding." They're like "hard to get" now. There are these digital guys who have these names now like "DJ Black Ninja Electron," you know, as if they'd come from the twenty-third century. And you actually look at the stuff they're using, and it's like this weird, flaking crap out of the mid-'70s that's held together with duct tape.

PDM: *It's definitely a kind of "back to the future" type situation in the DJ scene. I can tell ya some stories sometime, but I gotta finish my own books before that happens. But the whole obsolete equipment issue is definitely* *going to be a bugged-out reflection of culture in the early twenty-first century, 'cause class, social hierarchy, and info access seem to move so quickly but are all mutually reflective. It's a situation that the industry creates for its own built-in time frames, and it all just filters down into the other zones of contemporary culture.*

BS: Well, I think these issues are going to come up pretty strong. I mean, there are a lot of guys like Bureau of Low Technology. I think the history of electronics, the fact that a lot of electronics is old, and kind of fallen off the edge of the table. Time is on my side when it comes to the dead-media thing. And by the time the book comes out, I would expect this to be becoming an issue. Dealing with the legacies of this sort of frenetic electronic explosion we've had.

PDM: *Blank memory space filled with potential: think of Charles Babbage and Ada Lovelace's "Difference Engine" and the whole steam-engine calculating scene. I think it's great that you work with so many other writers and have created a forum that is pretty much a group of people who are all open to issues that a lot of other sci-fi writers can't hold a candle to.*

BS: I have written things with Gibson. The defining moment: What did Gibson, Sterling, and Neal Stephenson have in common? Okay, well, the thing that Gibson and Sterling have in common is that we are more or less, kinda the same age, and that we spend a lot of time sending faxes to each other. So, we share the same research material. Uh, Neal Stephenson, I don't know, he read my stuff, he read Gibson's stuff, but he's seven years younger than I am, and I'm seven years younger than Gibson. We certainly didn't have to bring this guy up by the seat of his pants; he just burst on the scene all by himself. I'm on good terms with Neal. I was over at Neal's house during my most recent signing tour, and I respect him very much, but there really isn't like a mafia linkage between us. The thing is, he is just looking at the same things we are, and drawing the same conclusions. Cause if you

look hard, it's hard to miss. I would have to say that the world, and especially the Soviet Union, the former Soviet Union, Russia, looks incredibly
like the world William Gibson was describing in 1984, in *Neuromancer*. I
mean, I remember when *Neuromancer* came out, people were saying, "You
know, how could this society possibly survive? There aren't any honest
people in this book. Nobody ever goes out in daylight! There's no working
stiffs!" It just seemed improbable and cartoon-like because every single
person in *Neuromancer* is some kind of criminal. You know, they've all
got some agenda and some hustle, and they just despise the government
and the law enforcement agencies, utterly and totally. These sort of formal
public entities just have received absolutely no respect whatsoever from
the population. Right?

Well, that's what Russia is right now, right? Everybody is a criminal
and all the real activity is going on in these sort of large, spooky, mafia-style
organizations, which aren't corporations exactly, but they're clearly behind
the scenes pulling the strings. And the ability of the common Joe in Russia
to get a handle on, let's say, Boris Berezovsky's media empire, is just as dis-
tant as, let's say, Automatic Jack in a Gibson story trying to raid Mitsubishi
Genetech, right? I mean, it's really a very, very, very Gibsonian milieu. And
it's not the United States. But, hey, it is a former super-power. So, if you look
at other science fiction that was being written at the time, and you try and
compare *Neuromancer* to *2001: A Space Odyssey*, it's a great science-fiction
movie and everything, but, hey, it's almost 2001, right? We ought to be on a
Pan Am clipper to the moon by now. We should be wearing Velcro shoes
and contacting aliens and monoliths. You seen any monoliths around
lately? You seen any zero-gravity stewardesses with Velcro moon boots?
No, you haven't seen any of those. Have you seen, like, down-and-dirty
guys in lofts who are making their living by like assembling big pieces of
semi-legal electronic equipment? Yeah, you've seen plenty of those guys!
Haven't you? They're kind of like pirates and, you know, they've got MP3

websites where you don't have to, like, pay for other people's music and shit. How many of those guys do you know?

PDM: *I know a lot of those types, but like you say, a lot of people don't.*
BS: Can you even count the number of guys like that that you know? You know, probably not. And every one of them looks like a character out of a Gibson novel. They're hanging around in their shirtsleeves; they're buying used equipment down at the junk store. There's a whole class of these characters! They don't necessarily break into banks, or steal data by penetrating the black ice or any of that kind of shit, but they certainly look a lot more . . . I mean the world of 1999 looks a hell of a lot more like a William Gibson novel than it does like an Arthur Clarke novel. It's that simple. And why? Because he was looking at things that Clarke wasn't looking at. Clarke was spending all his time with Wernher von Braun, and Gibson was spending all his time listening to Velvet Underground albums and haunting junk stores in Vancouver. And, you know, it's just a question of you are what you eat. And the guy had a different diet than science-fiction writers that preceded him.

PDM: *Like I've said earlier, the whole thing reminds me a little of how different themes pass from author to author, and then on through to the audience. Have you checked out Jack Womack's* Let's Put the Future Behind Us *(Atlantic Monthly Press, 1996)? Like you were saying,* Distraction *is about a fallen U.S.,* Let's Put the Future Behind Us *is kind of a fallen Russia story. Great piece of fiction, by the way.*
BS: Yeah, I know him. He's a good friend of Gibson's. They spend a lot of time together. He lives up in New York, a Kentucky guy. Wrote a pretty good Russian novel. Spent some time in Russia. That's a very good book. It's really like a Bulgakov novel. It's one of the best Russian novels a Russian never wrote.

PDM: *I'm really into the way you use art to highlight technology. Very few sci-fi writers do that. What makes a lot of your work a powerful description of tools we use to create imaginary objects that don't even exist yet is that I think you explore the psychology behind tool use. And that's what made cyberpunk so interesting when it first hit the scene. I think that* Holy Fire's *characters' interaction with art is some of the best stuff I've seen outside of Samuel Delaney. And I'm a huge Delaney fan.*

BS: Holy Fire is my art novel. It is kinda my valentine to the electronic arts crowd. Engineers have no taste, right? And science fiction is mostly written by and for engineers. That's really about gizmos and, like, "how do I get my hand on this gizmo?" But there are many things that are intriguing about art, and I take art very seriously, but the forms of art that I myself find most exciting are machine-mediated forms of art, like photography, which is an art form you can't do without a gizmo. And now there's all types of computer art, web art, net.art, which are all gizmo-oriented. So, in a way, art is very technosized now. It's all about the equipment, right? It's all about the return key and so forth. So this makes it possible to technically speculate about art. You can think about art the way an engineer would think now. And that's an exciting thing for me. I am interested in design, and I'm interested in areas in the crevasse between the arts and sciences, or between art and engineering. And I think that's where our society has kind of hidden all the oxygen. Now it's in that paradox, that paradoxical area between C.P. Snow's two cultures. There's a kind of ontological outlawry there. It interests me to see what artists choose to put their mitts on. So my experience there is that whenever a device falls off the back of a truck and kind of falls out of engineers' hands, that's when artists appropriate it. It's like guys who collect old medical instruments. You wouldn't want to go and collect modern medical instruments because, hey, they're for a doctor. But Victorian medical instruments, which are now kind of obsolete and mysterious, suddenly become very aestheticized. Their beauty

345

becomes apparent because they no longer have any use. It's like a dental instrument hasn't actually wrenched a bloody molar out of a guy's head in about a hundred years, so now the leather case is pretty, and the fact that you no longer know what certain devices are for, lends them a kind of mystery now, and they become kind of romanticized. I think that is an important phenomenon: things moving from the realm of the medical or the industrial or the engineering realm into the realm of the poetic, the abstract, and the arty. In a way it shows that the arty is carnivorous. In a weird kind of way it is stronger than the engineering because it gets to feed on the leavings of the other one. I mean, engineering doesn't feed on dead art, but art can feed on dead engineering. So there's something very provocative going on there. I mean, the strength of art is underestimated. So I think about art seriously, and I like to think about the future of art — the long-term future of art — like what might art be like 200 years from now. There's never been a time when we were without it. There are tremendous cave paintings from 20,000 years ago.

PDM: *Art is just another code, and those paintings were all ritual based, just like contemporary culture: different time, different tools. But they are amazing works.*

BS: Yeah, you know, fuckin'-A! They're good. So, I think that although the rhetoric of art changes over the years, the urge to do something arty is an enormously powerful, almost sexual urge, and that's something I take very seriously. My question is why do I write novels instead of just going out and getting a job at Dell? I mean, I could do that. Dell's the guy. Bill Gates is almost exactly my age. We're a few months apart. I'm of Gates's generation. Why didn't I go and join a tech startup and have an initial public offering and try and become a computer guy? The whole reason is because I am a fucking artist, okay? You know, that's what I want to do. That's what gratifies me.

Contributors

JOHN BROCKMAN is a cultural impresario whose career has encompassed the avant-garde art world, science, books, software, and the internet. In the 1960s he coined the word "intermedia" and pioneered "intermedia kinetic environments" in art, theatre, and commerce, while also consulting for clients such as General Electric, Columbia Pictures, Scott Paper, the Pentagon, and the White House.

In 1973, he formed Brockman, Inc., the international literary and software agency specializing in serious nonfiction. He is the founder of the nonprofit Edge Foundation, Inc. and editor of *Edge (www.edge.org)*, the highly acclaimed website devoted to discussions of cutting-edge science by many of the world's brilliant thinkers, the leaders of what he has termed "the third culture".

Included in his works as author and/or editor are *By the Late John Brockman* (Macmillan, 1969), *The Third Culture: Beyond the Scientific Revolution* (Simon & Schuster, 1995), *Digerati: Encounters with the Cyber Elite* (Hardwired, 1996), *The Greatest Inventions of the Past Two Thousand*

Years (Diane Publishing, 2000), *The Next Fifty Years: Science in the First Half of the Twenty-First Century* (Vintage, 2002), *The New Humanists: Science at the Edge* (Barnes & Noble, 2003), *What We Believe but Cannot Prove: Today's Leading Thinkers on Science in the Age of Certainty* (Harper Perennial, 2006), and *Intelligent Thought: Science Versus the Intelligent Design Movement* (Vintage, 2006).

Brockman has the distinction of being the only person to have been profiled on the front page of both *The New York Sunday Times* "Arts & Leisure" (1966), and *The New York Times* "Science Times" (1997).

ERIK DAVIS is an award-winning journalist, scholar, and "performance lecturer" based in San Francisco. He is the author, most recently, of *The Visionary State: A Journey Through California's Spiritual Landscape* (Chronicle, 2006), with photographs by Michael Rauner. Along with a critical volume on *Led Zeppelin IV* (Continuum, 2005), he also wrote *TechGnosis: Myth, Magic, and Mysticism in the Age of Information* (Harmony, 1998), a cult classic of visionary media studies that has been translated into five languages. Davis' essays on music, media, technoculture, and contemporary spirituality have appeared in over a dozen books, including *AfterBurn: Reflections on Burning Man* (University of New Mexico Press, 2005), *Zig Zag Zen* (Chronicle, 2002), *Book of Lies: The Disinformation Guide to Magick and the Occult* (Disinformation, 2003), *010101: Art in Technological Times* (SFMOMA, 2001), and *Prefiguring Cyberculture* (MIT Press, 2003). Davis has contributed articles and essays to a variety of publications, including *Bookforum, Artforum, Salon, Rolling Stone, Spin, Blender,* the *LA Weekly,* and *The Village Voice.* For many years he was a contributing writer at *Wired,* and he is now the executive editor of *Evolver* magazine.

A vital speaker, Davis has given talks at universities, media art conferences, and festivals around the world. He has taught workshops at the California Institute of Integral Studies, the New York Open Center, and

Esalen. He was one of the original minds behind Planetwork, an organization devoted to cross-fertilizing information technology and global
ecology. He has been interviewed by CNN and the BBC, and appeared in
Craig Baldwin's underground film, the sci-fi media critique *Specters of the
Spectrum*. He occasionally plays guitar in front of microphones. Some of
his work can be accessed at *www.techgnosis.com*.

MARK DERY is a cultural critic and professor at NYU, where he teaches
media studies in the Department of Journalism. He writes about fringe
thought, unpopular culture, the media environment, the politics of images,
and deviant sex in the Digital Age.

He edited the seminal anthology, *Flame Wars: The Discourse of
Cyberculture* (Duke University Press, 1994), in which he coined the term
"Afro-Futurism," a discursive zone now widely explored in cultural studies. His early essay, "Culture Jamming: Hacking, Slashing, and Sniping in
the Empire of the Signs," popularized the term "culture jamming" and
presaged the current interest in "tactical media" and "meme warfare."

His books include the critically acclaimed titles *Escape Velocity:
The Discourse of Cyberculture* (Grove Press, 1996) and *The Pyrotechnic
Insanitarium: American Culture on the Brink* (Grove Press, 1999). He's at
work on *Don Henley Must Die*, a cultural critique of San Diego, where he
grew up in the '70s, amid the borderlands and badlands of its suburban
sprawl. (More at *www.markdery.com*.)

TOM GEORGOULIAS is a systems engineer at a media company in Raleigh,
North Carolina. He spends a lot of his free time riding his skateboard,
hanging out with his wife and friends, and making things for his house.

MC PAUL BARMAN got more rimes than there's grains in wheat silo. He
put out 7" "Postgraduate Work," which found producer Prince Paul —

They made an EP that's berserk: *It's Very Stimulating* — followed by tours and LP *Paullelujah*. Fallujah of the mouth. Science Gang in the future. Publications include *Games Magazine, Spin, Nick Jr.,* and *Wired*. Idea is more perfect than the person it inspired.

PAUL D. MILLER AKA DJ SPOOKY THAT SUBLIMINAL KID is a conceptual artist, writer, and musician working in New York. His written work has appeared in *The Village Voice, The Source, Artforum, Raygun, Rap Pages, Paper Magazine,* and a host of other periodicals. Miller's first collection of essays, *Rhythm Science,* was published by MIT Press in April 2004, and was included in several year-end lists of the best books of 2004, including *The Guardian* (UK) and *Publishers Weekly*. In 2007, *Sound Unbound,* an anthology of writings on sound art and multimedia by contemporary cultural theorists will follow *Rhythm Science*.

But even with all this, Miller is most well known under the moniker of his "constructed persona" as DJ Spooky That Subliminal Kid. Miller has recorded a huge volume of music and collaborated with a wide variety of musicians and composers such as Iannis Xenakis, Ryuichi Sakamoto, Butch Morris, Kool Keith aka Doctor Octagon, Pierre Boulez, Killa Priest from Wu-Tang Clan, Steve Reich, Yoko Ono, and Thurston Moore from Sonic Youth among many others. He also composed and recorded the music score for the Cannes and Sundance award-winning film *Slam,* starring critically acclaimed poet Saul Williams.

As DJ Spooky, Miller continues his globe-trotting appearances. In 2004 he played at festivals from France to Mexico City, performed a DJ concerto in Oakland and at Yale, gave numerous talks at prominent universities, and participated in Microsoft's International DJ Summit. Miller's latest collaborative release *Drums of Death* (Thirsty Ear, 2005) features Dave Lombardo of Slayer, Chuck D. of Public Enemy, Vernon Reid of Living Color, and Jack Dangers of Meat Beat Manifesto. (More at *www.djspooky.com.*)

BRANDON PIERCE is currently living in Seattle, studying public health and genetics at the University of Washington. His current research deals with statistical approaches to studying the genetics of complex diseases. Other interests include science journalism, biking everywhere, solving the Rubik's Cube, playing with guitars and synths, and kicking soccer balls. He reads lots of science/media books, music biographies, a bit of sci-fi, and anything by Murakami.

MARK WIEMAN is an interactive producer living in Seattle, Washington. His early interest in information architecture guided his work on large-scale web site design. He is a graduate of the Master of Communication in Digital Media program at the University of Washington. Mark currently works as an independent producer of interactive features that educate and entertain. (More at *www.markwieman.com.*)

Bibliography

Abbott, Edwin A. *Flatland: A Romance of Many Dimensions*. New York: Signet Classics, 1984.

Adorno, Theodor. *Culture Industry*. New York: Routledge, 1991.

Alighieri, Dante. *Dante: Inferno*. Translated by Anthony Esolen. New York: Random House, 2002.

Archer-Straw, Petrine. *Negrophilia: Avant-Garde Paris and Black Culture in the 1920s*. New York: Thames & Hudson, 2000.

Aylett, Steve. *The Inflatable Volunteer*. London: Orion, 2000.

___. *Lint*. New York: Avalon, 2005.

___. *Tao Te Jinx*. London: Scar Garden, 2004.

Ballard, J. G. *Crash: A Novel*. New York: Picador, 1973.

Barabási, Albert-László. *Linked: The New Science of Networks*. New York: Perseus Books, 2002.

Bellamy, Edward. *Looking Backward*. New York: Signet, 1960.

Berger, John. *Ways of Seeing*. New York: Viking, 1973.

Bey, Hakim. *T.A.Z.: The Temporary Autonomous Zone*. Brooklyn: Autonomedia, 1998.

Bloom, Howard. *Global Brain: The Evolution of Mass Mind from the Big Bang to the 21st Century*. New York: J. Wiley & Sons, 2000.

___. "Instant Evolution: The Influence of the City on Human Genes: A Speculative Case," Paper presented at the Center for Human Evolution Fifth Workshop "Cultural Evolution," Seattle, May 11, 2000.

___. *The Lucifer Principle: A Scientific Expedition into the Forces of History*. London: Atlantic Monthly Press, 1995.

Bolter, Jay David. *Writing Space: The Computer, Hypertext and the History of Writing*. Mahwah: Lawrence Erlbaum Associates, 1991.

Bolter, Jay David, and Richard Grusin. *Remediation: Understanding New Media*. Cambridge: The MIT Press, 1999.

Borsook, Paulina. *Cyberselfish: A Critical Romp Through the Terribly Libertarian Culture of High Tech*. New York: PublicAffairs, 2000.

Bosma, Josephine. "To Not Be Satisfied with Just the Screenal Net Art: An Interview with Eugene Thacker," Nettime, www.nettime.org/Lists-Archives/nettime-l-0103/msg00175.html.

Brand, Stewart. *The Clock of the Long Now: Time and Responsibility: The Ideas Behind the World's Slowest Computer*. New York: Perseus, 1999.

Branwyn, Gareth. *Jamming the Media: A Citizen's Guide to Reclaiming the Tools of Communication*. San Francisco: Chronicle Books, 1997.

Breton, André. *Manifestoes of Surrealism*. Ann Arbor: University of Michigan Press, 1972.

Brown, Norman O. *Love's Body*. New York: Random House, 1966.

Burian, Al. *Burn Collector: Collected Stories from One Through Nine*. Brooklyn: Buddy System, 2000.

Capra, Fritjof. *The Tao of Physics: An Exploration of the Parallels between Modern Physics and Eastern Mysticism*. London: Wildwood House, 1975.

Carse, James P. *Finite and Infinite Games*. New York: Free Press, 1986.

Clarke, Arthur C. *2001: A Space Odyssey*. New York: Putnam, 1968.

Coleman, Brian. *Rakim Told Me: Hip-Hop Waxfacts, Straight from the Original Artist: The '80s*. Everett: Waxfacts, 2005.

Crawford, Ashley, and Edgar, Ray. *Transit Lounge: Wake-up Calls and Traveler's Tales from the Future*. Sydney: Craftsman House, 1997.

Danielewski, Mark Z. *House of Leaves*. New York: Random House, 2000.

Davis, Erik. *Techgnosis: Myth, Magic and Mysticism in the Age of Information*. New York: Harmony, 1998.

Dawkins, Richard. *The Selfish Gene*. New York: Oxford University Press (USA), 1976.

De Landa, Manuel. *A Thousand Years of Nonlinear History*. Cambridge: Zone Books, 1997.

___. *War in the Age of Intelligent Machines*. Cambridge: Zone Books, 1991.

Debord, Guy. *Comments on the Society of the Spectacle*. Verso, 1998.

___. *Considerations on the Assassination of Gerard Lebovici*. Los Angeles: TamTam, 2001.

___. *The Society of the Spectacle*. Cambridge: Zone Books, 1995.

Delaney, Samuel. *Dhalgren*. Boston: Gregg Press, 1977.

Deleuze, Gilles, and Guattari, Félix. *Anti-Oedipus: Capitalism and Schizophrenia*. Minneapolis: University of Minnesota Press, 1983.

___. *A Thousand Plateaus: Capitalism and Schizophrenia*. Minneapolis: University of Minnesota Press, 1987.

DeLillo, Don. *Underworld*. New York: Scribner, 1997.

___. *White Noise*. New York: Viking, 1985.

Derrida, Jacques. *Dissemination*, Translated by Barbara Johnson. Chicago: University of Chicago Press, 1981.

Dery, Mark. *Escape Velocity: Cyberculture at the End of the Century*. New York: Grove Press, 1996.

___. *The Pyrotechnic Insanitarium: American Culture on the Brink*. New York: Grove Press, 1999.

Dick, Philip K. *Do Androids Dream of Electric Sheep?* New York: Doubleday, 1968.

___. *Dr. Bloodmoney, or How We Got Along After the Bomb*. Boston: Gregg Press, 1977.

___. *Now Wait For Last Year*. New York: DAW, 1981.

___. *The Minority Report and Other Classic Stories*. Sacramento: Citadel Press, 2002.

Doctorow, Cory. *Down and Out in the Magic Kingdom*. New York: Tor Books, 2003.

Dunaway, David. *Huxley in Hollywood*. New York: HarperCollins, 1989.

Ellul, Jacques. *Propaganda: the Formation of Men's Attitudes*. New York: Alfred A. Knopf, 1965.

____. *The Technological Society.* New York: Alfred A. Knopf, 1964.

Eno, Brian. *A Year with Swollen Appendices.* London: Faber & Faber, 1996.

Erickson, Milton. *The February Man: Evolving Consciousness and Identity in Hypnotherapy.* New York: Brunner/Mazel, 1989.

Eshun, Kodwo. *More Brilliant Than the Sun: Adventures in Sonic Friction.* London: Quartet, 1998.

Fairey, Shepard. *Supply & Demand — The Art of Shepard Fairey.* Corte Madera: Gingko Press, 2006.

Feyerabend, Paul. *Against Method.* New York: Verso, 1975.

____. *Farewell to Reason.* New York: Verso, 1988.

Foucault, Michel. *Discipline and Punish: The Birth of the Prison.* London: Penguin, 1975.

____. *The Hermeneutics of the Subject: Lectures at the College de France 1981-82.* Translated by Graham Burchell. New York: Palgrave MacMillan, 2005.

____. *The History of Sexuality: An Introduction.* New York: Random House, 1978.

____. *"Society Must Be Defended": Lectures at the College de France, 1975-1976.* Translated by David Macey. New York: Picador, 2003.

Frank, Thomas. *One Market Under God: Extreme Capitalism, Market Populism, and the End of Economic Democracy.* New York: Doubleday, 2000.

Gainsbourg, Serge. *Evguenie Sokolov.* Los Angeles: TamTam, 1998.

Garreau, Joel. *Edge City: Life on the New Frontier.* New York: Random House, 1991.

Gates, Henry Louis. *The Signifying Monkey: A Theory of African-American Literary Criticism.* New York: Oxford University Press (USA), 1988.

Gibson, William. *All Tomorrow's Parties.* New York: Putnam, 1999.

____. *Neuromancer.* New York: Ace, 1984.

Gilroy, Paul. *The Black Atlantic: Modernity and Double-Consciousness.* Cambridge: Harvard University Press, 1993.

Gladwell, Malcolm. *The Tipping Point: How Little Things Can Make a Big Difference.* New York: Little, Brown & Co., 2000.

Gleick, James. *Chaos: Making a New Science.* New York: Viking, 1987.

Granovetter, Mark. "The Strength of Weak Ties," *American Journal of Sociology* 78 (1973): 1360-1380.

Harries, Dan, ed. *The New Media Book.* London: British Film Institute, 2002

Hayles, N. Katherine, ed. *Chaos and Order: Complex Dynamics in Literature and Science*. Chicago: University of Chicago Press, 1991.

____. *Writing Machines*. Cambridge: MIT Press, 2002.

Heim, Michael. "Heidegger On-line." In *Uncanny Networks*, edited by Geert Lovink. Cambridge: MIT Press, 2003.

Heidegger, Martin. *Being and Time*. Translated by John Macquarrie and Edward Robinson. New York: Harper & Row, 1962.

____. *Introduction to Metaphysics*. Translated by Gregory Fried and Richard Polt. New Haven: Yale University Press, 2000.

____. *The Question Concerning Technology and Other Essays*. New York: Harper Perennial: 1982.

Heraclitus. *Fragments: The Collected Wisdom of Heraclitus*. New York: Viking, 2001.

Hitchens, Christopher. *Letters to a Young Contrarian*. New York: Basic, 2001.

Hunt-Badiner, Allan, and Alex Grey, eds. *Zig Zag Zen: Buddhism and Psychedelics*. San Francisco: Chronicle, 2002.

Huxley, Aldous. *Brave New World*. New York: HarperCollins, 1932.

Jaynes, Julian. *Origins of Consciousness in the Breakdown of the Bicameral Mind*. Toronto: University of Toronto Press, 1978.

Johnson, Steven. *Emergence: The Connected Lives of Ants, Brains, Cities, and Software*. New York: Scribner, 2001.

____. *Everything Bad Is Good for You: How Today's Popular Culture Is Actually Making Us Smarter*. New York: Riverhead, 2005.

____. *Interface Culture: How New Technology Transforms the Way We Create and Communicate*. San Francisco: Harper San Francisco, 1997.

____. *Mind Wide Open: Your Brain and the Neuroscience of Everyday Life*. New York: Scribner, 2004.

Joy, Camden. *Lost Joy*. Seattle: TNI, 2002.

Jung, C. G. *Flying Saucers: A Modern Myth of Things Seen in the Sky*. New York: Fine Communications, 1997.

Kammerer, Paul. *The Inheritance of Acquired Characteristics*. New York: Boni and Liveright, 1924.

Kelly, Kevin. "Gossip is Philosophy: An Interview with Brian Eno," *Wired*, May 1995: 145-151, 204-209.

____. *Out of Control: The New Biology of Machines, Social Systems and the Economic World*. New York: Perseus, 1994.

357

Kerouac, Jack. *On the Road*. New York: Viking, 1959.

Kick, Russ, ed. *Everything You Know Is Wrong: The Disinformation Guide to Secrets and Lies*. New York: Disinformation, 2002.

Koestler, Arthur. *The Ghost in the Machine*. London: Arkana, 1989.

Kundera, Milan. *Unbearable Lightness of Being*. New York: Harper & Row, 1984.

Lakatos, Imre. *Criticism and the Growth of Knowledge*. Cambridge: Cambridge University Press, 1970.

Landau, Misia. *Narratives of Human Evolution*. New Haven: Yale University Press, 1991.

Laurel, Brenda, ed. *Design Research: Methods and Perspectives*. Cambridge: MIT Press, 2003.

____. *Utopian Entrepreneur*. Cambridge: MIT Press, 2001.

Lazzarato, Maurizio. *Puissances de l'invention: La Psychologie économique de Gabriel Tarde contre l'économie politique*. Paris: Les empêcheurs de penser en rond, 2002.

Leary, Timothy, Ralph Metzner, Richard Alpert, and Karma-Glin-Pa. *The Psychedelic Experience: A Manual Based on the Tibetan Book of the Dead*. New York: Citadel Press, 1995.

Leyner, Mark. *The Tetherballs of Bougainville*. New York: Harmony, 1997.

Locke, Christopher, Rick Levine, Doc Searls, and David Weinberger. *The Cluetrain Manifesto*. New York: Perseus Books, 2000.

Lovink, Geert. *Dark Fiber: Tracking Critical Internet Culture*. Cambridge: MIT Press, 2002.

____. *Uncanny Networks: Dialogues with the Virtual Intelligentsia*. Cambridge: MIT Press, 2003.

Lunenfeld, Peter. *The Digital Dialectic: New Essays on New Media*. Cambridge: MIT Press, 1999.

____. *Snap to Grid: A User's Guide to Digital Arts, Media and Cultures*. Cambridge: MIT Press, 2000.

Mander, Jerry. *Four Arguments for the Elimination of Television*. New York: William Morrow, 1978.

Manovich, Lev. *The Language of New Media*. Cambridge: MIT Press, 2001.

Marvell, Andrew. *The Complete Poems*. New York: Penguin, 1972.

McElroy, Joseph. *Plus*. New York: Carroll & Graf, 1987.

McKenna, Terence. *The Archaic Revival: Speculations on Psychedelic Mushrooms, the Amazon, Virtual Reality, UFOs, Evolution, Shamanism, the Rebirth of the Goddess, and the End of History.* New York: HarperCollins, 1992.

____. *Food of the Gods: The Search for the Original Tree of Knowledge: A Radical History of Plants, Drugs, and Human Evolution.* New York: Bantam, 1992.

____. *True Hallucinations: Being an Account of the Author's Extraordinary Adventures in the Devil's Paradise.* New York: HarperCollins, 1993.

McKenna, Terence and Dennis McKenna. *The Invisible Landscape: Mind, Hallucinogens, and the I Ching.* New York: Scribner, 1976.

McLuhan, Marshall. *The Gutenberg Galaxy: The Making of Typographic Man.* Toronto: University of Toronto Press, 1962.

____. *Understanding Media: The Extensions of Man.* New York: McGraw-Hill, 1964.

____. *Verbi-Voco-Visual Explorations.* New York: Something Else Press, 1967.

McLuhan, Marshall and Eric McLuhan. *Laws of Media: The New Science.* Toronto: University of Toronto Press, 1988.

McLuhan, Marshall and Quentin Fiore. *The Medium is the Massage: An Inventory of Effects.* New York: Bantam, 1967.

____. *War and Peace in the Global Village: An Inventory of Some of the Current Spastic Situations That Could Be Eliminated by More Feedforward.* New York: Bantam, 1968.

Miller, Paul D. *Rhythm Science.* Cambridge: MIT Press, 2004.

Naisbitt, John. *Megatrends: Ten New Directions Transforming Our Lives.* New York: Warner, 1982.

Negri, Antonio. *Global.* Buenos Aires: Ediciones Paidos Iberica, 2006.

Orwell, George. *1984.* New York: Signet, 1950.

Paglia, Camille. *Sexual Personae: Art & Decadence from Nefertiti to Emily Dickinson.* New Haven: Yale University Press, 1990.

Partch, Harry. *Genesis of a Music: An Account of a Creative Work, Its Roots and Its Fulfillments.* Cambridge: Da Capo, 1974.

Penfield, Wilder. *The Mystery of the Mind: A Critical Study of Consciousness and the Human Brain.* Princeton: Princeton University Press, 1975.

Persinger, Michael. *Neuropsychological Bases of God Beliefs.* New York: Praeger, 1987.

Pescovitz, David. "Live from Bedlam." *Wired,* September, 1998.

Pinker, Steven. *The Language Instinct: How the Mind Creates Language.* New York: William Morrow and Company, 1994.

Playboy Interview: Marshall McLuhan, *Playboy*, March 1969: 26-27, 45, 55-56, 61, 63.

Read Me! ASCII Culture & The Revenge of Knowledge. Brooklyn: Autonomedia, 1999.

Reed, Ishmael. *Mumbo Jumbo.* New York: Doubleday, 1972.

Rheingold, Howard. *Smart Mobs: The Next Social Revolution.* New York: Perseus Books, 2002.

___. *Virtual Reality: The Revolutionary Technology of Computer-Generated Artificial Worlds — and How It Promises to Transform Society.* Cambridge: MIT Press, 1990.

Roberts, Paul. *The End of Oil: On the Edge of a Perilous New World.* New York: Houghton Mifflin, 2004.

Ross, Andrew. *Strange Weather: Culture, Science, and Technology in the Age of Limits.* New York: Verso, 1991.

Rucker, Rudy. *As Above So Below.* New York: Forge Books, 2002.

___. *Freeware.* New York: Eos Books, 1998.

___. *The Hacker and The Ants: Version 2.0.* New York: Four Walls Eight Windows, 2002.

___. *Master of Space and Time.* New York: St. Martin's Press, 1984.

___. *Realware.* New York: Avon Books, 2000.

___. *Seek!.* New York: Four Walls Eight Windows, 1999.

___. *Saucer Wisdom.* New York: Forge Books, 1999.

___. *Software.* New York: Eos Books, 1987.

___. *Software Engineering and Computer Games.* Boston: Addison-Wesley, 2002.

___. *Spaceland.* New York: Tor Books, 2002.

___. *Wetware.* New York: Eos Books, 1997.

Rushkoff, Douglas. *Coercion: Why We Listen to What "They" Say.* New York: Riverhead, 1999.

___. *Cyberia: Life in the Trenches of Cyberspace.* New York: HarperCollins, 1994.

___. *Ecstasy Club: A Novel.* San Francisco: HarperEdge, 1997.

___. *Free Rides.* New York: Delta, 1991.

___, ed. *The GenX Reader.* New York: Ballantine, 1994.

___. *Media Virus! Hidden Agendas in Popular Culture.* New York: Ballantine, 1994.

___. *Playing the Future: What We Can Learn from Digital Kids.* New York: HarperCollins, 1996.

Ruskin, John. *The Stones of Venice.* Cambridge: Da Capo, 1985.

Sagan, Dorion. *Up From Dragons: The Evolution of Human Intelligence.* New York: McGraw-Hill, 2002.

Salen, Katie, and Eric Zimmerman, eds. *The Game Design Reader: A Rules of Play Anthology.* Cambridge: MIT Press, 2005.

___, eds. *Rules of Play: Game Design Fundamentals.* Cambridge: MIT Press, 2003.

Scholder, Amy, and Eric Zimmerman, eds. *Replay: Game Design and Game Culture.* New York: Peter Lang, 2003.

Schuyler, George S. *Black No More.* New York: Random House, 1999.

Shannon, Claude, and Warren Weaver. *The Mathematical Theory of Communication.* Champagne: University of Illinois Press, 1963.

Shaviro, Steven. *Connected, or What It Means to Live in the Network Society.* Minneapolis: University of Minnesota Press, 2003.

___. *Doom Patrols: A Theoretical Fiction about Postmodernism.* San Francisco: Serpent's Tail, 1997.

Sheldrake, Rupert. *The Presence of the Past: Morphic Resonance and the Habits of Nature.* New York: Crown, 1988.

Shenk, David. *Datasmog: Surviving the Information Glut.* New York: HarperCollins, 1997.

Shirley, John. *City Come a Walkin'.* New York: Four Walls Eight Windows, 2000.

Snow, C. P. *The Two Cultures.* Cambridge: Cambridge University Press, 1959.

Spivak, Gayatri Chakravorty. *Critique of Post-Colonial Reason.* New York: Routledge, 1990.

Stapledon, Olaf. *Star Maker.* Middletown: Wesleyan University Press, 2004.

Stephenson, Neal. *Cryptonomicon.* New York: Avon, 1999.

Sterling, Bruce. *Distraction.* New York: Spectra, 1999.

___. *Heavy Weather.* New York: Bantam, 1994.

___. *Holy Fire.* New York: Bantam, 1996.

Taylor, Mark C. *Confidence Games: Money and Markets in a World without Redemption.* Chicago: University of Chicago Press, 2004.

___. *The Moment of Complexity: Emerging Network Culture.* Chicago: University of Chicago Press, 2003.

___. *Mystic Bones*. Chicago: University of Chicago Press, 2006.

___. *The Picture in Question: Mark Tansey and the Ends of Representation*. Chicago: University of Chicago Press, 1999.

Teilhard de Chardin, Pierre. *The Phenomenon of Man*. New York: Harper Perennial, 1976.

Thacker, Eugene. *Biomedia*. Minneapolis: University of Minnesota Press, 2004.

___. *The Global Genome*. Cambridge: MIT Press, 2005.

Tipler, Frank J. "The Omega Point as Eschaton: Answers to Pannenberg's Questions for Scientists," *Zygon* vol. 24, no. 2 (June 1989).

___. *Physics of Immortality: Modern Cosmology, God and the Resurrection of the Dead*. New York: Doubleday, 1994.

Toffler, Alvin. *The Third Wave*. New York: Bantam, 1980.

Toop, David. *Rap Attack: African Jive to New York Hip-Hop*. Cambridge: South End Press, 1984.

Turcotte, Bryan Ray and Christopher T. Miller, (eds). *Fucked Up + Photocopied: Instant Art of the Punk Rock Movement*. Corte Madera: Gingko Press, 1999.

Ullman, Ellen. *Close to the Machine*. San Francisco: City Lights, 1997.

Vian, Boris. *I Spit on Your Graves*. Los Angeles: TamTam, 1998.

Vico, Giambattista. *The New Science*. Ithaca: Cornell University Press, 1984.

Virilio, Paul. *The Art of the Motor*. Translated by Julie Rose. Minneapolis: University of Minnesota Press, 1995.

___. *Polar Inertia*. Thousand Oaks: SAGE, 1999.

___. *Speed and Politics*. Cambridge: Semiotext(e), 1986.

Virno, Paolo. *A Grammar of the Multitude*. Translated by Isabella Bertoletti, James Cascaito, and Andrea Casson. Cambridge: Semiotext(e), 2004.

Voith, Adam. *Stand Up Ernie Baxter: You're Dead*. Seattle: TNI, 2003.

von Neumann, John. *The Computer and the Brain*. New Haven: Yale University Press, 1958.

Wardrip-Fruin, Noah, and Pat Harrigan, eds. *First Person: New Media as Story, Performance, and Game*. Cambridge: MIT Press, 2004.

Wark, McKenzie. *Celebrities, Culture and Cyberspace: The Light on the Hill in a Postmodern World*. North Melbourne: Pluto Press, 1999.

___. *Dispositions*. Cambridge: Salt Publishing, 2002.

___. *Virtual Geography: Living With Global Media Events*. Bloomington: Indiana University Press, 1994.

___. *The Virtual Republic: Australia's Culture Wars of the 1990s.* Crows Nest: Allen & Unwin, 1998.

Weinberger, David. *Small Pieces Loosely Joined: A Unified Theory of the Web.* New York: Perseus Books, 2002.

Whitehead, Alfred North. *Process and Reality.* New York: Free Press, 1978.

Wilber, Ken. *A Brief History of Everything.* Boston: Shambhala, 1996.

Wiener, Norbert. *Cybernetics: Or the Control and Communication in the Animal and the Machine.* Cambridge: MIT Press, 1965.

Wittgenstein, Ludwig. *The Blue and Brown Books.* New York: Harper & Row, 1958.

___. *Philosophical Investigations.* Malden: Blackwell, 1953.

Wolfram, Stephen. *A New Kind of Science.* Champaign: Wolfram Media, 2002.

Womack, Jack. *Let's Put the Future Behind Us.* London: Atlantic Monthly Press, 1996.

Wurman, Richard Saul. *Information Anxiety.* New York: Doubleday, 1989.

___. *Understanding USA.* New York: TED Conferences, 1999.

Xenakis, Iannis. *Formalized Music: Thought and Mathematics in Composition.* Hillsdale: Pendragon Press, 1992.

Photo Credits

Roy Christopher by Cynthia D. Hutto.
Eugene Thacker by Eugene Thacker.
Howard Rheingold by Robin Good.
Rudy Rucker by Tina Mills.
Eric Paulos by Jill Miller.
Richard Saul Wurman by Reven T.C. Wurman.
Eric Zimmerman by Natascha Stellmach.
McKenzie Wark by Ara Koopelian.
N. Katherine Hayles by Evan Gustanson.
Brenda Laurel by Steve Heller.
Erik Davis by Michael Rauner.
Gareth Branwyn by Jay Townsend.
Douglas Rushkoff by Gisela Torres.
Pete Miser by Chris Ho.

Yoni Wolf by Jessica Miller.
dälek by Herve Baudat.
Weasel Walter by Maria Fischinger.
Milemarker by Tim Owen.
Paul D. Miller by Tobin Poppenberg.
Paul Roberts by Karen Dickinson.
Hal Brindley by Meredith Mosely.
Tod Swank by Tod Swank.
Shepard Fairey from *obeygiant.com*.
Steven Shaviro by Steven Shaviro.
Mark Dery by Jorge Madrigal, Madrigal Studios: *www .madrigalphotography.com*.
Steve Aylett found his picture on the floor of his house.
Bruce Sterling by Jasmina Tesanovic.

Index